CLEVELAND
BROWNS
A TO Z

ROGER GORDON

SP

SPORTS
PUBLISHING
L.L.C.

ACKNOWLEDGMENTS

I would like to thank Mike Pearson of Sports Publishing, L.L.C., first and foremost, for giving me the opportunity to write this book. Without him, it never would have happened. Also from Sports Publishing, I would like to thank Jennifer Polson for the time and energy she put into the book, and Joe Bannon, Jr.

I also appreciate the assistance I received from the staff of the Pro Football Hall of Fame archives library, specifically Chad Reese for his diligent effort in furnishing me with much of the research material I needed.

Gratitude is also owed to the following in furnishing me with photos: the Cleveland Browns; the staff of the Cleveland State University Cleveland Press Collection department; Jim Tozzi, owner of Sports Archives in Canton, Ohio; and Ted Patterson.

Special thanks goes to Mike Pruitt for writing the foreword.

ISBN: 1-58261-240-4

Director of Production: Susan M. Moyer
Senior project manager, book design: Jennifer L. Polson
Cover design: K. Jeffrey Higgerson
Developmental Editors: Stephanie Fuqua and Mark E. Zulauf
Copy editor: Ashley Burum

SPORTS PUBLISHING LLC
www.sportspublishingllc.com

TABLE OF CONTENTS

Author's Note IV

Notes V

Abbreviations Key VI

Characters Key VII

Foreword VIII

Decade-by-Decade Timeline IX

A   ABC Television Network to Awards 1

B   Mike Baab to Earnest Byner 9

C   Reggie Camp to Isaac Curtis 24

D   Dallas Cowboys to Dumont TV Network 35

E   Eastern Conference to Steve Everitt 48

F   Paul Farren to The Fumble 50

G   Bob Gain to Lou Groza 56

H   Carl Hairston to Art Hunter 64

I   Indianapolis Colts to Interceptions Leaders 71

J   Michael Jackson to Tony Jones 73

K   Jim Kanicki to Bernie Kosar 79

L   Warren Lahr to Lowest-scoring Games Between Both
     Teams, Regular and Postseason 85

M   Kevin Mack to Najee Mustafaa 90

N   Gern Nagler to Numbers on Helmets 105

O   Oakland Raiders to Overtime 114

P   Chris Palmer to Jim Pyne 118

Q   Quarterbacks 129

R   Wali Rainer to Lou Rymkus 130

S   Lou Saban to Sunday Night Games 137

T   Tampa Bay Buccaneers to Two One-Thousand-Yard
     Rushers in One Season 153

U   Ed Ulinksi, USFL 161

W   Brian Wagner to Sam Wyche 162

X   X-Rays in '88 170

Y   John Yonakor to Glen Young 171

Z   Eric Zeier 172

Browns Trivia 173

Coaches and Assistant Coaches 179

Attendance Statistics 181

Individual Statistics 188

Team Statistics 204

AUTHOR'S NOTE

I look at the alphabet in a whole new way now.

That's what happens after countless hours of research and writing in compiling a book called *Cleveland Browns A to Z*.

Now, when I think of the letter "A," instead of a one-word article coming to mind, I think of the All-America Football Conference. When I think of the letter "D," rather than my college report cards coming to mind, I think of The Dawg Pound. When I think of the letter "H," I think of http://www.clevelandbrowns.com/.

When Sports Publishing L.L.C. approached me in the spring of 1999 to write *Cleveland Browns A to Z*, it was a no-brainer for me. Authoring an alphabetic history of the Browns was a project I could not resist. I have been a Browns fan for years—from the Kardiac Kids days of Brian Sipe, Greg Pruitt, and Reggie Rucker; to the Dawg Days of Bernie Kosar, Webster Slaughter, and Earnest Byner; to mainstays from both eras: Ozzie Newsome, Clay Matthews, and Hanford Dixon; to the new era that features Tim Couch, Kevin Johnson, and Jamir Miller.

In addition, I have always been an ardent researcher, fascinated not only by the history of the Browns from nearly the last quarter century, but also way back to their pre-National Football League days when they were members of the All-America Football Conference.

Cleveland Browns A to Z was at times a challenging work, but well worth it. I hope you enjoy the final result.

NOTES

1. Overtime in the regular season began in 1974.

2. Players' career statistics are comprised of regular-season play only unless indicated otherwise.

3. Preseason games are not included unless indicated otherwise.

4. Sacks have been an official NFL statistic since 1982.

5. The statistic "combined net yards" (also called all-purpose yards) comprises the following yardage totals: rushing, receiving, punt return, kickoff return, interception return, and fumble return.

6. The statistic "total net yards" comprises rushing yards and net passing yards.

7. When an individual is described as having led the league/conference in an "average yards per" category, it is assumed that individuals with higher averages, but a minute amount of attempts, are not included.

8. When a player is described as being drafted, it is the AAFC or NFL drafts only unless indicated otherwise.

9. When a team and/or league record being set is described, it is assumed that the record still stands unless indicated otherwise.

10. When there were two teams playing in the same city in lists that are rankings of particular games, the city's abbreviation is followed by the nickname.

11. When a touchdown (six points) is described, and the resulting game score results in seven points, the point after touchdown (PAT) is assumed successful unless indicated otherwise.

ABBREVIATIONS KEY

AAFC: All-America Football Conference

ABC: American Broadcasting Company

AFC: American Football Conference

AP: Associated Press

CBS: Columbia Broadcasting Company

CFL: Canadian Football League

C&O: Coaches & Officials

ESPN: Entertainment and Sports Programming Network

FD: *Football Digest*

FWA: Pro Football Writers Association

INS: International News Service

MAC: Mid-American Conference

MAX: Maxwell Club

NBC: National Broadcasting Company

NCAA: National Collegiate Athletic Association

NEA: Newspaper Enterprise Association

NFC: National Football Conference

NFL: National Football League

NYN: *New York Daily News*

OFF: official teams

PFI: *Pro Football Illustrated*

PFW: *Pro Football Weekly*

SI: *Sports Illustrated*

SN: *The Sporting News*

SP: Sportswriters Inc.

UP: United Press

UPI: United Press International

USFL: United States Football League

CHARACTERS KEY

The following notations denote their meanings:

#: Does not include Browns games against the Buffalo Bills Dec. 4, 1949, and Los Angeles Rams Dec. 24, 1950, for Otto Graham and Marion Motley, and the Browns game against the New York Giants Dec. 17, 1950, for Motley

##: Does not include Browns games against the New York Giants Dec. 17, 1950, and Los Angeles Rams Dec. 24, 1950, and a portion of the Browns game against the Buffalo Bills Dec. 4, 1949

###: Does not include the Browns game against the New York Giants Dec. 17, 1950, and a portion of Browns games against the Buffalo Bills Dec. 4, 1949, and Los Angeles Rams Dec. 24, 1950

####: Does not include a portion of Browns games against the Buffalo Bills Dec. 4, 1949, and Los Angeles Rams Dec. 24, 1950

#####: Does not include the Browns game against the Los Angeles Rams Dec. 24, 1950, and a portion of the Browns game against the Buffalo Bills Dec. 4, 1949

######: Does not include fumble return yardage for part of Browns history

#######: Does not include Browns games against the Brooklyn Dodgers Dec. 8, 1946, and Baltimore Colts Dec. 7, 1947

FOREWORD

The first time I ran onto the Cleveland Municipal Stadium field for a regular season game, I was in awe. We were playing the New York Jets. Joe Namath was on that team! I was thinking, 'I can't believe I'm actually here, competing with guys who I've watched for years!' And the Cleveland fans were remarkable. I'd never seen anything like it. Never had I seen a city so covet a team like Cleveland does the Browns.

I went on to enjoy a successful nine-year career as a running back with Cleveland, something I never dreamed would happen—and definitely not with the Browns. Not only was I taken aback when they selected me in the 1976 NFL Draft, I was in utter shock WHERE they picked me —No. 7 overall! I expected to be drafted, yes, but in the second or third round. Upon returning to earth, I realized I was headed to a team that, although having gone through recent tough times, had loads of tradition. Guys like Jim Brown, Leroy Kelly, and Marion Motley played for this team!

The Kardiac Kids days were the most thrilling times—moments like the Monday night shocker over the Cowboys in a rocking Stadium in 1979, the upset of the Oilers in the Astrodome the next year, and the division-clincher three weeks later in Cincinnati.

There were also moments I'd like to file away forever. The 1982 players' strike. The excruciating loss to the Vikings two years before that nearly cost us a playoff berth. The worst one, though, should come as no surprise to Browns fans—Red Right 88.

The moment I recall most, though was a good one. It occurred in 1978 in a home game against Buffalo. I scored on a 71-yard run. Benchwarming had been my calling for the most part during my two plus seasons with the Browns. I was beginning to doubt my abilities. That long run against the Bills gave me the confidence boost I desperately needed. For the first time, I truly believed I belonged in the NFL.

Whether pleasant memories or not, though, I'll always cherish my days with the Cleveland Browns.

Cleveland Browns A to Z offers fans the chance to re-live the rich history of the Browns franchise, from the glory days of yesteryear to the present that brims with hopes of a Super Bowl title.

—Mike Pruitt

DECADE-BY-DECADE TIMELINE

1940s

The 1940s began with the Browns' domination of the AAFC in their—and the conference's—first year of existence in 1946 under head coach Paul Brown, whom the team was named after. The Browns' dominance continued through 1949, when the AAFC folded. Cleveland won three Western Division Championships from 1946-48 and all four conference titles (in 1949, the two-division format was scratched). The Browns rolled through the 1946 season, finishing 12-2 (.857) and defeating the New York Yankees, 14-9, in Cleveland in the title game. The Browns were 12-1-1 (.893) in 1947 and beat New York again, 14-3. This time, Cleveland took the conference crown in Yankee stadium.

In 1948, the Browns put together a perfect 14-0 record and routed Buffalo, 49-7, in the AAFC title game at home. The Browns wound up 9-1-2 (.833) in 1949 and knocked off Buffalo at home, 31-21, in an opening-round playoff before dismantling the 49ers in the AAFC's final title contest, 21-7, in Cleveland. The Browns' all-time record in the 1940s was 47-4-3 (.898), with 24-2-1 (.907) at home and 23-2-2 (.889) on the road. Cleveland's all-time postseason record in the 1940s was 5-0, with 4-0 at home and 1-0 on the road.

Browns in action, 1946. Photo courtesy of the Cleveland Press Collection.

1950s

The Browns began the 1950s by continuing their stellar play upon joining the NFL. Under head coach Paul Brown, they finished 10-2 (.833), tying the Giants for first place in the American Conference in 1950. They beat the New Yorkers, 8-3, in a playoff to claim the conference title. They beat the Los Angeles Rams, 30-28, for the NFL title on Lou Groza's 16-yard field goal with 28 seconds left.

Cleveland won the American Conference title in 1951 and 1952, with 11-1 (.917) and 8-4 (.667) records, respectively, but were upended in the league title game each time—by the Rams in 1951 and Lions in 1952. The Browns won the renamed Eastern Conference in 1953, but lost to the Lions again in the league championship game. They won the Eastern Conference again in 1954 and 1955, and claimed NFL crown both years, beating the Lions in 1954 and Rams in 1955.

The Browns against the Rams, 1951. Photo courtesy of the Cleveland Press Collection.

After a down year in 1956, in which they finished 5-7 (.417) due in large part to several retirements, rookie running back Jim Brown led the Browns back to the NFL Championship game in 1957, but Cleveland was routed by the Lions, 59-14. The Browns had a chance to win the Eastern Conference crowns in 1958, but lost a heartbreaker to the Giants on the final Sunday, 13-10, in New York that forged a tie with the giants at 9-3 (.750). New York won a playoff, 10-0, the next week in Yankee Stadium. The Browns

Action from 1954. Photo courtesy of the Cleveland Press Collection.

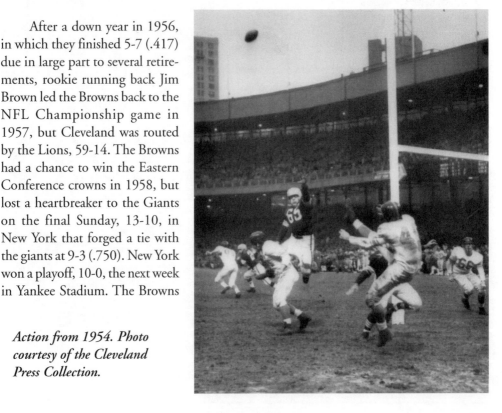

finished 7-5 (.583) in 1959. Cleveland's record in the 1950s was 88-30-2 (.742), with 45-15 (.750) at home and 43-15-2 (.733) on the road. The Browns' postseason record in the 1950s was 4-5 (.444), with 3-1 (.750) at home and 1-4 (.200) on the road.

1960s

The Browns began the 1960s as a team treading in mediocrity—at least for a franchise with the championship tradition that the Browns had built. They were 8-3-1 (.708) in 1960, 8-5-1 (.607) in 1961, and 7-6-1 (.536) in 1962, finishing second, third and third, respectively, in the Eastern Conference. Majority owner Art Modell, deciding a change was needed, fired the only head coach the franchise ever had, Paul Brown, Jan. 9, 1963. Modell replaced Brown with offensive backfield coach Blanton Collier.

Collier implemented a more wide-open offensive attack, and led by quarterback Frank Ryan and running back Jim Brown, Cleveland improved to 10-4 (.714) in 1963. However, the Browns still finished one game behind the Eastern Conference Champion Giants. In 1964, the team finished in first place at 10-3-1 (.750) and upset heavily favored Baltimore, 27-0, in the NFL Championship game in Cleveland. The Browns returned to the title game the following year but fell to the Packers in the snow and mud of Green Bay, 23-12. Cleveland finished 9-5 (.643) in 1966 but missed the postseason.

In 1967, the Eastern Conference split into two divisions, the Capitol and Century. The Browns won the Century, repeating their 9-5 mark from the year before, but were

Frank Ryan is taken down as Jim Brown (32) looks on in the background in 1962. Photo courtesy of the Cleveland Press Collection.

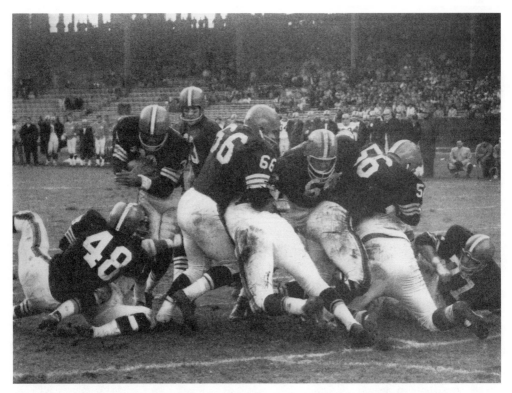

Jim Brown finds a hole against the Steelers Nov. 25, 1962. Photo courtesy of the Cleveland Press Collection.

creamed by the Cowboys in the Cotton Bowl, 52-14, in the conference championship game. Bill Nelsen replaced Ryan as the starting quarterback early in the 1968 season and directed the Browns on an offensive binge that Browns fans had never seen before - the team scored at least 30 points in seven straight games, winning them all. Cleveland wound up 10-4 (.714) and Century Division titlists once again. They upset the Cowboys in the Eastern Conference Championship game in Cleveland but were buried by Baltimore, 34-0, at home for the NFL Championship.

The Browns won their third straight Century championship in 1969, finishing 10-3-1 (.750). The team beat Dallas with ease in the conference title game in the Cotton Bowl, then fell to Vikings, 27-7, in the NFL Championship game Jan. 4, 1970, in frigid Minnesota. The Browns' record in the 1960s was 92-41-5 (.685), with 48-18-3 (.717) at home and 44-23-2 (.652) on the road. Their postseason record in the 1960s was 3-4 (.429), with 2-1 (.667) at home and 1-3 (.250) on the road.

1970S

The 1970s began with one of the biggest trades in Browns history. The team traded exceptional wide receiver Paul Warfield to the Miami Dolphins for the third pick in the next day's draft in order to select sensational Purdue University quarterback Mike Phipps.

Veteran Bill Nelsen, however, was the starter when the 1970 season began. That season got off to a rousing start as the Browns helped inaugurate the ABC *Monday Night Football* series by hosting its very first game, a 31-21 Browns victory over the Joe Namath-led New York Jets Sept. 21, 1970, in front of 85,703 fans, a Browns record (home and away). The Browns, though, were a model of inconsistency all season and finished 7-7, a game behind the Cincinnati Bengals in the first year of the AFC Central Division.

Under new head coach Nick Skorich, the Browns easily won the weak Central in 1971 with a 9-5 (.643) record, but lost to Baltimore in an AFC Divisional Playoff at home. In 1972, Phipps took over as the starter early in the season and directed Cleveland to a 10-4 (.714) finish and the AFC Wild Card spot. The Browns took the undefeated Dolphins down to the wire before falling, 20-14, in a divisional playoff in the Orange Bowl, a game in which Phipps was intercepted five times. The Browns seemed headed for the playoffs once again in 1973 but collapsed late in the season and finished in third place in the Central at 7-5-2 (.571).

The Browns won just seven games during the next two seasons, the second of which was under new head coach Forrest Gregg. They finished in last place both years. In 1976, the Browns rebounded by finishing 9-5 (.643) and were in playoff contention through the final weekend. Cleveland began 1977 with high hopes and came through in the first half of the season—they were 5-2 (.714) and in first place. Then the bottom fell out, and the team won just one of its last seven games, winding up 6-8 (.429) and in last place. Gregg was fired with one game left in the season (defensive coordinator Dick Modzelewski coached the season finale in Seattle).

Don Cockroft's punt is blocked by the Cowboys' Richmond Flowers in the Browns' 6-2 loss at home Dec. 12, 1970. Photo courtesy of the Cleveland Press Collection.

Cold Browns on the sidelines, 1974. Photo courtesy of the Cleveland Press Collection.

Longtime NFL assistant coach Sam Rutigliano came aboard in 1978 and instilled a more wide-open offensive philosophy. That, combined with the maturing of quarterback Brian Sipe, who replaced Phipps (who was traded May 3, 1977) as the starter in the opening game of the 1976 season, the Browns rose to 8-8 that season and 9-7 (.563) in 1979. The '79 team earned the nickname of "Kardiac Kids," due to several close finishes. The team barely missed the playoffs that year. The Browns' record in the 1970s was 72-70-2 (.507), with 41-30-1 (.576) at home and 31-40-1 (.438) on the road. Their postseason record in the 1970s was 0-2—0-1 at home and 0-1 on the road.

1980s

The 1980s began with a bang when the Browns—rather, the Kardiac Kids—won the AFC Central Division title in 1980 in thrilling fashion under head coach Sam Rutigliano, dethroning 1970s kingpin Pittsburgh in the process. Twelve games that year were decided by seven points or less en route to an 11-5 (.688) record. The Browns tied Houston for the best record in the division. The Browns, however, were awarded the division title on the basis of a better record within the AFC (8-4) than the Oilers (7-5). Quarterback Brian Sipe, a multi-award winner that year, passed for a team-record 4,132 yards. Cleveland's Super Bowl dreams came to a crashing end against Oakland in the AFC Divisional Play-offs, though, when Sipe was intercepted by Mike Davis in the end zone with less than a minute to play. The Browns lost to the Raiders, 14-12, in arctic-like temperatures.

The Browns fell on hard times during the next four seasons (5-11 in 1981, 4-5 in 1982, 9-7 in 1983, and 5-11 in 1984). The 1982 club actually qualified for the expanded playoff tournament (due to a players' strike) despite its losing record, but lost in Los Angeles to the Raiders, 27-10, in the first round. Paul McDonald replaced Sipe as the starting quarterback after six games that year. The 1983 squad just missed qualifying for the playoffs on tiebreakers, the only one of five 9-7 teams in the league that year that missed the postseason. The 83 team posted consecutive shutouts when it blanked Tampa Bay and New England in November, becoming the second Browns team ever—and first since 1951—to do so.

Defensive coordinator Marty Schottenheimer replaced the fired Rutigliano midway through the disastrous 1984 campaign that culminated in a 5-11 (.313) record should come after "campaign". With rookie hometown hero Bernie Kosar as the starting quarterback for part of the season and a pair of 1,000-yard running backs in Kevin Mack and Earnest Byner, the Browns won the Central Division title in 1985 despite an 8-8 record. They nearly upset heavily-favored Miami in the divisional playoffs, blowing a 21-3 third-quarter lead. The 1986 and 1987 Browns not only won the Central Division, but also advanced to the AFC Championship game, the first due to a remarkable comeback victory over the Jets in the divisional playoffs. The Browns lost in heartbreaking fashion to the John Elway-led Denver Broncos in both conference title tilts. (*See Drive, The and Fumble, The*).

Cleveland persevered through countless injuries that resulted in four starting quarterbacks in 1988, but lost to Houston in an AFC Wild Card game. Under new head coach Bud Carson (Schottenheimer had resigned soon after the 1988 season), the Browns recaptured the division title in 1989 but lost to the Broncos again in the conference title game. The Browns' record in the 1980s was 83-68-1 (.549), with 46-28-1 (.620) at home and 37-40 (.481) on the road. Their postseason record in the 1980s was 3-7 (.300), with 3-3 at home and 0-4 on the road.

1990s

The 1990s began in horrific fashion as the Browns finished just 3-13 (.188) in 1990—the worst season in team history to that point—after five straight playoff appearances. Head coach Bud Carson was replaced by assistant coach Jim Shofner nine games into the season, the day after a 42-0 home loss to Buffalo, the worst shutout loss and worst home defeat for the Browns up to that point. With Bill Belichick as head coach, the Browns improved to 6-10 (.375) in 1991 and 7-9 (.438) in both 1992 and 1993.

The mid-point of the 1993 season marked the release of hometown hero quarterback Bernie Kosar, who was reaised in nearby Boardman, Ohio. The Browns finally came through in 1994 with quarterback Vinny Testaverde, an ex-teammate of Kosar's at the University of Miami, finishing 11-5 (.688), mostly due to the fact they yielded just 204 points, the fewest in the league. A wild card win over New England was all but forgotten when the Browns were obliterated, 29-9, by Pittsburgh the next week in an AFC Divisional Playoff, Cleveland's third loss to the Steelers that season.

As bad as the decade began for the Browns with their miserable 1990 season, what happened in 1995 made that seem like nothing. Rumors circulated for the first two months of the season that Browns majority owner Art Modell was planning on relocating the franchise to Baltimore after the season, but the Browns still won three of their first four games. They hit a cold spell, but recovered as rookie quarterback Eric Zeier replaced the benched

Testaverde (who was actually leading the AFC in passing a the time) and led the team to a thrilling overtime victory against the Bengals in Cincinnati Oct. 29. On Nov. 5, in a home game against Houston, the uninspired Browns, aware that Modell's official announcement of the relocation would occur the next day, were crushed, 37-10. Modell made his team's impending move to Maryland official to the public the following day in Baltimore.

The rest of the season was basically a moot point, as the Browns won just one more game—a 26-10 victory over the Bengals Dec. 17 in what many thought to be the final home game in the history of the franchise. The Browns did leave, and move to Baltimore, where they were renamed the Ravens. Thus, football-crazed Cleveland was without a pro football team for three seasons from 1996-98.

However, on June 12, 1996, the city of Cleveland and the NFL announced terms of a historic public-private partnership that would continue the Browns franchise and guarantee a new state-of-the-art stadium in Cleveland in 1999. On March 23, 1998, at a league meeting in Orlando, NFL owners agreed that the Cleveland Browns would be an expansion team in 1999. On Sept. 8, 1998, the NFL awarded majority ownership of the franchise to Al Lerner. The Browns didn't have much time, but they spent months putting together a team through free agency, the expansion draft and the regular draft, in which University of Kentucky standout quarterback Tim Couch was their top pick and the first overall selection.

Under head coach Chris Palmer, the "reborn" Browns took the field for the first time Sept. 12, 1999, against the Pittsburgh Steelers in brand new Cleveland Browns Stadium for a nationally televised game broadcast on ESPN. The Browns not only lost, 43-0, but were only able to net 40 total yards—less than the Steelers' point total. The Browns, as expected, had a rough season in 1999, but at times showed flashes of a bright future. They finished 2-14 (.125) and in last place in the AFC Central. Cleveland's record in the 1990s was 41-71 (.366), with 22-34 (.393) at home and 19-37 (.339) on the road. The Browns' postseason record in the 1990s was 1-1, with 1-0 at home and 0-1 on the road.

1999 EXPANSION DRAFT

The 1999 expansion draft was held Feb. 9. The expansion draft gave the Browns an opportunity to stock up on players other teams believed were less important to their success and thus left "unprotected." The Browns selected 37 players. Their first choice was Detroit Lions guard Jim Pyne, who was a member of the Browns in 1999 and 2000. Other notable selections were No. 2 pick defensive lineman Hurvin McCormack from Dallas, who played for the Browns in 1999; No. 3 pick offensive lineman Scott Rehberg from New England, who was on the team in 1999; No. 6 pick linebacker Tarek Saleh from Carolina, who has been on the team since; No. 10 pick linebacker Lenoy Jones from Tennessee, who has also been on the team since; and No. 27 pick guard Orlando Bobo, who was a Brown in 1999.

2000s

The 2000s began roughly for the Browns, as they finished just 3-13 (.188) in 2000 after a 2-1 (.667) start. Things started going downhill and then got worse as quarterback

Tim Couch, the 1999 No. 1 overall pick in the draft, fractured his right thumb in a practice session Oct. 19, sidelining him for the year. With castoff Doug Pederson and the 2000 Browns' sixth-round draft choice Spergon Wynn calling the signals the rest of the way, Cleveland lost eight of nine.

The Browns got off to a surprisingly fine start in 2001 behind a strong defensive effort. The Browns led the NFL in interceptions with 33. After a season-opening home loss to Seattle on a field goal by Rian Lindell with three seconds left, the team won three straight, including an upset in Jacksonville Sept. 30, the Browns' first-ever win over the Jaguars. Cleveland dropped to 4-4 via consecutive overtime losses to the Bears and Steelers. Although the Browns were underdogs in Chicago, they suffered an astonishing defeat considering that they were in complete control, 21-7, with 28 seconds left. The Bears pulled off a miracle with the help of a recovered onside kick, a Hail Mary touchdown with no time left, and an interception return off a batted pass for another touchdown that secured the sudden death win. The Browns rebounded big time with consecutive victories over Baltimore and Cincinnati. The win in Baltimore was the second Browns victory over the defending Super Bowl Champions that season. The 18-0 win over the visiting Bengals was the Browns' first shutout since Sept. 18, 1994.

The playoffs seemed a distinct possibility until the Browns incurred three straight losses, including a bizarre home defeat to Jacksonville Dec. 16 that put to rest any realistic hopes of postseason dreams. Enraged fans hurled thousands of plastic bottles onto the field due to a controversial call by officials toward the end of the game. The Browns avoided a season-ending five-game losing streak with a thrilling 41-38 comeback win at Tennessee in the second-to-last game. Couch passed for a career-high 336 yards and also three touchdowns against the Titans for the Browns' first win over the Titans since they relocated from Houston.

The season was somewhat marred by the first-ever cancellation of NFL games when all week two games were cancelled due to terrorist attacks on the United States. In the Browns' case, the cancelled game was their Sept. 16 nationally televised Sunday night affair in Pittsburgh. The matchup was eventually rescheduled for Jan. 6, 2002, the weekend the wild card games were supposed to have been played. Thus, the postseason was pushed back a week, causing the first-ever Super played in February. Cleveland's record in the 2000s is 10-22 (.313), with 6-10 (.375) at home and 4-12 (.250) on the road.

A

ABC TELEVISION NETWORK

The ABC television network broadcast the NFL's first game Sept. 21, 1970. The Browns won, 31-21, over the New York Jets in front of 85,703 fans in Cleveland Municipal Stadium. ABC has aired several other Browns prime time games since, including other Monday games and special edition Thursday and Sunday games.

ABRAHAM, ABE

Abe Abraham was the man in the brown suit who used to catch field goals and extra points at Browns home games. Born in Lebanon, he came to the United States at age three. He was working at the pass gate in week four of the 1946 season and went on the field to watch the action. He was hit by the ball and knocked down on a field goal by Lou Groza. From that point until he passed away in 1982, Abraham caught all field goals and extra points at the closed end of Cleveland Municipal Stadium.

ACCORSI, ERNIE

Ernie Accorsi was executive vice president of football operations for the Browns from 1985-91 after spending 1984 as the assistant to the president. He was instrumental in the Browns obtaining quarterback Bernie Kosar in the 1985 supplemental draft.

ADAMLE, TONY

Tony Adamle was a Browns linebacker from 1947-51 and in 1954. A product of Ohio State University, he was acquired by the Browns as a free agent. He had four interceptions for 42 return yards in 1949 and intercepted seven passes for 96 return yards in his Browns career. He was voted to All-NFL defensive teams in 1951 by NYN and UP and was selected to play in the Pro Bowl in 1950 and 1951.

Tony Adamle.

ALL-AAFC

Various news organizations voted on players for the All-AAFC, a "team" comprised of outstanding players from across the All-America Football Conference. The organizations that voted are denoted after the players' names. *Please see the abbreviations key.*

1946   Otto Graham (OFF, UP), Dante Lavelli (AP, OFF), Marion Motley (AP, NYN, OFF, UP), Lou Rymkus (SP), Mike Scarry (NYN), Mac Speedie (NYN, UP), Bill Willis (OFF, SP)

1947   Otto Graham (AP, C&O, NYN, OFF, SP), Dante Lavelli (OFF), Marion Motley (AP, C&O, NYN, OFF), Lou Rymkus (C&O, NYN, OFF, SP), Mike Scarry (C&O), Mac Speedie (AP, C&O, NYN, OFF, SP), Bill Willis (OFF)

1948   Otto Graham (AP, OFF, UP), Marion Motley (AP, NYN, OFF, SN), Lou Rymkus (AP, OFF, UP), Lou Saban (NYN, UP), Mac Speedie (AP, NYN, OFF, SN, UP), Bill Willis (AP, NYN, OFF, UP)

1949   Otto Graham (AP, NYN, OFF, UP), Marion Motley (NYN), Lou Rymkus (UP), Lou Saban (AP, NYN, OFF, UP), Mac Speedie (AP, NYN, OFF, UP); Offense: Otto Graham (INS), Lou Rymkus (INS), Mac Speedie (INS); Defense: Lou Saban (INS)

ALL-AMERICA FOOTBALL CONFERENCE

The All-America Football Conference was home to the Browns from 1946-49. It also originally consisted of the Chicago Rockets, Los Angeles Dons and San Francisco 49ers in the Western Division, and the Brooklyn Dodgers, Buffalo Bisons, Miami Seahawks, and New York Yankees in the Eastern Division. The conference had shrunk to seven teams in a one-division format by 1949. The championship was won all four years by the Browns, who compiled an overall record of 47-4-3 (.898) and 5-0 mark in the postseason.

AAFC WESTERN DIVISION

The AAFC Western Division was home to the Browns from 1946-48. It dissolved in 1949 along with the Eastern Division, as the All-America Football Conference would have no divisions in its final season of 1949. The Browns won the division all three years, finishing 12-2 (.857) in 1946, 12-1-1 (.893) in '47, and a perfect 14-0 in '48.

ALL-AFC

Various news organizations voted on players for the All-AFC, a "team" comprised of outstanding players from across the American Football Conference. The organizations that voted are denoted after the players' names. *Please see the abbreviations key.*

1970   Offense: Gene Hickerson (FWA, UPI)
1971   Offense: Leroy Kelly (NEA), Milt Morin (AP, UPI)
1972   Defense: Don Cockroft (NEA)
1973   Defense: Clarence Scott (UPI)
1975   Defense: Jerry Sherk (SN)

1976   Defense: Jerry Sherk (AP, NEA, PFW, FWA, SN, UPI)
1978   Offense: Keith Wright (PFW); Defense: Thom Darden (NEA, PFW, FWA, SN, UPI)
1979   Offense: Ozzie Newsome (FWA, SN, UPI), Mike Pruitt (PFW, SN, UPI); Defense: Lyle Alzado (PFW), Thom Darden (PFW)
1980   Offense: Joe DeLamielleure (PFW, FWA, SN, UPI), Brian Sipe (AP, NEA, PFW, FWA, SN, UPI); Defense: Lyle Alzado (AP, UPI)
1983   Offense: Cody Risien (UPI); Defense: Chip Banks (AP, PFW, FWA, UPI), Tom Cousineau (UPI)
1984   Offense: Ozzie Newsome (AP, NEA, PFW, FWA, SN, UPI); Defense: Tom Cousineau (UPI), Clay Matthews (NEA, PFW, SN)
1985   Defense: Chip Banks (UPI), Bob Golic (SN)
1986   Offense: Cody Risien (PFW); Defense:: Chip Banks (PFW, UPI), Hanford Dixon (AP, NEA, PFW, FWA, SN, UPI)
1987   Defense: Hanford Dixon (AP, NEA, PFW, FWA, SN, UPI), Frank Minnifield (PFW, FWA, SN, UPI)
1988   Defense: Frank Minnifield (AP, NEA, PFW, FWA, SN, UPI)
1989   Offense: Webster Slaughter (UPI); Defense: Mike Johnson (PFW, UPI), Frank Minnifield (UPI), Michael Dean Perry (AP, PFW, FWA, SN, UPI)
1990   Defense: Michael Dean Perry (AP, NEA, PFW, FWA, SN, UPI)
1991   Defense: Michael Dean Perry (PFW, SN)
1992   Defense: Michael Dean Perry (SN)
1993   Offense: Eric Metcalf (AP, PFW, SN, UPI); Defense: Michael Dean Perry (SN)
1994   Offense: Tony Jones (PFW), Eric Metcalf (SN); Defense: Michael Dean Perry (UPI), Eric Turner (AP, PFW, UPI)
2001   Defense: Jamir Miller (PFW)

ALL-NFL

Various news organizations voted on players for the All-NFL, a "team" comprised of outstanding players from across the National Football League. The organizations that voted are denoted after the players' names. *Please see the abbreviations key.*

1950   Offense: Marion Motley (AP, NYN, UP), Mac Speedie (NYN, UP), Bill Willis (UP); Defense: Bill Willis (NYN)
1951   Offense: Frank Gatski (NYN, UP), Otto Graham (AP, NYN, UP), Lou Groza (NYN, UP), Dub Jones (AP, NYN, UP), Dante Lavelli (NYN, UP); Defense: Tony Adamle (NYN, UP), Len Ford (AP, NYN, UP), Warren Lahr (NYN, UP), Bill Willis (AP, NYN, UP)
1952   Offense: Frank Gatski (AP, NYN), Otto Graham (NYN, UP), Lou Groza (AP, NYN, UP), Mac Speedie (UP); Defense: Len Ford (AP, NYN, UP), Bill Willis (AP, NYN)
1953   Offense: Frank Gatski (AP, NYN, UP), Abe Gibron (NYN), Otto Graham (AP, NYN, UP), Lou Groza (AP, NYN, UP), Dante Lavelli (NYN, UP); Defense: Len Ford (AP, NYN, UP), Ken Gorgal (NYN, UP), Tommy Thompson (AP, UP), Bill Willis (AP)

1954   Offense: Otto Graham (AP, NYN, SN, UP), Lou Groza (AP, NYN, SN, UP); Defense: Len Ford (AP, NYN, UP)

1955   Offense: Frank Gatski (AP, NYN, NEA, UP), Abe Gibron (NYN, NEA, UP), Otto Graham (AP, NYN, UP), Lou Groza (AP, NYN, NEA, UP), Mike McCormack (NYN); Defense: Don Colo (NEA, UP), Len Ford (NYN, NEA, UP), Don Paul (UP)

1957   Offense: Jim Brown (AP, NYN, NEA, UP), Lou Groza (NYN, UP), Mike McCormack (NEA); Defense: Don Colo (NYN, NEA)

1958   Offense: Jim Brown (AP, NYN, NEA, UPI); Defense: Bob Gain (NEA)

1959   Offense: Jim Brown (AP, NYN, NEA, UPI), Jim Ray Smith (AP, NYN, NEA, UPI); Defense: Walt Michaels (NYN)

1960   Offense: Jim Brown (AP, NYN, NEA, UPI), Jim Ray Smith (AP, NYN, NEA, UPI)

1961   Offense: Jim Brown (AP, NYN, NEA, UPI), Jim Ray Smith (AP, NYN, NEA, PFI, UPI)

1962   Offense: Jim Ray Smith (NEA)

1963   Offense: Jim Brown (AP, NYN, NEA, UPI), Dick Schafrath (AP)

1964   Offense: Jim Brown (AP, NYN, NEA, UPI), Dick Schafrath (AP, NYN, UPI), Paul Warfield (NEA); Defense: Jim Houston (NEA)

1965   Offense: Jim Brown (AP, NYN, NEA, UPI), Gary Collins (NYN, UPI), Dick Schafrath (AP, NYN, UPI); Defense: Jim Houston (UPI)

1966   Offense: Gene Hickerson (NEA), Leroy Kelly (AP, NYN, NEA, UPI), John Wooten (NYN)

1967   Offense: Gene Hickerson (AP, NYN, NEA, UPI), Leroy Kelly (AP, NYN, NEA, UPI)

1968   Offense: Gene Hickerson (AP, NYN, NEA, PFW, FWA, UPI), Leroy Kelly (AP, NYN, NEA, PFW, FWA, UPI), Paul Warfield (NEA, PFW, UPI)

1969   Offense: Gary Collins (AP, UPI), Gene Hickerson (AP, NYN, OFF, PFW, FWA, SI, UPI), Leroy Kelly (NEA), Paul Warfield (NEA, OFF, PFW, SI)

2001   Defense: Jamir Miller (AP, FD [first team], PFW, SI)

ALZADO, LYLE

Lyle Alzado was a Browns defensive end from 1979-81. He was a Yankton product acquired by Cleveland on Aug. 12, 1979, in a trade with the Denver Broncos for second- and fifth-round draft picks in 1980. He was voted to All-AFC defensive teams in 1979 by PFW and in '80 by AP and UPI.

Lyle Alzado

Dick Ambrose breaks up a pass headed for Pittsburgh's John Stallworth in the Browns'
15-9 overtime loss in Three Rivers Stadium Sept. 24, 1978. Photo courtesy of the
Cleveland Press Collection.

AMBROSE, DICK

Dick Ambrose was a Browns linebacker from 1975-83. He was the Browns' 12th-round draft choice in 1975 out of the University of Virginia.

AMERICAN CONFERENCE

The American Conference was the Browns' home from 1950-52. It changed names in 1953 when it became known as the Eastern Conference. It also consisted of the Chicago Cardinals, New York Giants, Philadelphia Eagles, Pittsburgh Steelers, and Washington Redskins. It was won all three years by the Browns, who finished 10-2 (.833) in 1950. The Browns tied with the Giants but won a playoff, 8-3, Dec. 17 in Cleveland. The Browns finished 11-1 (.917) in 1951, one-and-a-half games ahead of second-place New York, and 8-4 (.667) in 1952, one game ahead of the Giants and Eagles, both of whom wound up 7-5 (.583).

AMERICAN FOOTBALL CONFERENCE

The American Football Conference was the Browns' home from 1970-95, and has been since 1999. It was formed in 1970 when the NFL and AFL merged to become the 26-team National Football League [evening the NFL's two conferences-the American Football Conference and the National Football Conference-at 13 teams apiece (in 1969, there had been 16 teams in the NFL and 10 in the AFL]. The Browns have never won the championship. They have come close three times by advancing to the title game in 1986, 1987, and 1989. Each time, though, they lost to the Broncos—23-20 in overtime in 1986, 38-33 in 1987 and 37-21 in 1989.

ANDREWS, BILLY

Billy Andrews was a Browns linebacker from 1967-74. He was a 13th-round draft choice by the Browns in 1967 out of Southeastern Louisiana University. The highlight of his career was when he made a diving interception of a Joe Namath pass, got up and returned the ball 25 yards for a touchdown with 35 seconds left in the first-ever ABC *Monday Night Football* game Sept. 21, 1970, in Cleveland Municipal Stadium. Andrews' touchdown was the clincher in a 31-21 triumph.

ARIZONA CARDINALS

The Arizona Cardinals were opponents of the Browns in the NFL from 1950-95 and have been since 1999. The franchise was based in Chicago through 1959 and in St. Louis from 1960-87. One of the more memorable games against the Browns occurred Sept. 20, 1964, in Cleveland Municipal Stadium when the teams ended their matchup in a 33-33 tie. The Cardinals' all-time record against the Browns is 11-32-3 (.272) overall, with 5-18-1 (.229) at home and 6-14-2 (.318) on the road.

ASSISTANT COACHES

John Brickels, Blanton Collier, William (Red) Conkright, Fritz Heisler, and Bob Voigts were the first assistant coaches for the Browns. *Please see Coaches and Assistant Coaches on page 179 for a full list of assistant coaches.*

Jim Brown gains seven yards behind the blocking of Art Hunter (56) and Jim Ray Smith (64) against the St. Louis Cardinals (now Arizona Cardinals). Photo courtesy of the Cleveland Press Collection.

Head coach Paul Brown is flanked by members of his 1952 coaching staff (left to right): Howard Brinker, Blanton Collier, Weeb Eubanks, and Fritz Heisler. Photo courtesy of the Cleveland Browns.

ATLANTA FALCONS

The Atlanta Falcons were Browns opponents in the NFL from 1966-95 and have been since 1999. Their all-time record against Cleveland is 2-8 (.200) overall, with 1-4 (.200) at home and 1-4 (.200) on the road.

ATTENDANCE

The highest home attendance figure recorded was Sept. 21, 1970, when the Browns beat the Jets, 31-21, in front of a crowd of 85,703. The lowest home attendance figure recorded was the 16,506 fans who watched the Browns beat Chicago, 35-2, Nov. 6, 1949. *For more attendance statistics (both regular season and postseason), please see Attendance Statistics on page 181.*

AUGUST
—30, 1946

The Browns beat the Brooklyn Dodgers, 35-20, in the Rubber Bowl in Akron, Ohio, in their first-ever exhibition game. *Please see "Rubber Bowl."*

—9, 1999

The Browns defeated the Dallas Cowboys, 20-17, in overtime in Canton, Ohio, in the "new era" team's first preseason game.

AWARDS

Various news organizations voted on individual player awards. The organizations that voted are denoted after the players names. *Please see the abbreviations key.*

1947   Otto Graham (AAFC Most Valuable Player by OFF)
        Paul Brown (AAFC Coach of the Year by PFI)
1948   Otto Graham (AAFC Most Valuable Player by UP; AAFC co-Most Valuable Player with San Francisco quarterback Frankie Albert by OFF)
        Paul Brown (AAFC Coach of the Year by NYN)
1949   Otto Graham (AAFC Most Valuable Player by OFF)
        Paul Brown (AAFC Coach of the Year by NYN, SN)
1951   Paul Brown (NFL Coach of the Year by NYN)
1953   Otto Graham (NFL Most Valuable Player by UP)
        Paul Brown (NFL Coach of the Year by NYN)
1954   Lou Groza (NFL Most Valuable Player by SN)
        Paul Brown (NFL Coach of the Year by UP)
1955   Otto Graham (NFL Most Valuable Player by SN, UP)
1957   Jim Brown (NFL Player of the Year by AP; NFL Rookie of the Year by AP, UP)
        Paul Brown (NFL Coach of the Year by NYN, UP)
1958   Jim Brown (NFL Most Valuable Player by NEA, UPI)
1963   Jim Brown (NFL Most Valuable Player by MAX, UPI; co-Most Valuable Player with New York quarterback Y.A. Tittle by NEA)
1965   Jim Brown (NFL Player of the Year by AP; NFL Most Valuable Player by NEA, SN, UPI)
1968   Leroy Kelly (NFL Most Valuable Player by MAX)
1976   Jerry Sherk (NFL Defensive Player of the Year by NEA)
        Forrest Gregg (AFC Coach of the Year by AP)
1979   Sam Rutigliano (AFC Coach of the Year by UPI)
1980   Brian Sipe (NFL Most Valuable Player by FWA, SN; NFL Player of the Year by AP; NFL Offensive Player of the Year by PFW; AFC Most Valuable Player by UPI)
        Sam Rutigliano (AFC Coach of the Year by UPI)
1982   Chip Banks (NFL Defensive Rookie of the Year by AP, PFW)
1985   Kevin Mack (AFC Rookie of the Year by UPI)
1986   Marty Schottenheimer (AFC Coach of the Year by FWA, UPI)
1989   Michael Dean Perry (AFC Defensive Most Valuable Player by UPI)

BAAB, MIKE

Mike Baab was a center for the Browns from 1982-87, and in 1990 and 1991. He was a fifth-round draft choice of the Browns in 1982 out of the University of Texas. He was traded to New England Aug. 29, 1988, and then re-acquired as a free agent March 6, 1990.

BABICH, BOB

Bob Babich was a linebacker for the Browns from 1973-78. He was a Miami University product. He was acquired by the Browns Sept. 6, 1973, in a trade with the San Diego Chargers for a first-round draft choice in 1974 and second-round pick in 1975.

BAHR, MATT

Matt Bahr was a Browns kicker from 1981-89. He was a Penn State University product obtained by the Browns Oct. 6, 1981, in a trade with San Francisco for a 1983 draft choice. Bahr replaced Dave Jacobs, who had supplanted long-time kicker Don Cockroft. Jacobs was released after a terrible start. Bahr connected on 87.5 percent of his field goal attempts in 1983 (21-of-24 attempts). He scored 101 points (10th all-time for the Browns) that year. He tallied 104 points (ninth all-time in team history) in 1988.

Bahr ranks fourth all-time for the Browns with 677 points and second all-time in team history with 46 postseason points. He kicked a pair of 52-yard field goals—one in the

Billy Andrews greets Bob Babich as the defense comes off the field in 1973. Photo courtesy of the Cleveland Press Collection.

regular season and one in the postseason. The regular-season field goal came Oct. 26, 1986, in a win against Minnesota, and the postseason one occurred Jan. 8, 1983, in an AFC First-Round Playoff loss to the Raiders in Los Angeles.

Bahr was as tough as kickers come, as evidenced by his courage on Nov. 23, 1986, at home against Pittsburgh. He tore ligaments in his right knee while making a game-saving tackle off a return of his own kickoff with the Browns leading, 31-28. The Browns eventually won in overtime, 37-31.

BAKER, AL

Al Baker was a Browns defensive end in 1987, 1989 and 1990. He was a Colorado State University product obtained by Cleveland Sept. 3, 1987, in a trade with the St. Louis Cardinals for a fifth-round 1988 draft pick. The Browns waived him Aug. 29, 1988, before he returned as a free agent Mar. 31, 1989. Baker's 14.5 sacks rank ninth all-time for the Browns.

BALDWIN, RANDY

Randy Baldwin was a Browns running back from 1991-94. He was a University of Mississippi product. He was picked up by the Browns as a free agent Nov. 13, 1991. Baldwin was best known for his kickoff return duties, leading the Browns in kickoff returns and kickoff return yardage every season from 1992-94. He had an 85-yard kickoff return for a touchdown in a 28-20 opening-day victory over the Bengals in Cincinnati Sept. 4, 1994. That year, he totaled 753 return yards, which ranks 10th all-time for the Browns. His 1,872 kickoff return yards rank fourth in team history.

BALTIMORE COLTS (ORIGINAL)

The original Baltimore Colts were Browns opponents in the AAFC from 1947-49 and in the NFL in 1950. They were the forerunners of the Colts franchise that became quite successful in later years. Their all-time record against the Browns was 0-7, with 0-4 at home and 0-3 on the road.

BALTIMORE RAVENS

The Baltimore Ravens have been Browns opponents in the NFL since 1999. They were members of the AFC Central Division through 2001. The Ravens were the original Browns franchise before their relocation in 1996. The Ravens easily defeated the Browns in the four games in 1999 and 2000 before the Browns gained many measures of revenge with two upsets of the Ravens in 2001. Baltimore's record against Cleveland is 4-2 (.667) overall, with 2-1 (.667) at home and 2-1 (.667) on the road.

BANKS, CHIP

Chip Banks was a Browns linebacker from 1982-86. He was a Browns first-round draft choice in 1982 from the University of Southern California. He was second on the team with three interceptions in 1983, including a 65-yard return for a touchdown in a 30-0 victory Nov. 20 in New England in a crucial matchup of AFC wild card contenders. Banks led the Browns with 11 sacks in 1985, tying for fifth all-time for the Browns. His 28 sacks all-time rank seventh in team history. AP and PFW named him NFL Defensive Rookie of the Year in 1982. He was voted to All-AFC defensive teams in 1983 by AP, PFW, FWA and UPI, in 1985 by UPI; and in 1986 by PFW and UPI. He was voted to the Pro Bowl in 1982, 1983, 1985, and 1986.

BARNES, ERICH

Erich Barnes was a Browns defensive back from 1965-71. He was a product of Purdue University acquired by

Chip Banks. Photo courtesy of the Cleveland Browns.

Cleveland Aug. 30, 1965, in a trade with the New York Giants. The deal also included a trade to the Detroit Lions for Mike Lucci and a draft choice. On Oct. 1, 1967, against New Orleans, Barnes intercepted a pass and threw a lateral pass to Ross Fichtner, who raced 88 yards deep into Saints territory en route to a 42-7 rout for the Browns' first win of the year after two defeats. Barnes was the team leader with five interceptions in 1970, including a 38-yard return for a touchdown that sealed Cleveland's 15-7 victory over Pittsburgh Oct. 3 in Cleveland Municipal Stadium. He had 18 career interceptions with the Browns and was a Pro Bowl pick in 1968.

BELICHICK, BILL

Bill Belichick was the Browns' head coach from 1991-95. He took over a 3-13 (.188) team from 1990. He was previously the New York Giants' defensive coordinator the year before when the Giants won Super Bowl XXV. Belichick led the Browns to a 6-10 (.375) finish in 1991 and two 7-9 (.438) finishes in 1992 and 1993 before directing the team to a playoff berth in 1994 and a wild-card win over New England. He was fired following a 5-11 (.313) finish in 1995 when the franchise announced it would be relocating to Baltimore. Belichick's all-time record as Browns head coach was 36-44 (.450), with 20-20 at home and 16-24 (.400) on the road. His

Bill Belichick. Photo courtesy of the Cleveland Browns.

all-time postseason mark as Browns head coach with the team was 1-1, with 1-0 at home and 0-1 on the road.

BEREA

Berea is a small Ohio town near Cleveland that was the home of the Browns' training and administrative complex from 1991-95 and has been since 1999.

BERNIE, BERNIE

Bernie, Bernie is a song named after quarterback and hometown hero Bernie Kosar. It was popular during the Browns' playoff run in 1986.

BERNIE'S INSIDERS

Bernie's Insiders is a publication that has been around since 2001 and offers news, views, features, and many other things regarding the Browns.

BIG DAWG

Big Dawg is Browns fan John Thompson who attires himself in canine paraphernalia. This behavior stems from the enormous popularity of The Dawg Pound at old Cleveland Stadium. He became known nationwide. *See "Dawg Pound, The."*

BLOOM, TOM

Tom Bloom was a sixth-round draft choice of the Browns in 1963 out of Purdue University. He was the Boilermakers' Most Valuable Player as a running back in 1962. He was killed in an automobile accident soon after draft day while driving the car he had purchased with the bonus money received for signing with the Browns. He had hoped to win a spot in the defensive backfield.

BOLDEN, LEROY

Leroy Bolden was a Browns running back in 1958 and 1959. He was a sixth-round draft selection for the Browns in 1955 out of Michigan State University. Bolden spent 1956 and 1957 in the military. In addition to playing running back, he also returned kickoffs, including a 102-yarder for a touchdown Oct. 26, 1958, in a 38-24 victory over the Chicago Cardinals.

BOLDEN, RICKEY

Rickey Bolden was a Browns offensive tackle from 1984-89 and a fourth-round draft choice by the Browns in 1984 out of Southern Methodist University.

Leroy Bolden fumbles in preseason action in Detroit against the Lions on Aug. 22, 1958. Photo courtesy of the Cleveland Press Collection.

BOLTON, RON

Ron Bolton was a Browns defensive back from 1976-82 and a Norfolk State University product. Cleveland acquired him on April 8, 1976, in a trade with the Patriots for Bob McKay. He intercepted 17 passes in his career. One of his most memorable occurred in an AFC divisional playoff on Jan. 4, 1981, when he returned a Jim Plunkett pass 42 yards for a touchdown. This gave the Browns a 6-0 second-quarter lead on the frozen field of Cleveland Stadium, but the Browns eventually lost, 14-12.

Ron Bolton. Photo courtesy of the Cleveland Browns.

BOTTLEGATE

"Bottlegate" was a bizarre incident that occurred Dec. 16, 2001, toward the end of the Browns' 15-10 loss to Jacksonville in Cleveland Browns Stadium. Angry fans threw thousands of plastic bottles from the stands, littering large parts of both end zones in response to the following scenario: with the Browns, trailing by five and still in playoff contention, deep in Jaguars territory late in the game, quarterback Tim Couch passed to Quincy Morgan.

The rookie wide receiver was hit by safety James Boyd and struggled to hold onto the ball. After making an apparent catch, Morgan lost the ball temporarily when he hit the ground but recovered his own fumble, which would have made it a catch and given the Browns a first down. That would have given them time for four attempts to get into the end zone. Couch quickly spiked the ball to stop the clock, which by rule ends the option for an instant replay challenge. Referee Terry McAulay, though, ruled the replay buzzer on his belt went off prior to the snap.

Jacksonville's request for a review was honored, and the ruling of a completion was overturned, causing the bottle-throwing escapade. Due to the danger of this, McAulay ruled the game over and ordered both teams to their respective locker rooms with 48 seconds still left on the clock. Nearly 30 minutes later, however, both sides returned to the field for one more snap to officially complete the game, via orders from NFL commissioner Paul Tagliabue.

BOUSMA, BOB

Bob Bousma was a Browns radio broadcaster in 1952 and 1953.

BOWLING GREEN STATE UNIVERSITY

Bowling Green State University acted as the Browns' training-camp site from 1946-51. The Browns drafted nine players from the university over the years.

BRADLEY, HENRY

Henry Bradley was a Browns defensive tackle from 1979-82. He was an Alcorn State University product acquired by Cleveland as a free agent in July 1979. He was released on Aug. 27, 1979, and re-signed in November of that year when Jerry Sherk went down with a staph infection.

BRANDON, DAVID

David Brandon was a Browns linebacker from 1991-93. A Memphis State University product, he was acquired in 1991 by the Browns as a free agent. Brandon was second on the Browns in interceptions in 1991 and 1992. Two were returned for touchdowns—a 30-yarder in overtime that gave the Browns a 30-24 win in San Diego on Oct. 20, 1991, and a 92-yarder on the Bears' opening drive that fueled the Browns' 27-14 home victory on Nov. 29, 1992.

BRENNAN, BRIAN

Brian Brennan was a Browns wide receiver from 1984-91. He was a fourth-round draft selection of the Browns in 1984 out of Boston College. His most productive season was 1986, when he led the team with 55 receptions and 838 receiving yards, and had six touchdown catches. He had 315 receptions (sixth all-time for the Browns) for 4,148 yards and 19 touchdowns in his Browns career. Quite possibly, Brennan's most memorable moment came against Denver in the AFC Championship game on Jan. 11, 1987, when he was on the receiving end of a 48-yard touchdown pass from Bernie Kosar that gave the

Browns a 20-13 lead with 5:43 left in the game. The Browns eventually lost, 23-20, in double overtime. His 12 points in the Browns' AFC title game loss in Denver on Jan. 14, 1990, are tied for fourth most all-time in team postseason history. Six of those points came on a spectacular, diving 10-yard pass from Kosar. Brennan also returned punts, and ranks 10th all-time for the Browns with 435 return yards, including a 37-yarder for a touchdown against the Jets on Dec. 22, 1985.

Brian Brennan. Photo courtesy of the Cleveland Browns.

BREWER, JOHNNY

Johnny Brewer was a tight end/linebacker for the Browns from 1961-67. He was a fourth-round draft choice of the Browns in 1960 out of the University of Mississippi with one year of college eligibility remaining. He returned an interception 70 yards for a touchdown in a 42-37 home victory over Washington on Nov. 26, 1967. He was selected to play in the Pro Bowl in 1966.

BREWSTER, DARREL

Darrel Brewster was a Browns wide receiver from 1952-58. He was a Purdue University product acquired by the team on July 12, 1952, in a trade with the Chicago Cardinals for Burl Toler. Brewster was the team leader in receptions and receiving yards every season from 1955-57. He was second on the team in touchdown receptions in 1954 and 1955. His 183 yards receiving on Dec. 6, 1953, against the New York Giants rank seventh all-time in team history. He was a Pro Bowl pick in 1955 and 1956.

BROADCASTS, RADIO

The following are the Browns' radio broadcasters and the flagship stations Browns games have been broadcast on:

1946	Bob Neal and Stan Gee (WGAR-AM 1220)
1947-49	Bob Neal and Bill Mayer (WGAR-AM 1220)
1950	Bob Neal and Don Cordray (WERE-AM 1300)
1951	Bob Neal and Phil McLean (WERE-AM 1300)
1952-53	Ken Coleman and Bob Bousma (WTAM-AM 1100)
1954	Bill McColgan and Bill Mayer (WGAR-AM 1220)
1955	Bill McColgan and Jim Graner (WTAM-AM 1100)
1956-60	Bill McColgan and Jim Graner (WGAR-AM 1220)
1961	Gib Shanley and Les Clark (WGAR-AM 1220)
1962	Gib Shanley and Ray Tannehill (WERE-AM 1300)

1963-67   Gib Shanley and Jim Graner (WERE-AM 1300)
1968-74   Gib Shanley and Jim Graner (WHK-AM 1420)
1975-84   Gib Shanley and Jim Mueller (WHK-AM 1420)
1985   Nev Chandler, Doug Dieken, and Jim Mueller (WHK-AM 1420)
1986-89   Nev Chandler, Doug Dieken, and Jim Mueller (WWWE-AM 1100,
            WDOK-FM 102.1)
1990-93   Nev Chandler, Doug Dieken, and Jim Mueller (WHK-AM 1420,
            WMMS-FM 100.7)
1994-95   Casey Coleman, Doug Dieken, and Jim Mueller (WKNR-AM 1220,
            WDOK-FM 102.1)
1999-2001   Jim Donovan and Doug Dieken (WMJI-FM 105.7, WTAM-AM 1100)

BROADCASTS, TELEVISION

The following are the Browns' television broadcasters and the network/stations Browns road games have been broadcast on:

1948   Bob Neal and Stan Gee (Dumont Network)
1949-51   Bob Neal and Bill Mayer (Dumont Network)
1952   Don Wattrick and Lou Saban (WXEL-Channel 9)
1953   Bill McColgan and John Fitzgerald (WXEL-Channel 9)
1954-55   Ken Coleman (WJW-Channel 8)
1956   Ken Coleman and Otto Graham (WJW-Channel 8)
1957-60   Ken Coleman and Jimmy Dudley (WJW-Channel 8)
1961-62   Ken Coleman and Cliff Lewis (WJW-Channel 8)
1963-65   Ken Coleman and Warren Lahr (WJW-Channel 8)
1966-67   Frank Glieber and Warren Lahr (WJW-Channel 8)

In 1968, CBS began broadcasting NFL games on a regional and national basis, until it lost its NFL package in 1994 to FOX. FOX, like CBS from 1970-93, broadcast Browns Sunday afternoon home games when their opponent was an NFC team. From 1970-95, NBC beamed Browns games on Sunday afternoon and selected Saturday afternoon and Thanksgiving games, when they were on the road or at home against a fellow AFC team. ABC started with its *Monday Night Football* package in 1970 with the very first game in Cleveland against Joe Namath and the New York Jets on Sept. 21. The *Monday Night Football* package also included special edition games on other nights, of which the Browns appeared on Thursday and Sunday. ESPN joined the fray in 1987 with a Sunday night package on which the Browns have appeared, including special edition games on Thursday and Saturday.

BROOKLYN DODGERS

The Brooklyn Dodgers were Browns opponents in the AAFC from 1946-48. They were blown out at home by the Browns, 66-14, on Dec. 8, 1946, the largest point total ever for the Browns. The Dodgers were the Browns' first-ever exhibition opponents, when on

Aug. 30, 1946, they lost to Cleveland, 35-20, in the Rubber Bowl in Akron, Ohio. The Dodgers merged with the New York Yankees following the 1948 season. Brooklyn's all-time record against the Browns was 0-6. Their home record was 0-3, and their road record was 0-3.

BROOKLYN–NEW YORK YANKEES

The Brooklyn-New York Yankees were opponents of the Browns in the AAFC in 1949. The team was the result of a merger by the New York Yankees and the Brooklyn Dodgers of the AAFC. Their all-time record against Cleveland was 0-2, 0-1 at home and 0-1 on the road.

BROWN BLUES, THE

The Brown Blues was a half-hour program hosted by Jerry Sherk and Brian Sipe that originally aired on WKYC TV-3 in 1996, not long after the final game in Cleveland Stadium. The show was a retrospective about the two ex-Browns' days with the team in the Stadium.

BROWN, COURTNEY

Courtney Brown has been a defensive end for Cleveland since 1999. He was a first-round draft choice of the Browns in 2000 out of Penn State University. He was the first overall selection in the draft. Brown returned a fumble 25 yards for a touchdown in a 27-21 overtime defeat in Chicago on Nov. 4, 2001.

BROWN, JIM

Jim Brown was a Cleveland running back from 1957-65. He was a first-round draft choice of the Browns in 1957 out of Syracuse University. He rushed for 942 yards his rookie year while leading the Browns back to the NFL title game after their first losing season ever the year before. Included was his first 100-yard game when he gained 109 in a 21-17 victory over Washington on Nov. 3 in Cleveland Municipal Stadium, a game in which he also scored two touchdowns rushing. Three weeks later, he set an NFL record that was not broken until 14 years later, when he rushed for 237 yards in a 45-31 triumph over Los Angeles at home. He rushed for four touchdowns in that game, including an early 69-yarder.

Brown rushed for 1,527 yards in 1958, including nine 100-yard games, in leading the Browns to an Eastern Conference Playoff against the New York Giants. He rushed for 1,329 yards in 1959, including five rushing touchdowns that helped the Browns to a 38-31 victory at Baltimore on Nov. 1. He rushed for 1,257 yards in 1960, including a 71-yard touchdown run against the Eagles on Nov. 23. He gained 1,403 yards in 1961 and matched his 237-yard performance from four years earlier when he did it on Nov. 19 in a 45-24 home win over Philadelphia, a game in which he scored four touchdowns rushing.

Brown had a "down" year in 1962 when he gained "just" 996 yards on the ground, the only year he failed to lead the league. He rebounded big time in 1963 under a more

Jim Brown gains five yards to the Steelers' 38-yard line in 1960. Photo courtesy of the Cleveland Press Collection.

wide-open offense with new head coach Blanton Collier, scorching opposing defenses for 1,863 yards—an NFL record until O.J. Simpson broke it 10 years later. In the season opener at home against Washington on Sept. 15, Brown had quite a day, scoring on an 83-yard play off a short pass from Frank Ryan, a 10-yard run, and an 80-yard run en route to a 37-14 victory. One week later on Sept. 22, Brown scored on a 71-yard run in a victory over the Cowboys in Dallas.

A year later, on Oct. 18, 1964, he had another 71-yard run in another victory over the Cowboys in Dallas. That year, he gained 1,446 yards and in 1965 he gained 1,544 in leading the Browns to consecutive NFL title-game appearances, the first of which they won (defeating the Colts in '64).

Brown retired in the summer of 1966 to pursue an acting career in the movies. All seven of his 1,000-yard rushing seasons rank in the top eight all-time in Browns history. He was the team leader in rushing yards every year and rushed for a team record 12,312 yards overall, an astonishing 5.2-yards per game average, also a team record. He averaged a remarkable 104.3 yards per game. He scored 106 rushing touchdowns, another team mark. He also holds four of the top five, and five of the top 10 spots in team history for most rushing yards in one game (the two 237-yard performances are Nos. 1 and 2). He also had 262 receptions for 2,499 yards and 20 touchdown catches in his career. His 756 points are third all-time in team history, and his 15,459 combined net yards rank first all-time (######) in team history.

In addition, Brown holds five of the top nine spots in Browns history for most combined net yards in one season, including the No. 1 spot with 2,131 in 1963. He holds three of the top eight positions for most points scored in team history, including the No. 1 spot (126 in 1965). His 114 rushing yards in the Browns' 27-0 victory over Baltimore in the 1964 NFL Championship game rank as the fourth most in team history.

Brown's awards include: NFL Player of the Year in 1957 (AP), NFL Rookie of the Year in 1957 (AP, UP), NFL Most Valuable Player in 1958 (NEA, UPI), NFL Most Valuable Player in 1963 (MAX, UPI) NFL co-Most Valuable Player with New York Giants quarterback Y.A. Tittle in 1963 (NEA), NFL Player of the Year in 1965 (AP), NFL Most Valuable Player in 1965 (NEA, SN, and UPI). Brown was named to All-NFL offensive teams in 1957 (AP, NYN, NEA, and UP) and from 1958-61 and 1963-65 (AP, NYN, NEA, and UPI). He was a Pro Bowl pick from 1957-65. His uniform No. 32 is retired by the Browns. He was inducted into the Pro Football Hall of Fame in 1971.

Jim Brown in action against the Cowboys in 1964. Photo courtesy of the Cleveland Press Collection.

BROWN, ORLANDO

Orlando Brown was an offensive tackle with the Browns in 1994, 1995, and 1999. He was a South Carolina State University product acquired by the Browns as a free agent on May 13, 1993. He spent the 1993 season on injured reserve with a shoulder problem. He signed with Cleveland as a free agent again on Feb. 28, 1994, again on July 19, 1995, and finally on Feb. 17, 1999.

He was the center attraction in one of the more unusual plays in NFL history when he was hit in his open right eye with a penalty flag thrown by referee Jeff Triplett. This happened during the second quarter of a home game against Jacksonville on Dec. 19 in the second-to-last game of the season. After much confusion as to whether or not Brown should have left the game for a play, he returned to the field and shoved Triplett to the ground. He was kicked out of the game and suspended indefinitely by the NFL.

The suspension eventually was shortened to one game—that year's season finale. Brown's eye suffered direct trauma that affected his vision and could develop into glaucoma. He never played again and was cut by the Browns in Sept. 2000. At the time, he had a six-year, $27 million contract from which he collected a $7.5 million signing bonus. Brown filed a $200 million lawsuit against the NFL. U.S. District Judge Gerard E. Lynch ruled on Mar. 18, 2002, that the NFL could not force the lawsuit into arbitration by saying that a union contract governs a player's claim that his career was ruined. The case was moved from federal to state court and is still pending.

BROWN, PAUL

Paul Brown was Cleveland's first head coach. He held the position from 1946-62. His surname is the reason behind the team's nickname, and he is the only pro football coach for whom a team has been named. Brown led Cleveland to four straight championships in the AAFC from 1946-49 and six straight title-game appearances in the NFL from 1950-55, three of which his team won (1950, 1954, and 1955).

He was an innovator when it came to the game of football, as he was the first head coach to hire a full-time coaching staff, utilize classroom study to such a broad extent, use intelligence tests, grade his players from individual film clips, and develop a messenger-guard system so he could call plays from the sideline. Brown had much to do in inventing, or improving, plays such as the screen pass, draw play, and trap plays. He also invented the first single-bar facemask.

His days as head football coach and athletic officer at the Great Lakes Naval Training Center had much to do with his firing by Browns majority owner Art Modell on Jan. 9, 1963. Toward the end of his reign as head coach, many players were growing tired of his military-like approach to dealing with them. They also believed the game was passing him by, that his play-calling had become too conservative for the changing times. He was constantly in disagreement with Modell over how the team should be run.

Brown was voted AAFC Coach of the Year in 1947 (PFI), in 1948 (NYN), and in 1949 (NYN and SN). He won NFL Coach of the Year honors in 1951 and 1953 (NYN), in 1954 (UP), and in 1957 (NYN and UP). He was inducted into the Pro Football Hall of Fame in 1967, two months before he and his family were awarded an AFL franchise that would turn out to be the Cincinnati Bengals. (The Bengals would later become bitter rivals of the Browns in the NFL.) Brown's all-time record as Browns head coach was 158-48-8 (.757). That includes 81-24-2 (.766) at home and 77-24-6 (.748) on the road. His all-time postseason record as Browns head coach was 9-5 (.643), with 7-1 (.875) at home and 2-4 (.333) on the road.

Paul Brown (left) and Lou Groza. Photo courtesy of the Cleveland Press Collection.

*The Brownie Elf.
Photo courtesy of
the Cleveland
Press Collection.*

BROWNIE ELF

The Brownie Elf was a character used to represent the Browns that surfaced in advertisements, game programs, and on the back of players' parkas, among other places.

BROWNS BACKERS WORLDWIDE

Browns Backers Worldwide is the official Browns fan club that surfaced in Mar. 1984. It is the largest organized fan club in professional sports, some say. There are 258 clubs throughout the world with more than 20,000 members. Browns Backers Worldwide grew with the help of *Browns News/Illustrated*, a publication that received letters from transplanted Browns fans throughout the country requesting other Browns fans in their locales to contact them.

BROWNS NEWS/ILLUSTRATED

Browns News/Illustrated was a publication that lasted from 1981-2001 and offered news, views, features, and many other things concerning the Browns.

BUFFALO BILLS (CURRENT)

The Buffalo Bills were opponents of the Browns in the NFL from 1970-95 and have been since 1999. The most memorable game between the two teams occurred in the postseason, when on Jan. 6, 1990, the Browns won a 34-30 barnburner in an AFC divisional playoff in Cleveland Stadium. Buffalo's all-time record against Cleveland is 4-7 (.364), with 1-3 (.250) at home and 3-4 (.429) on the road. The Bills' all-time postseason record against Cleveland is 0-1 (home).

BUFFALO BISONS/BILLS (ORIGINAL)

The original Buffalo Bisons/Bills were Browns opponents in the AAFC from 1946-49. The team's nickname was changed from "Bisons" to "Bills" (no relation to the current Buffalo Bills) in 1947. They lost both postseason matchups in Cleveland—49-7 in the AAFC Championship game on Dec. 19, 1948, and 31-21 in an AAFC First-Round Play-off on Dec. 4, 1949. Their all-time record against the Browns was 0-6-2 (.125), with 0-3-1 (.125) at home and 0-3-1 (.125) on the road. Buffalo's all-time postseason record against Cleveland was 0-2 (home).

BURNETT, ROB

Rob Burnett was a defensive end for the Browns from 1990-95. He was a fifth-round draft choice of the Browns in 1990 out of Syracuse University. He had a team-high 10 sacks in 1994, ranking seventh in team history for most in one season. He had nine sacks in both 1992 and 1993, the former tying Clay Matthews for the team lead and the latter leading the team. Both totals are tied with Matthews's 1992 total for eighth most in one season in team history. Burnett's 40.5 sacks all-time are third most in Browns history. He was a Pro Bowl pick in 1994.

BURRELL, CLINTON

Clinton Burrell was a Browns defensive back from 1979-84. He was a sixth-round draft choice of the Browns in 1979 out of Louisiana State University. He was second on the team with five interceptions in 1980. He returned a Ken Anderson pass 14 yards for the Browns' only touchdown in a 23-10 defeat to the Bengals on Dec. 12, 1982, in Cincinnati.

Clinton Burrell sends Buffalo's Dan Fulton (a future teammate of Burrell's with the Browns) to the ground during a scrimmage in 1979. Photo courtesy of the Cleveland Press Collection.

BYNER, EARNEST

Earnest Byner was a Browns running back from 1984-88 and in 1994 and 1995. He was a 10th-round draft choice by the Browns in 1984 out of East Carolina University. He was part of one of the worst trades in franchise history when he was shipped to Washington for Mike Oliphant on draft day 1989. Byner went on to lead the Redskins in rushing yards for three straight years, including two 1,000-yard seasons and a 998-yard season, respectively, and helped them to the 1991 NFL Championship. Meanwhile, Oliphant gained 188 combined net yards in three seasons with the Browns, with all of the yardage coming in 1989. Byner was re-acquired by the Browns on May 5, 1994, as a free agent.

One highlight of Byner's rookie year occurred on Nov. 4, 1984, when he recovered a fumble and raced 55 yards for a touchdown in a 13-10 victory at Buffalo. Another highlight happened on Dec. 16 when he rushed for 188 yards (tied for eighth in Browns history) in a 27-20 triumph at Houston in the season finale.

In 1985, Byner became part of only the third running-back tandem in NFL history in which both backs rushed for 1,000 yards in the same season. (He totaled 1,002, while Kevin Mack had 1,104.) He set a Browns record for most rushing yards in a postseason game, with 161 in an AFC divisional playoff loss in Miami on Jan. 4, 1986. He

Earnest Byner. Photo courtesy of the Cleveland Browns.

also holds the No. 3 spot in the same category with his 122-yard performance against the Colts on Jan. 9, 1988.

Byner was injured for most of the 1986 season. His crucial fumble in the 1987 AFC Championship game in Denver will always offset his titanic performance leading up to it, including the fourth-highest receiving yardage total (120) in one playoff game (####) in team history. His seven catches in the Broncos game are tied for second in team history (#####). He is seventh on the Browns' all-time rushing yardage list with 3,364 and 10th on the team's all-time combined net yardage list with 6,564 (######). His 36 postseason points are tied with Otto Graham for third all-time in team history. He ranks second all-time for the Browns with 480 postseason rushing yards (#) and is tied for fourth in team history for most points scored in a postseason game with 12, doing it three times.

C

CAMP, REGGIE

Reggie Camp was a Browns defensive end from 1983-87. He was a third-round draft choice of the Browns in 1983 out of the University of California, Berkeley. He had 14 sacks in 1984, a Browns record. Camp's 35.5 sacks all-time rank fifth in team history.

CAROLINA PANTHERS

The Carolina Panthers were opponents of the Browns in the NFL in 1995 and have been since 1999. Their all-time record against the Browns is 1-0 (away).

Ken Carpenter. Photo courtesy of the Cleveland Browns.

CARPENTER, KEN

Ken Carpenter was a Browns running back from 1950-53. He was a first-round draft choice of Cleveland's in 1950 out of Oregon State University. He was picked for the Pro Bowl in 1951.

CARSON, BUD

Bud Carson was the Browns' head coach in 1989 and 1990. He was fired after nine games in 1990. He coached the Browns to an appearance in the 1989 AFC Championship game. His all-time record as Browns head coach was 11-13-1 (.460), with a record of 6-5-1 (.542) at home and 5-8 (.385) on the road. His all-time postseason record with Cleveland was 1-1, 1-0 at home and 0-1 on the road.

CBS TELEVISION NETWORK

The CBS television network broadcast Browns games in 1968 and 1969, and Sunday afternoon home games when their opponent was an NFC team from 1970-93.

CENTRAL DIVISION

The Central Division was Cleveland's home from 1970-99 and 1999-2001. The division was formed in 1970 when the NFL and AFL merged to become one National Football League consisting of 26 teams. The Central Division was one of three divisions in the AFC that consisted of the Cincinnati Bengals, Houston Oilers, and Pittsburgh Steelers from its inception through 1994. It was joined in 1995 by the expansion Jacksonville Jaguars and in 1996 by the Baltimore Ravens (former relocated Browns team). Houston relocated to Tennessee in 1997 and became known as the Titans in 1999. The Browns won six times–in 1971, 1980, from 1985-87, and in 1989.

CENTURY DIVISION

The Century Division was home to the Browns from 1967-69. It was formed in 1967 when the NFL's Eastern Conference split into two divisions (the other was the Capitol). It lasted through 1969 as the NFL merged with the AFL the following season. The Century was won by the Browns all three years. They finished 9-5 (.643), 10-4 (.714), and 10-3-1 (.750), respectively. The division was also made up of the New York Giants, Pittsburgh Steelers, and St. Louis Cardinals in 1967 and 1969, and New Orleans Saints, Pittsburgh, and St. Louis in 1968.

CHANDLER, NEV

Nev Chandler was a Browns radio broadcaster from 1985-93.

CHICAGO BEARS

The Chicago Bears were opponents of the Browns in the NFL from 1950-95 and have been since 1999. Four of the more memorable games between the two teams occurred on Nov. 25, 1951, Sept. 7, 1986, Oct. 23, 1989, and Nov. 4, 2001. The Browns won the 1951 game in Cleveland, 42-21, as Dub Jones set a Cleveland record, and tied an NFL mark, by scoring six touchdowns. NFL single-game records were set that day for most penalties against both teams (37) and most yards penalized against both teams (374). Several players had to be helped off the field, and Browns quarterback Otto Graham suffered a broken nose.

The Bears escaped the 1986 game in Chicago with a wild 41-31 victory in a contest that left the Browns looking like a MASH unit. The game also marked the first time in NFL history a team had a play reviewed by instant replay when, on the third play of the game, Al Gross appeared to recover an errant Chicago snap in the Bears' end zone. The debate was whether Gross gained possession of the ball before sliding across the end line. After a review, referees ruled that Gross did indeed gain possession of the ball in time for a touchdown and a 7-0 Browns lead.

The Browns won the 1989 game, 27-7, in Cleveland on *Monday Night Football,* as they shook off recent offensive doldrums. The key play was a 97-yard touchdown strike from Bernie Kosar to Webster Slaughter, the second-longest pass play in team history. The Bears won the 2001 game, 27-21, in overtime in Chicago in miracle fashion. The Bears trailed, 21-7, but scored a touchdown, recovered an onside kick, and scored another touchdown (on a Hail Mary play) in the final 28 seconds of regulation before Mike Brown returned a batted interception of a Tim Couch pass 16 yards for the winning score on Cleveland's third play from scrimmage in overtime. Chicago's all-time record against Cleveland is 4-8 (.667), with 3-2 (.600) at home and 1-6 (.143) on the road.

CHICAGO ROCKETS

The Chicago Rockets were opponents of the Browns in the AAFC from 1946-49. Their all-time record against the Browns was 0-8, with 0-4 at home and 0-4 on the road.

CINCINNATI BENGALS

The Cincinnati Bengals were Browns opponents in the NFL from 1970-95 and have been since 1999. The Bengals were rivals of the Browns in the AFC Central Division from 1970-95 and 1999-2001. The "Interstate 71" rivalry was fueled by bad blood between former Browns head coach Paul Brown and majority owner Art Modell. Brown was fired by Modell on Jan. 9, 1963, after 17 years as head coach of the Browns. With Brown now head coach the Bengals, Cincinnati lost its first meeting with the Browns, 30-27, on Oct. 11, 1970, in Cleveland. The Bengals beat the Browns for the first time, 14-10, in Cincinnati on Nov. 15 of the same season.

Another memorable Browns win against the Bengals came on Nov. 23, 1975, in Cleveland, a game the Bengals entered with an 8-1 record to the Browns' 0-9 mark. The Browns upset the Bengals, 35-23.

The Bengals administered a 10-7 setback to the Browns on Nov. 6, 1977, in Cleveland that brought the first-place Browns back to earth and headed them towards their final destination of the basement of the AFC Central Division.

The Bengals beat the Browns, 12-9, on Oct. 21, 1984, in Cincinnati on a last-second field goal in a battle of 1-6 teams that cost Browns head coach Sam Rutigliano his job.

The Browns annihilated Cincinnati, 34-3, on Dec. 14, 1986, in Cincinnati, a

Browns head coach Blanton Collier (left) shakes hands with his former mentor and the man he replaced seven years earlier, Cincinnati Bengals head coach Paul Brown, prior to the start of the first meeting between the Browns and the Bengals on Oct. 11, 1970. Photo courtesy of the Cleveland Press Collection.

game in which the Bengals were favored despite a 9-5 (.643) record to the Browns' 10-4 (.714) mark. The Bengals' loss that afternoon not only gave the Browns the AFC Central Division title but also ultimately kept them from qualifying for the postseason.

The Bengals won, 23-21, on Nov. 3, 1991, in Cincinnati in a game in which the Browns handed them their first win of the year in nine games, wasting numerous scoring opportunities and committing mistakes galore, the last of which was Matt Stover's 34-yard field goal try that was blocked as time expired.

In the 1994 season opener on Sept. 4 in Cincinnati, Randy Baldwin and Eric Metcalf led the way to a 28-20 victory over the Bengals with some second-quarter magic. Baldwin returned a kickoff 85 yards for a touchdown, and some three minutes later Metcalf raced 92 yards for a score off a punt return. It was the first time the Browns had both a kickoff return and punt return for touchdowns in the same game

Greg Pruitt tries to elude a Bengals defender on Oct. 13, 1974. Photo courtesy of the Cleveland Press Collection.

Mike Phipps is surrounded by fans after the Browns' shocking 35-23 victory at home over the Bengals on Nov. 23, 1975. Photo courtesy of the Cleveland Press Collection.

since Bobby Mitchell had one of each in a victory over the Eagles on Nov. 23, 1958. It was the first time any team accomplished the feat since the Lions' Eddie Payton did both against the Vikings on Dec. 17, 1977 (ironically, Payton had played for the Browns earlier that year).

The Bengals lost to the Browns, 26-10, on Dec. 17, 1995, in the final game in Cleveland Stadium on a day where emotions on and off the field ran high on the Browns' side, due to the fact that many believed it to be the final home game in franchise history because of the Browns'; impending move to Baltimore.

One remarkable aspect of the rivalry is that the wins and losses are so close. Cincinnati leads in scoring by just two points, 1,158-1,156. The Bengals' all-time record against the Browns is 28-29 (.491), with 18-11 (.621) at home and 10-18 (.357) on the road.

CLARK, LES

Les Clark was a Browns radio broadcaster in 1961.

CLARK, MONTE

Monte Clark was a Browns offensive tackle from 1963-69. He was a University of Southern California product acquired by the Browns on April 30, 1963, in a trade with Dallas for Jim Ray Smith.

CLEVELAND BROWNS FOUNDATION

The Cleveland Browns Foundation has existed since 1998. It was founded by Browns majority owner Al Lerner. It supports the local community by giving money to programs that better the lives of those at risk, mainly children, in Northeast Ohio.

CLEVELAND BROWNS STADIUM

Cleveland Browns Stadium has been home to the Browns since 1999. It was built on the site of old Cleveland Stadium. It has a seating capacity of more than 73,200.

CLEVELAND BROWNS TRUST

The Cleveland Browns Trust kept the Browns organization afloat during the three seasons absent of Browns football from 1996-98. It originated on July 1, 1996, and undertook numerous tasks, including helping plan Cleveland Browns Stadium, organizing alumni events, and producing television and radio programs. Its president was Bill Futterer.

Monte Clark. Photo courtesy of the Cleveland Press Collection.

CLEVELAND INDIANS

The Cleveland Indians were the Major League Baseball team that shared the use of Cleveland Municipal/Cleveland Stadium with the Browns from 1947-95.

CLEVELAND MUNICIPAL/CLEVELAND STADIUM

Cleveland Municipal/Cleveland Stadium was home to the Browns from 1946-95. Its name changed from "Cleveland Municipal Stadium" to "Cleveland Stadium" in 1978. Its seating capacity was exactly 80,000 in 1946. The seating capacity then fluctuated for years before reaching a high of 80,385 from 1978-80. In 1995, the Browns' final season there, capacity was 78,512.

CLEVELAND MUNICIPAL/CLEVELAND STADIUM
SEATING CAPACITIES

1946	80,000
1947	77,563
1948-51	77,707
1952-61	78,207
1962-64	78,166

The bright lights of Cleveland Municipal Stadium shine down on action on the field in 1951. Photo courtesy of the Cleveland Press Collection.

1965	77,096
1966	77,124
1967-74	79,282
1975-76	80,165
1977	80,233
1978-80	80,385
1981-82	80,322
1983-91	80,098
1992-95	78,512
1999	72,500
2000-01	73,200

COACH OF THE YEAR

Various news organizations voted for Coach of the Year designations. Those organizations that voted are denoted after the coach's names. *Please see the abbreviations key.*

1947	Paul Brown (AAFC by PFI)
1948	Paul Brown (AAFC by NYN)
1949	Paul Brown (AAFC by NYN, SN)
1951	Paul Brown (NFL by NYN)
1953	Paul Brown (NFL by NYN)
1954	Paul Brown (NFL by UP)
1957	Paul Brown (NFL by NYN, UP)
1976	Forrest Gregg (AFC by AP)
1979	Sam Rutigliano (AFC by UPI)
1980	Sam Rutigliano (AFC by UPI)
1986	Marty Schottenheimer (AFC by FWA, UPI)

HEAD AND ASSISTANT COACHES

For a complete list of head coaches and assistant coaches, please see Coaches and Assistant Coaches on page 179 for a full list of assistant coaches.

COCKROFT, DON

Don Cockroft was a Browns kicker/punter from 1968-80. He was a third-round draft choice of the Browns in 1967 out of Adams State College. He spent the 1967 season on the practice squad before beating out veteran Lou Groza for the kicking position in the 1968 training camp. Cockroft ranks second all-time in Browns history in scoring with 1,080 points. He was the team's leading scorer each season from 1969-80. His longest field goal was a 57-yarder in Denver on Oct. 29, 1972. He kicked a 51-yarder in a 38-20 victory in St. Louis on Oct. 28, 1979.

One game Cockroft might like to forget happened Jan. 4, 1981, when his two missed field goals and failed extra point had much to do with the Browns' 14-12 defeat to the Oakland Raiders in an AFC Divisional Playoff in a frozen Cleveland Stadium.

Twice, he had punts that traveled 71 yards on Nov. 22, 1970, against Houston and on Dec. 2, 1973, against Kansas City. He holds three of the top 11 spots for most punting yards in one season in team history. He is No. 1 all-time in punting yards for the Browns with 26,362. His 965 postseason punting yards rank second in team history. Cockroft was named to the All-AFC defensive team in 1972 by NEA.

Don Cockroft. Photo courtesy of the Cleveland Browns.

COLELLA, TOM

Tom Colella was a punter/defensive back with the Browns from 1946-48. He was a Canisius College product acquired by the team as a free agent. His 10 interceptions in 1946 are tied with two other players for the most in one Browns season. Colella also returned punts and scored an 82-yard return off one on Sept. 12, 1947, in a 55-7 Browns victory against the Dodgers in Brooklyn.

COLEMAN, CASEY

Casey Coleman was a Browns radio broadcaster in 1994 and 1995 and is the son of Ken Coleman, another Browns broadcaster who did television and radio.

COLEMAN, KEN

Ken Coleman was a Browns television broadcaster from 1954-65 and radio broadcaster in 1952 and 1953. He is also the father of Casey Coleman, another Browns broadcaster who did radio.

Tom Colella. Photo Courtesy of Ted Patterson.

COLLEGE ALL-STAR GAME

The College All-Star Game was an annual summer exhibition contest matching the previous season's NFL Champion and the college all-star team. The Browns participated four times, and won each time—33-0 in 1951, 30-27 in 1955, 26-0 in 1956, and 24-16 in 1965. Each of those four games was played in Soldier Field in Chicago.

COLLIER, BLANTON

Blanton Collier was the Browns' head coach from 1963-70. He led the Browns to the 1964 NFL Championship. His all-time record as Browns head coach was 76-34-2 (.688), with 40-14-2 (.732) at home and 36-20 (.643) on the road. His all-time postseason record as head coach of the team was 3-4 (.429), 2-1 (.667) at home and 1-3 (.250) on the road. Collier was also a Browns assistant coach from 1946-53 and in 1962, 1975, and 1976.

COLLINS, GARY

Gary Collins was a wide receiver for the Browns from 1962-71. He was a first-round draft pick by the Browns in 1962 out of the University of Maryland. He ranks fifth in team all-time receiving yards with 5,299 and fourth in team all-time receptions with 331. His highest receptions and receiving yards totals came in 1966 when his 56 catches went for 946 yards.

Collins will always be remembered for his performance in the 1964 NFL title game at home against heavily-favored Baltimore. After a scoreless first half, he was on the receiving end of three scoring strikes from Frank Ryan for 18, 42, and 51 yards en route to a 27-0 upset. His 18 points in that game are tied for first all-time, and his 130 receiving yards against the Colts are the most ever by a Browns player in a postseason game (####).

Gary Collins.

Collins also punted and holds the Browns' all-time record for highest average yards per punt for one season with 46.7 in 1965. His 420 all-time points rank seventh in team history, and his 30 postseason points are tied for fifth all-time in team history. His 13,764 punting yards rank fourth all-time for the Browns, and his 595 postseason punting yards rank fourth in team history. Collins had a 73-yard punt against the Steelers on Oct. 5, 1963, and a 71-yarder against the Eagles on Oct. 2, 1965. He was named to All-NFL offensive teams in 1965 by NYN and UPI and in 1969 by AP and UPI, and was selected for the Pro Bowl in 1965 and 1966.

COLO, DON

Don Colo was a Browns defensive tackle from 1953-58. A Brown University product, Colo was acquired by the Browns on Mar. 26, 1953, as part of a 15-player deal with Baltimore. He was voted to All-NFL defensive teams in 1955 by NEA and UP and in 1957 by NYN and NEA. He was a Pro Bowl selection in 1954, 1955, and 1958.

COMBINED NET YARDS LEADERS

Please see Individual Statistics on page 188.

COMPOSITE WON-LOSS-TIED RECORDS

Please see Team Statistics on page 204.

CONFERENCE CHAMPIONSHIP GAMES (NFL)

Dallas 52, Cleveland 14 (Eastern Conference, Dec. 24, 1967, at Dallas)
Cleveland 31, Dallas 20 (Eastern Conference, Dec. 21, 1968, at Cleveland)
Cleveland 38, Dallas 14 (Eastern Conference, Dec. 28, 1969, at Dallas)
Denver 23, Cleveland 20 (OT) (AFC, Jan. 11, 1987, at Cleveland)
Denver 38, Cleveland 33 (AFC, Jan. 17, 1988, at Denver)
Denver 37, Cleveland 21 (AFC, Jan. 14, 1990, at Denver)

Overall 2-4 (.333)
Home   1-1 (.500)
Away   1-3 (.250)

CORDRAY, DON

Don Cordray was a Browns radio broadcaster in 1950.

CORNER BROTHERS

Browns cornerbacks Hanford Dixon and Frank Minnifield were known as the "Corner Brothers." They teamed up to stifle opposing wide receivers as the Browns' starters together from 1985-89. "Top Dawg" Dixon played on the right side from 1981-89. "Mighty Minnie" Minnifield played on the left side from 1984-92. One of the Corner Brothers' finest performances came in the Browns' 24-21 loss to the Miami Dolphins in the AFC

Frank Minnifield. Photo courtesy of the Cleveland Browns.

Hanford Dixon. Photo courtesy of the Cleveland Browns.

Divisional Playoffs on Jan. 4, 1986, in South Florida. Dixon and Minnifield held the "Marks Brothers," Miami's vaunted wide receivers duo of Mark Clayton and Mark Duper, to one catch between the two.

Vince Costello.

COSTELLO, VINCE

Vince Costello was a Browns linebacker from 1957-66. He was an Ohio University product acquired by the Browns as a free agent in 1956 after he had toiled in baseball's minor leagues for awhile. He was out of action in '56 due to a pulled muscle. He intercepted 18 passes in his Browns career, with a high of seven in 1963 when he tied for the team lead with Larry Benz.

COUCH, TIM

Tim Couch has been a Browns quarterback since 1999 when he was a first-round draft pick of the Browns out of the University of Kentucky. He was the first overall selection in the draft. Couch established all-time Browns rookie records and led all NFL rookie quarterbacks in completions, pass attempts, yards passing, touchdown passes, and quarterback rating. He completed 223 of 399 passes for 2,447 yards (55.9 completion percentage), 15 touchdown passes, and 13 interceptions that year, becoming just the sixth rookie quarterback in the NFL since 1952 to have more touchdown passes than interceptions. He replaced starter Ty Detmer in the fourth quarter of the Browns' season-opening 43-0 loss at home to Pittsburgh on Sept. 12.

Couch gave the Browns their first victory of the "new era" when he completed a 56-yard Hail Mary bomb with no time left that was tipped into the hands of Kevin Johnson, as the Browns beat New Orleans in the Superdome, 21-16. He left the Dec. 19 home game against Jacksonville in the second quarter with an ankle sprain, causing him to miss the final game of the season the next week against the Colts.

Couch got off to a fine start in 2000 with 259 yards passing in a win over the Bengals and 316 yards through the air in a win over Pittsburgh. In the Steelers game, he connected with Johnson on a 79-yard pass play. He completed a 67-yarder to Johnson on Nov. 26 against Baltimore. However, he played in just seven games that season due to a fractured right thumb suffered in a practice session during the season.

He came back strong in 2001 by passing for 3,040 yards (ninth all-time in team history) on 272-for-454 and a 59.9 completion percentage. His completion total ranks eighth all-time for the Browns. He had 17 touchdown passes and 21 interceptions in 2001. With Couch's fine year, the Browns improved to 7-9 (.438) and were talking playoffs into Dec. after 2-14 and 3-13 seasons in 1999 and 2000, respectively. Couch directed three fourth-quarter comeback wins in 2001, including a thriller at Tennessee on December 30 in which he threw for a career high 336 yards on 20-for-27, including a 78-yarder to

Quincy Morgan. Couch's 6,970 passing yards rank ninth all-time in team history, and his 632 completions rank seventh all-time for the Browns.

COUSINEAU, TOM

Tom Cousineau was a Browns linebacker from 1982-85. He was an Ohio State University product acquired by Cleveland on Apr. 23, 1982, in a trade with the Bills for a first-round draft choice in 1983, third-round pick in '84, and fifth-round pick in '85. He was the overall No. 1 pick in the 1979 draft by the Bills, for whom he never played (he spent three years in the CFL). Cousineau led the Browns with four interceptions in 1983 and was voted to All-AFC defensive teams that year and in 1984 by UPI.

Tim Couch

COWHER, BILL

Bill Cowher was a Browns linebacker from 1980-82. He was a North Carolina State University product acquired in 1980 by the Browns as a free agent. He was an assistant coach from 1985-88. As special teams coach in 1985, he was a major factor in the Browns going from worst to first in the NFL in kickoff coverage.

COX, STEVE

Steve Cox was a punter/kicker for the Browns from 1981-84. He was a fifth-round draft choice of the Browns in 1981 out of the University of Arkansas. He ranks eighth all-time for the Browns in punting yards with 7,984. He also holds the top two spots in the category of longest field goal in team history—a 60-yarder in Cincinnati on Oct. 21, 1984, and a 58-yarder in Denver on Dec. 4, 1983. Cox's 291 yards punting in a 27-10 loss to the Raiders in Los Angeles in an AFC First-Round Playoff game on Jan. 8, 1983, rank fifth all-time in team history.

CURTIS, ISAAC

Isaac Curtis was a Cincinnati Bengals wide receiver from 1973-84. He not only caused havoc on Browns defensive backs throughout his career but also on the team's front office. Cleveland had a chance to draft Curtis from San Diego State University in 1973 but instead opted for wide receiver Steve Holden from Arizona State University. Holden played with the Browns until 1976 and ended his career with 62 receptions for 927 yards and four touchdowns. Curtis wound up with 416 catches for 7,101 yards and 53 touchdowns in a career that lasted through 1984.

D

DALLAS COWBOYS

The Dallas Cowboys were Browns opponents in the NFL from 1960-95 and have been since 1999. They were co-members of the Eastern Conference from 1960-69. Dallas lost 11 of its first 12 meetings with the Browns. One of the more memorable contests between the Cowboys and Browns occurred Dec. 12, 1970, in Cleveland Municipal Stadium, when the Cowboys won a mudfest, 6-2, severely denting the Browns' AFC Central Division title hopes.

Another memorable game between the two teams was a 26-7 Browns victory Sept. 24, 1979, on *Monday Night Football,* in front of 80,123 crazed fans in Cleveland Stadium. The last game between the teams was a 19-14 Browns upset win Dec. 10, 1994, in Dallas that was finalized when Cowboys tight end Jay Novacek slipped and fell inside the Browns'

The Browns defend against the Cowboys at Cleveland Municipal Stadium Dec. 12, 1970. Photo courtesy of the Cleveland Press Collection.

one-yard line after a short reception from Troy Aikman with no time left on the clock.

The Browns and Cowboys played three times in the postseason in the Eastern Conference Championship game from 1967-69. Dallas blew the Browns out of the Cotton Bowl, 52-14, Dec. 24, 1967. However, the Browns came back to win the next two games, 31-20, Dec. 21, 1968, in Cleveland and 38-14 Dec. 28, 1969, in Dallas. The Cowboys' all-time record against the Browns is 9-15 (.375), with 6-6 at home and 3-9 (.250) on the road. Their all-time postseason record against Cleveland is 1-2 (.333), with 1-1 at home and 0-1 on the road.

DANIELSON, GARY

Gary Danielson was a Browns quarterback in 1985, 1987, and 1988. He was a product of Purdue University obtained by Cleveland May 1, 1985, in a trade with Detroit for a third-round draft pick in 1986. He was on the injured reserve list in 1986 after sustaining a fractured left ankle in the final preseason game Aug. 28. He was acquired to stand in for Bernie Kosar until the rookie was ready to take over.

Danielson directed the Browns to a 2-2 start that year before suffering a severe right shoulder injury at home against New England Oct. 6. He returned to action against the Bengals Nov. 24 and hooked up with Clarence Weathers for a perfect 72-yard pass play that went for a touchdown (the Browns' only pass of the entire second half) in a key 24-6 victory.

The next week against the Giants in the Meadowlands, Danielson re-injured his shoulder, but was gutsy in leading two late drives that were major factors in a thrilling upset of New York, 35-33. This win was the impetus for Cleveland's AFC Central Division title. The Giants game was Danielson's last action of the season. He ended his Browns career with 1,879 yards passing on 153 completions out of 248 attempts, 12 touchdown passes, and seven interceptions.

Thom Darden reaches, and knocks down a pass intended for Pittsburgh's Lynn Swann in the Cleveland end zone. The Browns eventually upset the two-time Super Bowl Champions, 18-16, Oct. 10, 1976. Photo courtesy of the Cleveland Press Collection.

DARDEN, THOM

Thom Darden was a Browns defensive back from 1972-74 and 1976-81. He was a first-round draft choice of the Browns in 1972 from the University of Michigan. He missed the entire 1975 season due to preseason knee surgery. He is the Browns' all-time interceptions leader with 45. His 10 picks in 1978 led the league and tie him with Tom Colella (1946) and Anthony Henry (2001) for Cleveland's all-time single-season record. His eight thefts in 1974 are tied for eighth all-time in team history. Darden was named to All-AFC defensive teams in 1978 by NEA, PFW, FWA, SN and UPI, and in 1979 by PFW. He was a Pro Bowl selection in 1978.

DAVIS, BEN

Ben Davis was a Cleveland defensive back in 1967 and 1968, and from 1970-73. He was a 17th-round draft choice of the Browns in 1967 from Defiance College. He missed the 1969 season because of two knee operations from an injury in a preseason game Aug. 23 in San Diego. Davis's eight interceptions in 1968 are tied for eighth all-time in team history. He returned punts and kickoffs early in his career and led the Browns in punt returns, punt return yards, kickoff returns, and kickoff return yards in 1967.

Ben Davis. Photo courtesy of the Cleveland Press Collection.

DAVIS, BUTCH

Butch Davis has been head coach of the Browns since 2001. He led the Browns to more victories (seven) in 2001 than they had in 1999 and 2000 combined (five). Davis's all-time record as head coach of Cleveland is 7-9 (.438), with 4-4 at home and 3-5 (.375) on the road.

DAVIS, ERNIE

Ernie Davis was acquired by the Browns Dec. 14, 1961, in a trade with Washington for running back Bobby Mitchell and rights to 1962 first-round draft pick Leroy Jackson, a defensive back. He was the Redskins' first-round—and the first overall—pick in that draft. He had speed and power as a running back that helped him break most of legendary Browns running back Jim Brown's records at Syracuse University. Davis won the 1961 Heisman Trophy. He contracted leukemia, however, and never played for the Browns. He died on May 18, 1963. His uniform No. 45 is retired by the Browns.

DAWG POUND, THE

The Dawg Pound was the name originally given to the Cleveland Stadium bleachers section in 1984 that lasted through the Browns' last season there in 1995. The Dawg Pound has been the official name of the Cleveland Browns Stadium bleachers section since the stadium opened in 1999. The Dawg Pound originated from the antics of cornerbacks Hanford Dixon and Frank Minnifield, and linebacker Eddie Johnson, when they began barking at fans in the bleachers of Cleveland Stadium late in the 1984 season. Johnson was actually barking at teammates who made big defensive plays during training camp, but this led to the crazy canine antics of fans in the bleachers such as woofing, wearing dog masks, painting their faces brown, orange, and white and even eating dog biscuits. Fans became a little too enthusiastic at times, as some would hurl objects such as biscuits, batteries, and eggs at opposing players. Born at a time when the Browns were starting to win again after some down years, The Dawg Pound was a nice complement to the success of the team in the late 1980s and remained in force during the down times of the early 1990s.

DAWSON, LEN

Len Dawson was a Browns quarterback in 1960 and 1961. A product of Purdue University, he was obtained by Cleveland Dec. 31, 1959, in a trade with the Pittsburgh Steelers as part of a four-player deal. Dawson attempted just 28 passes, completing 15 before jumping to the AFL's Dallas Texans (who became the Kansas City Chiefs in 1963) and enjoying a Hall of Fame career there.

DAWSON, PHIL

Phil Dawson has been a kicker for the Browns since 1999. He was a product of the University of Texas acquired by the team Mar. 25, 1999, as a free agent. He was successful on 24 of 25 extra point attempts and eight of 12 field goal tries in 1999. He converted 14 of 17 treys in 2000 and 22 of 25 in 2001. He made good on his final 15 field goal attempts and 19 of his last 20 in 2001.

DECEMBER
—2, 1946

The Browns game in Miami against the Seahawks was postponed until the next day due to heavy rain. The Browns won, 34-0.

—22, 1946

Cleveland beat the New York Yankees, 14-9, on a 16-yard pass from Otto Graham to Dante Lavelli late in the AAFC Championship game in Cleveland.

—19, 1948

The Browns routed the Buffalo Bills, 49-7, in the AAFC Championship game in Cleveland.

—11, 1949

The Browns defeated the San Francisco 49ers, 21-7, in the AAFC Championship game in Cleveland.

—17, 1950

Cleveland defeated the New York Giants, 8-3, in an American Conference Playoff in Cleveland.

—24, 1950

The Browns defeated the Los Angeles Rams, 30-28, on Lou Groza's late 16-yard field goal in the NFL Championship game in Cleveland.

—26, 1954

The Browns routed the Detroit Lions, 56-10, in the NFL Championship game in Cleveland.

—26, 1955

The Browns defeated the Los Angeles Rams, 38-14, in the NFL Championship game in Los Angeles.

—27, 1964

The Browns upset the Baltimore Colts, 27-0, in the NFL Championship game in Cleveland.

Otto Graham, Dante Lavelli, Paul Brown, and Mac Speedie (left to right) pose after Cleveland's 14-9 victory over the New York Yankees in the AAFC title game at Cleveland Municipal Stadium Dec. 22, 1946. Photo courtesy of the Cleveland Press Collection.

Frank Ryan is mobbed as he leaves the Cleveland Municipal Stadium field after leading the Browns to a 27-0 upset of the Baltimore Colts in the NFL Championship game Dec. 27, 1964. Photo courtesy of the Cleveland Press Collection.

—29, 1968

The Browns were obliterated by the Baltimore Colts, 34-0, in the NFL Championship game in Cleveland.

—14, 1980

The Browns lost to the Vikings, 28-23, in Minnesota when Ahmad Rashad caught a game-winning 46-yard Hail Mary touchdown pass from Tommy Kramer with no time showing on the clock. The heartbreaking defeat kept the Browns from clinching their first playoff berth in eight years.

—17, 1995

Cleveland defeated Cincinnati, 26-10, in Cleveland in the final home game before the Browns relocated to Baltimore, where they became the Ravens.

—24, 1995

The Browns fell to the Jacksonville Jaguars, 24-21, in Jacksonville in Cleveland's final game prior to its relocation to Baltimore.

DEFENSIVE BACKS

Notable Browns defensive backs include Cliff Lewis, Tommy James, Warren Lahr, Ken Konz, Don Paul, Junior Wren, Jim Shofner, Bernie Parrish, Ross Fichtner, Don Fleming, Bobby Franklin, Larry Benz, Erich Barnes, Mike Howell, Ernie Kellerman, Ben Davis, Walt Sumner, Clarence Scott, Thom Darden, Tony Peters, Ron Bolton, Clinton Burrell, Hanford Dixon, Al Gross, Frank Minnifield, Don Rogers, Felix Wright, Ray Ellis, Thane Gash, Eric Turner, Stevon Moore, Antonio Langham, Earl Little, Daylon McCutcheon and Anthony Henry.

DEFENSIVE LINEMEN

Notable Browns defensive linemen include Bill Willis, Len Ford, John Kissell, Don Colo, Willie Davis, Bob Gain, Paul Wiggin, Bill Glass, Walter Johnson, Jim Kanicki, Jerry Sherk, Bob Golic, Reggie Camp, Carl Hairston, Michael Dean Perry, Rob Burnett, Anthony Pleasant, Courtney Brown, and Gerard Warren.

DEFENSIVE MOST VALUABLE PLAYER

1989—Michael Dean Perry (AFC by UPI)

DEFENSIVE PLAYER OF THE YEAR

1976—Jerry Sherk (NFL by NEA)

DEFENSIVE ROOKIE OF THE YEAR

1982—Chip Banks (NFL by AP, PFW)

DELAMIELLEURE, JOE

Joe DeLamielleure was a Browns guard from 1980-84. A product of Michigan State University, DeLamielleure was acquired by Cleveland Sept. 1, 1980, in a trade with the Buffalo Bills for a second-round draft choice in 1981 and third-round pick in 1982. PFW, FWA, SN, and UPI named him to All-AFC offensive teams in 1980. He was also voted to the Pro Bowl in 1980.

DELEONE, TOM

Tom DeLeone was a Browns center from 1974-84. A product of Ohio State University, he was obtained by the Browns in 1974 as a free agent. He was a Pro Bowl selection in 1979 and 1980.

DEMARCO, BOB

Bob DeMarco was a Browns center from 1972-74. He was a product of the University of Dayton. Cleveland acquired him in a trade with the Dolphins in late Sept. 1972 in exchange for a draft choice after starter Jim Copeland went down with a dislocated hip.

Tom DeLeone (left) and Brian Sipe run through a play in practice in 1980. Photo courtesy of the Cleveland Press Collection.

DEMARIE, JOHN

John DeMarie was a Browns guard and offensive tackle from 1967-75. He was a Browns sixth-round draft choice in 1967 out of Louisiana State University.

DENVER BRONCOS

The Denver Broncos were Browns opponents in the NFL from 1970-95 and have been since 1999. The Broncos lost three of their first four games against the Browns before winning the next eight games. The streak was broken Oct. 1, 1989, in thrilling fashion when the Browns finally beat the Broncos, 16-13, on a last-second 48-yard field goal by Matt Bahr.

Cleveland followed that up with an equally—and possibly more—exciting win the next season Oct. 8 when Bernie Kosar led a re-

John DeMarie (left) and Blanton Collier. Photo courtesy of the Cleveland Press Collection.

markable comeback from nine points down late to a 30-29 triumph on Jerry Kauric's last-second field goal. The most memorable aspect of the Browns-Broncos rivalry has come in the postseason in the form of three AFC title games in a four-year period.

Denver won each time, 23-20, in overtime in 1986 in Cleveland *(See Drive, The)*, 38-33 in 1987 in Denver *(See Fumble, The)*, and 37-21 in 1989 in Denver. The Broncos' all-time record against the Browns is 14-5 (.737), with 7-3 (.700) at home and 7-2 (.778) on the road. Their all-time postseason record against them is 3-0, with 2-0 at home and 1-0 on the road.

DETROIT LIONS

The Detroit Lions were a Browns opponent in the NFL from 1950-95 and have been since 1999. The Lions played the Browns four times in six years from 1952-57 in the NFL Championship game, winning three. They won 17-7, at home, Dec. 28, 1952, and 17-16 at home Dec. 27, 1953, before getting trashed, 56-10, in Cleveland Dec. 26, 1954.

Detroit won the fourth game in a blowout of their own, 59-14, in Detroit Dec. 29, 1957. Detroit's all-time record against the Browns is 12-4 (.750), with 8-1 (.889) at home and 4-3 (.571) on the road. The Lions' all-time postseason record against the Browns is 3-1 (.750), with 2-0 at home and 1-1 on the road.

Action from the NFL Championship game between the Browns and the Detroit Lions Dec. 29, 1957. Photo courtesy of the Cleveland Press Collection.

DIEKEN, DOUG

Doug Dieken was a Browns offensive tackle from 1971-84. A sixth-round draft choice of the Browns in 1971 from the University of Illinois, Dieken carried on the fine tradition of Browns left tackles when he replaced veteran Dick Schafrath during the 1971 season. One of Dieken's more memorable moments actually came as a receiver. On Oct. 30, 1983, at home against Houston, he caught a short touchdown pass from Paul McDonald on a fake field goal late in the first half that tied score at 10. It was the only touchdown of his career. Dieken was selected to play in the Pro Bowl in 1980. He was a Browns radio broadcaster from 1985-95 and has been since 1999.

Doug Dieken. Photo courtesy of the Cleveland Browns.

DIVISIONAL PLAYOFF GAMES

Baltimore 20, Cleveland 3 (AFC, Dec. 26, 1971, at Cleveland)
Miami 20, Cleveland 14 (AFC, Dec. 24, 1972, at Miami)
Oakland 14, Cleveland 12 (AFC, Jan. 4, 1981, at Cleveland)
Miami 24, Cleveland 21 (AFC, Jan. 4, 1986, at Miami)
Cleveland 23, N.Y. Jets 20 (2OT) (AFC, Jan. 3, 1987, at Cleveland)
Cleveland 38, Indianapolis 21 (AFC, Jan. 9, 1988, at Cleveland)
Cleveland 34, Buffalo 30 (AFC, Jan. 6, 1990, at Cleveland)
Pittsburgh 29, Cleveland 9 (AFC, Jan. 7, 1995, at Pittsburgh)

Overall	3-5 (.375)
Home	3-2 (.600)
Away	0-3 (.000)

DIXON, HANFORD

Hanford Dixon was a Cleveland cornerback from 1981-89. A first-round draft choice of the Browns in 1981 from the University of Southern Mississippi, he teamed with Frank Minnifield to form the "Corner Brothers" duo in the mid- to late-1980s. Dixon is tied with Felix Wright for ninth on the all-time Browns interceptions list with 26. One of his finest games came Dec. 19, 1982, when he picked off three passes in a 10-9 victory over visiting

Pittsburgh. He was named to All-AFC defensive teams in 1986 and 1987 by AP, NEA, PFW, FWA, SN, and UPI. He was picked for the Pro Bowl from 1986-88.

DOMES RECORD

When playing in domes, the Browns are 26-29 overall. *For a complete list of scores, please see Team Statistics on page 204.*

DONOVAN, JIM

Jim Donovan has been a Browns radio broadcaster since 1999.

DOUBLE-HEADERS

Double-headers were held in Cleveland Municipal Stadium once each preseason from 1962-71 with the Browns playing an opponent after a game between two other teams. The first double-header was held Aug. 18, 1962, when the Browns beat the Pittsburgh Steelers, 33-10, after the Detroit Lions defeated the Dallas Cowboys, 35-24, in the opener. The last double-header was held Sept. 4, 1971, when the Browns topped the New York Giants, 30-7, in the nightcap following the Steelers' 35-21 victory over the New York Jets.

Erich Barnes (left) and Joe Jones (right) defend against the Vikings in preseason action and the second game of a double-header Sept. 5, 1970. Photo courtesy of the Cleveland Press Collection.

DRAFTS

The Browns took part in the AAFC college player draft from 1947-49, and the NFL college player draft from 1950-95, and have taken part in it since 1999. *(See First-Round Draft Choices.)*

DRIVE, THE

The Drive was a 98-yard march that Denver quarterback John Elway led late in the 1986 AFC Championship game against the Browns in Cleveland. The Drive began with the Broncos trailing, 20-13, with 5:43 left. The final salvo of the long march was Elway's five-yard scoring strike to wide receiver Mark Jackson with 37 seconds left to tie the score. The key play of The Drive was when Elway connected with Jackson on a 20-yard pass play on third-and-18. Denver won in overtime, 23-20.

DUDLEY, JIMMY

Jimmy Dudley was a Browns television broadcaster from 1957-60.

DUMONT TV NETWORK

The Dumont TV Network broadcast Browns road games from 1948-51.

E

EASTERN CONFERENCE

The Eastern Conference was home to the Browns from 1953-69. The conference was re-named in 1953 after being known as the American Conference from 1950-52. The Eastern Conference was won by the Browns from 1953-55 and in 1957. The Browns tied the Giants in 1958 as both teams finished 9-3 (.750). The Browns lost to New York in a playoff, 10-0, Dec. 21 in Yankee Stadium.

From 1959-63, Cleveland finished in the upper echelon of the conference but failed to win it. The Browns came back, however, to claim titles in 1964 and 1965. In 1966, they tied Philadelphia for second place at 9-5 (.643), behind the 10-3-1 (.750) Cowboys.

The conference was divided into two divisions in 1967—the Capitol and Century. The Browns were placed in the Century with the Giants, Pittsburgh Steelers, and St. Louis Cardinals (the New Orleans Saints replaced the Giants in '68, and the Giants took the Saints' place in the Capitol that year). The Browns won the conference in 1968 and 1969, as they defeated the Cowboys in title games.

EIGHTY THOUSAND FANS

The attendance mark has been at least 80,000 for 53 Browns home games, the largest being 85,703 in the first *Monday Night Football* game Sept. 21, 1970, against the New York Jets. Twice, the Browns had home attendance marks of at least 80,000 in the postseason, as both occurred in 1968. Once, the Browns played in front of a crowd of at least 80,000 in a postseason game on the road during the 1955 NFL Championship game against the Los Angeles Rams.

ELWAY, JOHN

John Elway was the Denver Broncos' quarterback who caused havoc on the Browns throughout a 16-year career that lasted from 1983-98. He led the Broncos to seven wins in nine games against Cleveland. Even in the two games the Browns won, it took last-second field goals to do it.

However, Elway shined even more in the postseason, when he really gave the Browns headaches. He directed Denver to three AFC Championship game victories in four years— in 1986, 1987 and 1989, the first one in Cleveland. In 1986, he led the Broncos on The

Drive in which his team trailed by seven points with possession of the ball at its own two-yard line with 5:43 remaining. Denver traveled 98 yards with the help of several remarkable passing and running plays by Elway to the tying touchdown with 37 seconds left. The Broncos won, 23-20, in overtime.

Elway passed for three touchdowns in a 38-33 win in the 1987 game in which the Browns rallied from an 18-point, third-quarter deficit. The Browns rebounded and tied the Broncos late in the game, but Elway drove his team to the winning touchdown once again. Earnest Byner's fumble deep in Broncos territory on the Browns' ensuing drive sealed the Browns' fate. Elway passed for 385 yards and three touchdowns en route to a 37-21 Denver triumph in the 1989 title game.

ESPN

ESPN broadcast five Browns prime-time games from 1987-95 and has since 1999. They are the following:

San Francisco 38, Cleveland 24 (Sunday, Nov. 29, 1987, at San Francisco)
Cleveland 24, Houston 20 (Saturday, Dec. 23, 1989, at Houston)
Houston 28, Cleveland 24 (Sunday, Nov. 17, 1991, at Houston)
Cleveland 11, Houston 8 (Thursday, Oct. 13, 1994, at Houston)
Pittsburgh 43, Cleveland 0 (Sunday, Sept. 12, 1999, at Cleveland)

Overall   2-3 (.400)
Home   0-1 (.000)
Away   2-2 (.500)

EVANS, JOHNNY

Johnny Evans was a Browns quarterback and punter from 1978-80. He was a second-round draft choice of the Browns in 1978 from North Carolina State University. He was used mainly as a punter, and his 8,463 punting yards rank seventh all-time for the Browns.

EVERITT, STEVE

Steve Everitt was a Browns center from 1993-95. He was a Browns first-round draft choice in 1993 from the University of Michigan.

F

FARREN, PAUL

Paul Farren was a Browns offensive tackle from 1983-91. He was a Browns 12th-round draft choice in 1983 from Boston University.

FAST FACTS

For fascinating facts on Browns history, please see Browns Trivia on page 173.

FEACHER, RICKY

Ricky Feacher was a Browns wide receiver from 1976-84. He was a product of Mississippi Valley State University acquired by the Browns in Oct. 1976 as a free agent. One of Feacher's finest performances came Dec. 21, 1980, in the season-ending AFC Central Division-clinching 27-24 triumph over the Bengals in which he caught two long touchdown passes from Brian Sipe. He tied with Ozzie Newsome for the team lead in touchdown catches in 1982 with three. His 124 receiving yards in a 27-10 loss to the Raiders in an AFC First-Round Playoff game in Los Angeles Jan. 8, 1983, rank second all-time for the Browns (####).

Ricky Feacher pulls in a 35-yard touchdown grab from Brian Sipe in the Browns' 27-24 AFC Central Division-clinching win in Cincinnati Dec. 21, 1980. Photo courtesy of the Cleveland Press Collection.

FICHTNER, ROSS

Ross Fichtner was a defensive back for the Browns from 1960-67. A third-round draft selection of the Browns in 1960 from Purdue University, he had a team-leading seven interceptions in 1962. His eight picks in 1966 tied for the team lead and are tied with six others for eighth most in one season in team history. Fichtner's four interceptions in 1967 tied for the team lead. On Oct. 1 that year, he took a lateral from Erich Barnes, who had intercepted the ball, and raced 88 yards deep into New Orleans territory en route to a 42-7 rout of the Saints. It was the Browns first win of the year after two defeats. Fichtner's 27 interceptions are tied for seventh all-time in Browns history.

FIKE, DAN

Dan Fike was a Browns guard from 1985-92. He was a product of the University of Florida obtained by Cleveland as a free agent in 1985.

FINALES

For a listing of the scores of the season finales, please see Team Statistics on page 204.

For a listing of the scores of the season finales, please see Team Statistics on page 204.

FIRST-ROUND DRAFT CHOICES

1947	Dick Hoerner (University of Iowa)
1948	Jeff Durkota (Penn State University)
1949	Jack Mitchell (University of Oklahoma)
1950	Ken Carpenter (Oregon State University)
1951	Ken Konz (Louisiana State University)
1952	Bert Rechichar (University of Tennessee)
	Harry Agganis (Boston University)
1953	Doug Atkins (University of Tennessee)
1954	Bobby Garrett (Stanford University)
	John Bauer (University of Illinois)
1955	Kurt Burris (University of Oklahoma)
1956	Preston Carpenter (University of Arkansas)
1957	Jim Brown (Syracuse University)
1958	Jim Shofner (Texas Christian University)
1959	Rich Kreitling (University of Illinois)
1960	Jim Houston (Ohio State University)
1961	Bobby Crespino (University of Mississippi)
1962	Gary Collins (University of Maryland)
	Leroy Jackson (Western Illinois University)
1963	Tom Hutchinson (University of Kentucky)
1964	Paul Warfield (Ohio State University)
1966	Milt Morin (University of Massachusetts)
1967	Bob Matheson (Duke University)
1968	Marvin Upshaw (Trinity University)

1969   Ron Johnson (University of Michigan)
1970   Mike Phipps (Purdue University)
        Bob McKay (University of Texas)
1971   Clarence Scott (Kansas State University)
1972   Thom Darden (University of Michigan)
1973   Steve Holden (Arizona State University)
        Pete Adams (University of Southern California)
1975   Mack Mitchell (University of Houston)
1976   Mike Pruitt (Purdue University)
1977   Robert L. Jackson (Texas A&M University)
1978   Clay Matthews (University of Southern California)
        Ozzie Newsome (University of Alabama)
1979   Willis Adams (University of Houston)
1980   Charles White (University of Southern California)
1981   Hanford Dixon (Southern Mississippi University)
1982   Chip Banks (University of Southern California)
1984   Don Rogers (UCLA)
1987   Mike Junkin (Duke University)
1988   Clifford Charlton (University of Florida)
1989   Eric Metcalf (University of Texas)
1991   Eric Turner (UCLA)
1992   Tommy Vardell (Stanford University)
1993   Steve Everitt (University of Michigan)
1994   Antonio Langham (University of Alabama)
        Derrick Alexander (University of Michigan)
1995   Craig Powell (Ohio State University)
1999   Tim Couch (University of Kentucky)
2000   Courtney Brown (Penn State University)
2001   Gerard Warren (University of Florida)

FIRSTS

* Denotes only time

Majority owner—Arthur "Mickey" McBride
Head coach—Paul Brown
Training camp site—Bowling Green State University in Bowling Green, Ohio
Player signed to a contract—Otto Graham
Draft choice—Dick Hoerner
Preseason opponent—Brooklyn Dodgers
Opponent—Miami Seahawks
Road opponent—Chicago Rockets
Opponent the Browns lost to—San Francisco 49ers
Postseason opponent—New York Yankees
Postseason road opponent—New York Yankees
Starting quarterback—Cliff Lewis

Points scored by—Mac Speedie
Field goal by—Lou Groza
ABC Monday Night Football opponent—New York Jets
ABC Monday Night Football road opponent—Houston Oilers
Overtime opponent—New England Patriots
Overtime opponent the Browns lost to—Pittsburgh Steelers
Season the Browns missed the postseason—1956
Season with a losing record—1956
Player to rush for 1,000 yards in one season—Jim Brown
Player to pass for 3,000 yards in one season—Brian Sipe
*Player to pass for 4,000 yards in one season—Brian Sipe
Player to total 1,000 yards receiving in one season—Mac Speedie
Players selected for the Pro Bowl—Tony Adamle, Otto Graham, Lou Groza, Weldon
    Humble, Marion Motley, Mac Speedie, Bill Willis
Most Valuable Player—Otto Graham
Rookie of the Year—Jim Brown
Coach of the Year—Paul Brown
Player of the Year—Jim Brown

FISS, GALEN

Galen Fiss was a Browns linebacker from 1956-66. He was a 13th-round Browns draft choice in 1953 from the University of Kansas. He spent 1953-55 in the military. He was a Pro Bowl selection in 1962 and 1963.

FITZGERALD, JOHN

John Fitzgerald was a Browns television broadcaster in 1953.

FLEMING, DON

Don Fleming was a Browns defensive back from 1960-62. He was a University of Florida product obtained by the Browns May 12, 1960, in a trade with the St. Louis Cardinals. He intercepted 10 passes for 160 yards in his Cleveland career. He was killed in the spring of 1963 when electrocuted on a construction project in Florida. His uniform No. 46 is retired by the Browns.

Galen Fiss. Photo courtesy of the Cleveland Browns.

FONTENOT, HERMAN

Herman Fontenot was a Browns running back from 1985-88. A product of Louisiana State University, Fontenot was acquired by the Browns May 4, 1985, as a free agent. His most productive season came in 1986 when he was second on the team with 47 receptions, for 559 yards including a 72-yard catch-and-run from Bernie Kosar that went for a touchdown in a 24-9 win in Indianapolis Nov. 2.

He scored the first points in both playoff games that year—on a 37-yard reception from Kosar in the first quarter that tied the AFC Divisional Playoff at home against the Jets Jan. 3, 1987, and on a six-yard pass from Kosar that gave Cleveland a 7-0 first-quarter lead over the Broncos in the AFC Championship Jan. 11, also in Cleveland.

Fontenot's seven receptions in the Broncos game are tied for second all-time for the Browns (#####). He also returned kickoffs, and his 879 return yards in 1988 rank seventh all-time in team history. He had kickoff returns of 81 and 84 yards, respectively—the first at home against Houston Dec. 15, 1985, and the second at home against Cincinnati Oct. 30, 1988.

*Len Ford. Photo courtesy of the
Cleveland Browns.*

FORD, LEN

Len Ford was a Browns defensive end from 1950-57. A product of the University of Michigan, Ford was an early-round choice of the Browns in the 1950 special allocation draft that consisted of players (other than those from the New York Yankees, who were split among the New York Giants and New York Bulldogs) from the folded AAFC. He returned a fumble 54 yards in a 33-17 loss to the Eagles in Philadelphia Nov. 13, 1955. Ford was named to All-NFL defensive teams from 1951-54 by AP, NYN, and UP and in 1955 by NYN, NEA, and UP. He played in the Pro Bowl from 1951-54 and was inducted into the Pro Football Hall of Fame in 1976.

FOUR-THOUSAND-YARD PASSER

Brian Sipe is the only Browns quarterback to pass for more than 4,000 yards in a single season. His official record was 4,132 in 1980.

FOX TELEVISION NETWORK

The FOX television network broadcast Browns Sunday afternoon home games when their opponent was an NFC team in 1994, 1995, and has since 1999.

FRANKLIN, BOBBY

Bobby Franklin was a Cleveland defensive back from 1960-66. An 11th-round draft choice of the Browns in 1960 from the University of Mississippi, Franklin made eight interceptions his rookie year that tied him with Jim Shofner for the team lead and with six other players for eighth most in one season.

FRIDAY NIGHT GAMES

(Local starting times of 5 p.m. or later)

Cleveland 44, Miami 0 (Sept. 6, 1946, at Cleveland)
Cleveland 20, Chicago 6 (Sept. 13, 1946, at Chicago)
Cleveland 30, Buffalo 14 (Sept. 5, 1947, at Cleveland)
Cleveland 55, Brooklyn 7 (Sept. 12, 1947, at Brooklyn)
Cleveland 41, Chicago 21 (Sept. 26, 1947, at Chicago)
Cleveland 19, Los Angeles 14 (Sept. 3, 1948, at Cleveland)
Cleveland 28, Chicago 7 (Sept. 17, 1948, at Chicago)
Cleveland 61, Los Angeles 14 (Oct. 14, 1949, at Los Angeles)

Overall   8-0 (1.000)
Home   3-0 (.750)
Away   5-0 (1.000)

FUMBLE, THE

The Fumble occurred during the AFC title game against the Denver Broncos in Mile High Stadium Jan. 17, 1988. Earnest Byner was headed for the end zone late in the fourth quarter with the Browns trailing, 38-31. The play began at the Broncos' eight-yard line. Byner, bursting off left tackle, was stripped of the football by cornerback Jeremiah Castille, who then fell on the ball at the three-yard line. Denver deliberately took a safety and won, 38-33.

G

GAIN, BOB

Bob Gain was a Browns defensive tackle in 1952 and from 1954-64. A product of the University of Kentucky, Gain was acquired by Cleveland Sept. 20, 1951, in a trade with Green Bay for four players. He played in the CFL in 1951. After spending the 1953 season and most of the 1954 campaign in the military, he re-joined the team in time for the last two games and the 1954 NFL title game. Gain was voted to the All-NFL defensive team in 1958 by NEA. He was picked for the Pro Bowl from 1957-59 and in 1961 and 1962.

GAMES IN WHICH BOTH TEAMS SCORED FEWER THAN 10 POINTS

See Team Statistics on page 204.

Bob Gain.

GARDOCKI, CHRIS

Chris Gardocki has been a Browns punter since 1999. He was a product of Clemson University acquired by Cleveland Feb. 16, 1999, as a free agent. Gardocki set a Browns' record for most punting yards in one season with 4,645 in 1999. He broke it a year later with 4,919. He had 4,249 punting yards in 2001, which rank third all-time in team history. Gardocki's 13,813 all-time punting yards rank third all-time in Browns history. He holds the NFL record for most consecutive punts without being blocked with a streak of 825 that dates to 1991 and included his days with the Bears and Colts.

GARLINGTON, JOHN

John Garlington was a Browns linebacker from 1968-77. He was a second-round draft choice of the Browns in 1968 from Louisiana State University.

Joe Jones (left) and John Garlington chase Dallas's Bob Hayes in the end zone for a safety. It was the Browns' only score in a 6-2 home loss Dec. 12, 1970. Photo courtesy of the Cleveland Press Collection.

GATSKI, FRANK

Frank Gatski was a Browns center from 1946-56. He was a product of Marshall University acquired by Cleveland as a free agent. He was voted to All-NFL offensive teams in 1951 by NYN and UP; in 1952 by AP and NYN; in 1953 by AP, NYN and UP; and in 1955 by AP, NYN, NEA, and UP. He was picked to play in the Pro Bowl in 1954 and was enshrined into the Pro Football Hall of Fame in 1985.

GEE, STAN

Stan Gee was a Cleveland radio broadcaster in 1946 and a television broadcaster in 1948.

GIBRON, ABE

Abe Gibron was a Browns guard from 1950-56. A product of Purdue University, he was obtained by Cleveland prior to the 1950 season as one of three players in a merger deal with the folded AAFC's Buffalo Bills. He was voted to All-NFL offensive teams in 1953 by NYN and in 1955 by NYN, NEA and UP. He was a Pro Bowl selection from 1952-55.

Frank Gatski.

GILLOM, HORACE

Horace Gillom was a punter and wide receiver for the Browns from 1947-56. He was a product of rhe University of Nevada obtained by Cleveland as a free agent. He ranks second all-time for the Browns in punting yards with 21,207. His 3,321 punting yards in 1951 tie him with Don Cockcroft for 10th all-time. Gillom holds the Browns' all-time postseason record for most punting yards with 1,943. He holds the team record for most punting yards in one postseason game with 363 against the Giants Dec. 17, 1950, in New York. He had a 74-yard punt on Sept. 21, 1947, against Baltimore; a 75-yarder Oct. 29, 1950, against Pittsburgh; a 73-yarder Oct. 26, 1952, against the Redskins; and an 80-yarder against New York Nov. 28, 1954. He was a Pro Bowl pick in 1952.

GLASS, BILL

Bill Glass was a Browns defensive end from 1962-68. A product of Baylor University, he was acquired by Cleveland Mar. 28, 1962, as part of a six-player trade with the Detroit Lions. He was a Pro Bowler from 1962-64 and in 1967.

GLIEBER, FRANK

Frank Glieber was a Browns television broadcaster in 1966 and 1967.

GOLIC, BOB

Bob Golic was a Browns defensive tackle from 1982-88. He was a product of the University of Notre Dame acquired by Cleveland via waivers Sept. 2, 1982.

Bill Glass. Photo courtesy of the Cleveland Browns.

He returned a Lynn Dickey dead-duck pass seven yards for a touchdown Nov. 6, 1983, in a 35-21 loss to the Packers in Milwaukee. His 13.5 sacks all-time rank 10th in Browns history. Golic was voted to the All-AFC defensive team in 1985 by SN. He was selected to the Pro Bowl from 1985-87.

Bob Golic. Photo courtesy of the Cleveland Browns.

GORGAL, KEN

Ken Gorgal was a Cleveland defensive back in 1950, 1953, and 1954. He was a sixth-round draft choice of the Browns in 1950 from Purdue University. After two years in the Army, he re-joined the team in 1953 and was voted to All-NFL defensive teams that year by NYN and UP.

GOSSETT, JEFF

Jeff Gossett was a Browns punter in 1983 and from 1985-87. An Eastern Illinois University product, Gossett was acquired by the Browns via waivers Aug. 31, 1983. After two years in the USFL, he was re-acquired as a free agent in 1985. His 10,307 punting yards rank fifth all-time for the Browns, his 3,423 punting yards in 1986 rank eighth all-time in team history, and his 792 postseason punting yards rank third all-time in team history. Gossett's 310 punting yards in Cleveland's 23-20 double overtime victory over the Jets in an AFC Divisional Playoff Jan. 3, 1987, in Cleveland also rank third all-time for the Browns.

Ken Gorgal attempts to tackle the Chicago Cardinals' John Olszweski during the Browns' 31-7 victory Oct. 10, 1954. Photo courtesy of the Cleveland Press Collection.

GRAHAM, OTTO

Otto Graham was a Browns quarterback from 1946-55. A product of Northwestern University, Graham was acquired by Cleveland as a free agent and was the first player to be signed by the Browns. He led Cleveland to every AAFC Championship from 1946-49. In 1946, he had 17 touchdown passes and just five interceptions; in 1947, 25 touchdown passes and 11 interceptions; in 1948, 25 touchdown passes and 15 interceptions; and in 1949, 19 touchdown passes and 10 interceptions. Overall from 1946-49, he totaled 86 touchdown passes and 41 interceptions.

Graham led the Browns to three NFL Championships from 1950-55. He announced prior to the 1954 season that the 1954 campaign would be his last. The Browns won the NFL title that year. He changed his mind and returned for one more season, and led the Browns to their second straight NFL title in 1955 with a 38-14 destruction of the Rams in Los Angeles Dec. 26.

Graham ranks second behind Brian Sipe in Browns all-time passing yards with 23,584 and third all-time in team history in pass completions with 1,464. He holds four of the top 10 rankings for most passing yards in one game in team history. His highest total was 401 yards in a 21-20 win at Pittsburgh Oct. 4, 1952. Graham holds Cleveland's record for the

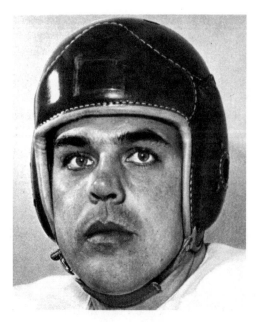

Otto Graham. Photo courtesy of the Cleveland Browns.

longest completion when his screen pass to Mac Speedie turned into a 99-yard touchdown play Nov. 2, 1947, against the Buffalo Bills.

Graham made more notable connections, including a 70-yard touchdown pass to Speedie Sept. 26, 1947, against the Chicago Rockets and a 78-yard touchdown pass to Speedie Nov. 3, 1946, against the Los Angeles Dons. He hit Dante Lavelli on a 72-yard touchdown strike Nov. 9, 1947, in Brooklyn, Speedie for an 82-yard pass in a 28-28 tie with the New York Yankees two weeks later Nov. 23, and Lewis Mayne for a 69-yard scoring strike that helped beat Los Angeles in Los Angeles four days later on Thanksgiving day. Graham hooked up with Bob Cowan on a 68-yard scoring strike in a 35-7 win over the Yankees Oct. 24, 1948. He connected with Bill Boedecker on a 79-yard pass play for a touchdown in a 42-7 rout of the Dons Oct. 2, 1949, in Cleveland. Graham also connected with Dub Jones on an 81-yard pass play for a score Sept. 30, 1951, against the 49ers.

He passed for a team record six touchdowns in a 61-14 destruction of Los Angeles Oct. 14, 1949, in Los Angeles. He ranks first in all-time Browns postseason passing yards with 2,001 and pass completions with 159. He ranks fifth in all-time Browns postseason rushing yards with 247 (#). He is tied for most points scored in one postseason game with 18 against Buffalo Dec. 19, 1948, and tied for fourth in the same category with 12 points against the Rams in the 1955 NFL title game. Graham holds the third- and fourth-place rankings for most passing yards in one Browns postseason game and three of the top eight positions for most pass completions a postseason affair. He ranks third all-time for the Browns with 36 postseason points.

Graham was voted AAFC Most Valuable Player in 1947 and 1949 by OFF, and in 1948 by UP. He was named AAFC co-Most Valuable Player with San Francisco 49ers quarterback Frankie Albert in 1948 by OFF. He was voted NFL Most Valuable Player in 1953 by UP and in 1955 by SN and UP.

He was voted to All-AAFC teams in 1946 by OFF and UP, in 1947 by AP, C&O, NYN, OFF, and SP; in 1948 by AP, OFF, and UP; and in 1949 by AP, NYN, OFF, and UP. INS voted him to the All-AAFC offensive team in 1949. He was voted to All-NFL offensive teams in 1951 by AP, NYN, and UP; in 1952 by NYN and UP; in 1953 by AP, NYN, and UP; in 1954 by AP, NYN, SN, and UP; and in 1955 by AP, NYN, and UP.

He was a Pro Bowl selection from 1950-54. His No. 32 uniform is retired by the Browns (he also wore No. 60). Graham was inducted into the Pro Football Hall of Fame in 1965. He was a Browns television broadcaster in 1956.

GRANER, JIM

Jim Graner was a Browns radio broadcaster from 1955-60 and 1963-74.

GRAYSON, DAVID

David Grayson was a Browns linebacker from 1987-90. A product of Fresno State University, he was acquired by Cleveland as a free agent during the 1987 players' strike. He returned an interception 14 yards for a touchdown in the Browns' 51-0 opening-day rout of the Steelers in Pittsburgh Sept. 10, 1989.

GREEN, BOYCE

Boyce Green was a Cleveland running back from 1983-85. He was an 11th-round draft choice of the Browns in 1983 from Carson-Newman College. Green was the Browns' rushing yards leader in 1984 with 673. His best game came the year before, on Oct. 16 against Pittsburgh. Despite the Browns' crushing loss, 44-17, in a battle for first place, he rushed for 137 yards, becoming the first running back to top the century mark against the Steelers in Three Rivers Stadium in six years.

GREEN, ERNIE

Ernie Green was a Cleveland running back from 1962-68. He was a product of the University of Louisville obtained by the Browns Aug. 13, 1962, in a trade with the Green Bay Packers for a seventh-round draft choice in 1963. His longest rush was a 73-yarder in a 38-10 loss in Detroit Dec. 8, 1963. He was second on the team in rushing yards behind Jim Brown from 1963-65 and Leroy Kelly in 1966 and 1967. He was second on the team in touchdowns rushing from 1964-67, and also was tops on the team with 39 receptions in 1967. Green returned kickoffs and punts, too, and had team highs of 13 and 18 kickoff returns in 1962 and 1963, respectively. His 3,204 rushing yards rank eighth all-time in team history. He was selected to play in the Pro Bowl in 1966 and 1967.

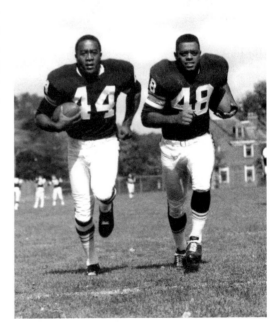

Leroy Kelly (left) and Ernie Greene. Photo courtesy of the Cleveland Browns.

GREEN BAY PACKERS

The Green Bay Packers were a Browns' opponent in the NFL from 1950-95 and have been since 1999. The Packers handed the Browns one of their two most lopsided defeats, 55-7, Nov. 12, 1967, in Milwaukee. The two met once in the postseason—a 23-12 Packers win in the 1965 NFL title game in Lambeau Field. Green Bay's all-time record against Cleveland is 9-6 (.600), with 4-2 (.667) at home and 5-4 (.556) on the road. They are 1-0 (home) against the Browns all-time in the postseason.

Forrest Gregg watches the game as Mike Phipps hangs his head in the background in 1975. Photo courtesy of the Cleveland Press Collection.

GREGG, FORREST

Forrest Gregg was Cleveland's head coach from 1975-77. He began his first season 0-9 en route to a 3-11 (.214) finish. The Browns improved to 9-5 (.643) in 1976, barely missing the playoffs. The team started the 1977 season 5-2 but lost six of their last seven to finish 6-8 (.429). Gregg was fired with one game left that season, although his departure was announced publicly as a resignation. Defensive coordinator Dick Modzelewski coached the last game in Seattle. Gregg was voted AFC Coach of the Year in 1976 by AP. His all-time record was 18-23 (.439), with 11-10 (.524) at home and 7-13 (.350) on the road. He was a Browns assistant coach in 1974.

GREGORY, JACK

Jack Gregory was a Browns defensive end from 1967-71 and in 1979. He was a ninth-round draft choice of the Browns in 1966 from Delta State University while he still had college eligibility left. He was traded to the Giants June 15, 1972, and then re-acquired Aug. 1, 1979, in another trade with New York for a 1980 draft choice. Gregory was a Pro Bowl pick in 1969.

GROSS, AL

Al Gross was a Browns safety from 1983-87. A product of the University of Arizona, Gross was acquired by the Browns Aug. 3, 1983, off waivers. He intercepted five passes in both 1984 and 1985, tying for the team lead in 1984 and leading the team outright in 1985. He returned a 37-yard pass for a touchdown that was instrumental in Cleveland's 35-33 upset of the Giants Dec. 1, 1985, in the Meadowlands.

GROZA, LOU

Lou Groza was a Cleveland offensive tackle and kicker from 1946-59 and 1961-67. A product of Ohio State University, Groza was acquired by the Browns as a free agent. He retired for one season—1960—due to a back injury during training camp. Upon his return in 1961, Groza focused solely on his kicking duties, leaving his left tackle position in the hands of Dick Schafrath.

Groza is the Browns' all-time leading scorer with 1,608 points. His 108 points in 1953 are tied for sixth-most in one Browns season, and his 115 in 1964 rank third all-time in team history. He led the Browns in scoring every year from 1950-57, and in 1961 and 1964. He ended his career with 810 extra points and 264 field goals in 481 attempts. His 83 postseason points rank first all-time for the Browns. He kicked a 53-yard field goal Oct. 10, 1948, against the Brooklyn Dodgers. He nailed 52-yarders against the Rams in the NFL Championship game Dec. 23, 1951, and the Giants Oct. 12, 1952. He connected on 51-yarders against the Chicago Rockets Nov. 17, 1946, Los Angeles Dons Sept. 3, 1948, Chicago Cardinals Dec. 16, 1956, and the Steelers Oct. 28, 1962.

He was voted NFL Most Valuable Player in 1954 by SN. He was named to All-NFL offensive teams in 1951 by NYN and UP in 1952; in 1953 by AP, NYN, and UP; in 1954 by AP, NYN, SN, and UP; in 1955 by AP, NYN, NEA, and UP; and in 1957 by NYN and UP. He was picked for the Pro Bowl from 1950-55 and 1957-59. Groza's No. 76 uniform is retired by the Browns (he also wore No. 46). He was voted into the Pro Football Hall of Fame in 1974.

Lou Groza in action against the Rams Sept. 28, 1958. Photo courtesy of the Cleveland Press Collection.

H

HAIRSTON, CARL

Carl Hairston was a Cleveland defensive end from 1984-89. A product of the University of Maryland Eastern Shore, Hairston was acquired by the Browns Feb. 9, 1984, in a trade with the Eagles for an undisclosed draft choice. His 37.5 sacks are fourth all-time in Browns history. He was part of one of the most memorable plays in Browns history Dec. 13, 1987, against the Bengals in Cleveland Stadium. With the Browns leading in the second quarter, 21-3, Hairston was on the receiving end of a lateral pass from Clay Matthews following Matthews's interception of a Boomer Esiason pass at the Browns' four-yard line. When Matthews got to the Browns' 40, he threw the ball to Hairston, who was the only Brown in the vicinity. The big guy lumbered 40 yards before he was taken down at the Bengals' 20-yard-line.

HALL, CHARLIE

Charlie Hall was a Browns linebacker from 1971-80. He was a Browns third-round draft choice in 1971 from the University of Houston. He tied for the team lead in interceptions in 1975. One memorable interception occurred Nov. 4, 1979, when he picked off a Ron Jaworski pass with no time left on the clock and Philadelphia at the Browns' one-yard line, thus preserving the Browns' 24-19 win.

HALL, DINO

Dino Hall was a Browns kickoff returner and running back from 1979-83. A product of Glassboro State College, Hall was acquired by Cleveland as a free agent June 14, 1979. He was released Aug. 21, 1979, and then re-signed Oct. 2, 1979, when Keith Wright injured a knee in week five. Hall led the Browns in kickoff returns and kickoff return yardage every year from 1979-82. He also returned punts, leading the team in returns and return yardage in 1979, 1981 and 1983. His 1,014 kickoff return yards in 1979 rank second for the most in one Browns season, and his 813 in 1981 rank eighth. His 295 punt return yards in 1979 rank ninth for the most in one Browns season. His 3,185 kickoff

Charlie Hall (right) knocks down a pass during training camp in July 1974. Photo courtesy of the Cleveland Press Collection.

return yards all-time rank first in team history, and his 901 all-time punt return yards rank fourth.

HALL OF FAME GAME

The Browns have played in the Hall of Fame Game, the annual exhibition contest in Canton, Ohio, five times. The following are the results:

Pittsburgh 16, Cleveland 7 (Sept. 8, 1963)
Philadelphia 28, Cleveland 13 (Aug. 5, 1967)
Cleveland 24, Atlanta 10 (Aug. 1, 1981)
Chicago 13, Cleveland 0 (Aug. 4, 1990)
Cleveland 20, Dallas 17 (OT) (Aug. 9, 1999)

Overall   2-3 (.400)

HALL OF FAMERS

Fourteen Browns have been inducted into the Hall of Fame. The year the individuals were inducted is in parentheses.

Otto Graham (1965)
Paul Brown (1967)

Marion Motley (1968)
Jim Brown (1971)
Lou Groza (1974)
Dante Lavelli (1975)
Len Ford (1976)
Bill Willis (1977)
Bobby Mitchell (1983)
Paul Warfield (1983)
Mike McCormack (1984)
Frank Gatski (1985)
Leroy Kelly (1994)
Ozzie Newsome (1999)

HANSEN, BRIAN

Brian Hansen was a Browns punter from 1991-93. A product of the University of Sioux Falls, Hansen was acquired by Cleveland Apr. 1, 1991, as a free agent. He had punts of 73 *Six Hall of Famers pose together: (From left to right, front to back) Dante Lavelli, Paul Brown, Frank Gatski, Marion Motley, Lou Groza, and Otto Graham.*

yards Sept. 27, 1992, at home against Denver and 72 yards Oct. 17, 1993, in Cincinnati. His 3,632 punting yards in 1993 rank sixth all-time for the Browns, and his 3,397 punting yards in 1991 rank ninth all-time for one Browns season. Hansen ranks sixth all-time in team history with 10,112 punting yards.

HEAD COACHES

For a list of Browns head coaches, please see Coaches and Assistant Coaches on page 179 for a full list of head coaches.

HEAD COACHES' COMPOSITE WON-LOST-TIED RECORDS

Paul Brown—158-48-8 (.757)
Blanton Collier—76-34-2 (.688)
Nick Skorich—30-24-2 (.554)
Forrest Gregg—18-23 (.439)
Dick Modzelewski—0-1 (.000)
Sam Rutigliano—47-50 (.485)
Marty Schottenheimer—44-27 (.620)
Bud Carson—11-13-1 (.460)

Jim Shofner—1-6 (.143)
Bill Belichick—36-44 (.450)
Chris Palmer—2-14 (.125)
Butch Davis—7-9-0 (.438)

HEISMAN TROPHY WINNERS

The following winners of the Heisman Trophy in college went on to play for the Browns:

Howard Cassady
Les Horvath
Vinny Testaverde
Charles White

HENRY, ANTHONY

Anthony Henry has been a Browns defensive back since 2001. A fourth-round draft choice by the Browns in 2001 from the University of South Florida, Henry intercepted 10 passes in 2001, tying him with Tom Colella's 1946 total and Thom Darden's 1978 total for the all-time team record. He led the AFC in interceptions, and tied for first in the NFL, becoming the first NFL rookie to lead the league in picks since 1995.

He became the first Browns player to have a pair of three-interception games, the first player in the NFL to accomplish the feat since 1989, and the first rookie to do so since 1962. Henry's three-interception games came Sept. 23 at home against Detroit and Nov. 18 at Baltimore. His 97-yard interception return for a touchdown late in the third quarter against Jacksonville kept the Browns within striking distance in what turned out to be a harrowing loss at home on Dec. 16.

HICKERSON, GENE

Gene Hickerson was a Browns guard from 1958-60 and 1962-73. He was Cleveland's seventh-round draft choice in 1957 from the University of Mississippi with one year of eligibility in school left. He missed the 1961 season due to a broken leg suffered in the first preseason game at Detroit Aug. 11. He fractured the leg again late in the season while watching a game from the sideline. Hickerson was voted to All-NFL offensive teams in 1966 by NEA, in 1967 by AP, NYN, NEA, and UPI; in 1968 by AP, NYN, NEA, PFW, FWA, and UPI; and in 1969 by AP, NYN, OFF, PFW, FWA, SI, and UPI. He was voted to All-AFC offensive teams in 1970 by FWA and UPI. He was selected to play in the Pro Bowl from 1965-70.

Gene Hickerson. Photo courtesy of the Cleveland Browns.

HIGHEST-SCORING GAMES

The highest-scoring game for the Browns occurred in 1946, when the Browns stomped Brooklyn, 66-14. *For more highest-scoring games by the Browns and Browns' opponents, please see Team Statistics on page 204.*

HILL, CALVIN

Calvin Hill was a Browns running back from 1978-81. A Yale University product, he was acquired by the Browns four weeks into the 1978 season as a free agent. He was used mostly as a receiver out of the backfield. He had 25 receptions for 334 yards and six touchdowns (second on the team) in 1978, 38 catches for 381 yards and a pair of touchdowns in 1979, and 27 receptions for 383 yards and a team-leading six touchdowns in 1980.

HIRAM COLLEGE

Hiram College acted as the Browns' training camp site from 1952-74.

Calvin Hill. Photo courtesy of the Cleveland Browns.

Cleveland rookies practice at training camp at Hiram College in July 1970. Photo courtesy of the Cleveland Press Collection.

HOAGLIN, FRED

Fred Hoaglin was a Cleveland center from 1966-72. He was a Browns sixth-round draft choice in 1966 from the University of Pittsburgh. He was picked to play in the Pro Bowl in 1969.

HOARD, LEROY

Leroy Hoard was a Cleveland running back from 1990-95. He was a second-round draft choice by the Browns in 1990 from the University of Michigan. He had a team-leading 11 touchdowns in 1991—nine receiving and two rushing with many completed in spectacular fashion. He was tops for the Browns in rushing yards in 1994 with 890 and 1995 with 547. His 1994 rushing yards total was the highest for a Browns player in nine years. Hoard was a Pro Bowl selection in 1994.

HOME WON-LOST-TIED RECORDS

Please see Team Statistics on page 204.

HOOKER, FAIR

Fair Hooker was a Browns wide receiver from 1969-74. Cleveland's fifth-round draft choice in 1969 from Arizona State University, Hooker led the Browns in receptions (45) and receiving yards (649) in 1971. He totaled 129 catches for 1,845 yards and eight touchdown catches in his Browns career. He was on the receiving end of a 27-yard touchdown pass from Mike Phipps that gave the Browns a surprising 14-13 lead over the undefeated Miami Dolphins late in an AFC Divisional Playoff Dec. 24, 1972, in the Orange Bowl. The Browns eventually lost, 20-14. Hooker had three catches for 53 yards that day.

HORVATH, LES

Les Horvath was a Cleveland running back in 1949. He was a product of Ohio State University. He returned a fumble 84 yards for a touchdown that gave the Browns their winning touchdown in a 14-3 victory over the New York Yankees Sept. 18, 1949, in Cleveland.

HOUSTON, JIM

Jim Houston was a Browns defensive end and line-backer from 1960-72. A first-round draft choice by the Browns in 1960 from Ohio State University, he was the younger brother of Lin Houston, who was a Cleveland guard from 1946-53. Houston returned an interception 44 yards for a touchdown in the Browns' 38-24 victory over visiting Philadelphia Nov. 29, 1964. He returned a Fran Tarkenton pass 79 yards for a score Dec. 3, 1967, in a 24-14 win over

Jim Houston. Photo courtesy of the Cleveland Browns.

the visiting Giants, and a week later returned a Jim Hart pass 18 yards for Cleveland's final score in a key 20-16 victory over the Cardinals in St. Louis. Houston was named to All-NFL defensive teams in 1964 by NEA and in 1965 by UPI. He was selected to play in the Pro Bowl in 1964, 1965, 1969, and 1970.

Lin Houston. Photo courtesy of Ted Patterson.

HOUSTON, LIN

Lin Houston was a guard for the Browns from 1946-53. He was a product of Ohio State University obtained by the Browns as a free agent. He was the older brother of Jim Houston, a defensive end and linebacker for the Browns from 1960-72.

HOWELL, MIKE

Mike Howell was a Browns defensive back from 1965-72. Cleveland's eighth-round draft choice in 1965 from Grambling State University, Howell had eight interceptions in 1966 that tied for the team lead and for eighth all-time in team history. His six picks in 1969 were tops on the team. He returned a Billy Kilmer pass 68 yards in the Browns' season-ending 20-13 triumph in Washington Dec. 19, 1971. Howell's 27 interceptions are tied for seventh all-time in Browns history.

HTTP://WWW.CLEVELANDBROWNS.COM/

Http://www.clevelandbrowns.com/ is the official Browns web site. It features several interactive elements for fans, updated information before each game, and is updated with activity from both on and off the field.

HUFF, SAM

Sam Huff was a linebacker for the New York Giants from 1956-63 and the Washington Redskins from 1964-69. Memorable were his hard-hitting confrontations with Jim Brown, especially during his days with the Giants.

HUMBLE, WELDON

Weldon Humble was a Cleveland linebacker from 1947-50. A product of Rice University, Humble was acquired by the Browns Aug. 14, 1947, in a trade with the Baltimore Colts for four players. He was a Pro Bowl pick in 1950.

HUNTER, ART

Art Hunter was a center for the Browns from 1956-59. He was a product of the University of Notre Dame acquired by the Browns Sept. 8, 1955, in a trade with Green Bay for two players. He was in the military in 1955 and for the first month of the 1956 season. He was a Pro Bowl selection in 1959.

I

INDIANAPOLIS COLTS

The Indianapolis Colts were NFL opponents of the Browns from 1953-95 and have been since 1999. The team was located in Baltimore from 1953-83 as a holding of the defunct Dallas Texans (no relation to the future AFL Dallas Texans). One of the more memorable Browns victories against the Colts occurred Nov. 1, 1959, in Baltimore when Jim Brown rushed for a team-record five touchdowns in a 38-31 win.

Another notable Cleveland victory came at home Oct. 25, 1981, when the team defeated Baltimore, 42-28, as Brian Sipe passed for a team-record 444 yards. The last meeting between the teams was an exciting Colts victory Dec. 26, 1999, in snowy Cleveland, when Mike Vanderjagt's 21-yard field goal with four seconds left gave Indianapolis a 29-28 victory.

The Colts and Browns have clashed four times in the postseason, all in Cleveland. Each team has won twice—once in the NFL Championship game and once in the AFC Divisional Playoffs. The heavily-favored Colts were upset by the Browns, 27-0, in the 1964 NFL Championship game in Cleveland. Baltimore easily won, 34-0, in the 1968 NFL title game in Cleveland. Baltimore defeated

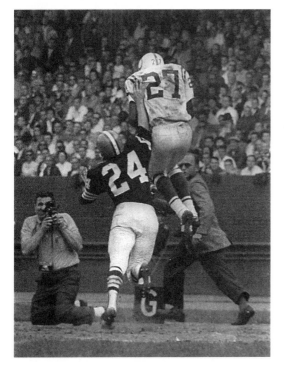

Bobby Franklin defends as Baltimore's R.C. Owens catches a pass on the goal line during the Colts' 36-14 rout of the Browns in Cleveland Oct. 14, 1962. Photo courtesy of the Cleveland Press Collection.

the Browns, 20-3, in a 1971 AFC Divisional Playoff, and the Browns won, 38-21, in a 1987 AFC Divisional Playoff. The Colts' all-time record against Cleveland is 8-14 (.364), with 4-9 (.308) at home and 4-5 (.444) on the road. Their all-time postseason record is 2-2 (away).

INDIVIDUAL TOP FIVES (POSTSEASON)

Please see Individual Statistics on page 188.

INDIVIDUAL TOP TENS

Please see Individual Statistics on page 188.

INTERCEPTIONS LEADERS

Please see Individual Statistics on page 188.

J

JACKSON, MICHAEL

Michael Jackson was a Browns wide receiver from 1991-95. He was a sixth-round draft choice of the Browns in 1991 from the University of Southern Mississippi. He tied Eric Metcalf for the Browns' lead in receptions in 1992 with 47. He was also the team leader that year in receiving yards (755) and touchdown receptions (seven). He also led the team in receiving yards and touchdown catches in 1993 (756, eight) and 1995 (714, nine).

Jackson's 122 receiving yards in Cleveland's 20-13 win over New England at home in an AFC Wild Card game Jan. 1, 1995, rank third all-time in Browns history. His seven receptions in the Patriots game are tied for second all-time.

JACKSON, ROBERT E.

Robert E. Jackson was a Browns guard from 1975-85. He was a product of Duke University acquired by Cleveland as a free agent in 1975.

Robert E. Jackson (left) and Cody Risen head for the showers in 1979. Photo courtesy of the Cleveland Press Collection.

Robert L. Jackson in 1978.
Photo courtesy of the
Cleveland Press Collection.

JACKSON, ROBERT L.

Robert L. Jackson was a Browns linebacker from 1978-81. He was a first-round draft pick of Cleveland's from Texas A&M University in 1977. A serious knee injury suffered at the outset of training camp forced him to miss the entire 1977 season.

JACKSONVILLE JAGUARS

The Jacksonville Jaguars were Browns opponents in the NFL in 1995 and have been since 1999. They administered one of the Browns' most embarrassing losses in their 23-15 win Oct. 22, 1995, in Cleveland during Jacksonville's initial season. The most memorable game in the series came Dec. 16, 2001, in Cleveland in a 15-10 Jaguars victory amid a frightening bottle-throwing episode by thousands of fans caused by a controversial call by the officials in the late stages of the game. *(See Bottlegate.)* Jacksonville's all-time record against the Browns is 7-1 (.875), with 3-1 (.750) at home and 4-0 on the road.

JAGADE, HARRY

Harry Jagade was a Browns running back from 1951-53. A product of Indiana University, he was acquired by Cleveland as a free agent in 1951. Jagade rushed for a team-high 104 yards on 15 carries and scored the Browns' only touchdown, a seven-yard run in the third quarter, during a 17-7 loss to the Lions in the 1952 NFL Championship game in Cleveland. Remarkably, Jagade gave a repeat performance with the exact same rushing statistics in the 1953 NFL title game against the same Lions, but this time in the Motor City. Once again, he totaled 104 yards on 15 carries in the Browns' 17-16 loss. He even scored on a third-quarter run, but this time it was a nine-yard run, two yards longer than his touchdown the year before. Jagade was picked for the Pro Bowl in 1953.

JAMES, TOMMY

Tommy James was a Browns defensive back from 1948-55. He was a product of Ohio State University obtained by the Browns as a free agent. His nine interceptions in 1950 led the Browns and are tied for the fourth-most picks in one Browns season. He ranks fourth all-time for the Browns in interceptions with 34, and was a Pro Bowl selection in 1953.

(Left to right) Jim Houston, Dale Lindsey, and Jack Gregory during the late stages of the Browns' 27-7 loss to the Vikings in the NFL Championship game in Metropolitan Stadium Jan. 4, 1970. Photo courtesy of the Cleveland Press Collection.

JANUARY
—9, 1963

Art Modell fired Coach Paul Brown.

—2, 1966

The Browns fell to the Green Bay Packers, 23-12, in the snow and mud of Lambeau Field in Green Bay in the NFL title game.

—4, 1970

Cleveland lost to the Minnesota Vikings, 27-7, in the NFL Championship game in Minnesota.

—26, 1970

The Browns traded sensational wide receiver Paul Warfield to Miami in exchange for the Dolphins' first-round pick—and third overall—in the next day's draft. The Browns did this in order to draft Purdue University quarterback Mike Phipps. Many believe this trade was the main reason behind the Browns' mediocrity in the mid-1970s.

—7, 1995

The Browns were obliterated by the Pittsburgh Steelers, 29-9, in an AFC Divisional Playoff in Pittsburgh.

JOHNSON, EDDIE

Eddie Johnson was a Browns linebacker from 1981-90. He was a seventh-round draft choice by the Browns in 1981 from the University of Louisville. Johnson was partly responsible for the birth of the famous Dawg Pound due to his barking ways during the 1984 training camp when a defensive teammate would make a big play. *(See Dawg Pound.)*

JOHNSON, KEVIN

Kevin Johnson has been a Browns wide receiver since 1999. He was a second-round draft choice of Cleveland's in 1999 from Syracuse University. He led all NFL rookies in 1999 in receptions (66), receiving yards (986), and touchdown receptions (eight). He set Browns rookie records for receptions and receiving yards. His yardage total (2,572) ranks eighth in team history and his receptions total (207) ranks sixth. Johnson was the receptions leader for the Browns with 57 and the receiving yards leader with 669 in 2000. He had a 79-yard reception from Tim Couch in a home game against Pittsburgh Sept. 17 that year and a 67-yarder from Couch at Baltimore Nov. 26. Johnson's 84 receptions in 2001 were tops on the team and rank third all-time for the Browns behind only Ozzie Newsome's 89 in both 1983 and 1984. His nine touchdown receptions in 2001 led the team and tied for third in the AFC and fifth in the NFL. His 1,097 receiving yards that year rank third in team history behind only Webster Slaughter's 1,236 in 1989 and Mac Speedie's 1,146 in 1947. Johnson has been the only Brown to start all 48 games since 1999.

JOHNSON, MIKE

Mike Johnson was a Browns linebacker from 1986-93. He was a first-round supplemental draft choice of the Browns in 1984 from Virginia Tech University. He spent 1984 and 1985 in the USFL. He returned an interception 64 yards for a touchdown Sept. 23, 1990, in a 24-14 home loss to the San Diego Chargers. Johnson was voted to All-AFC defensive teams in 1989 by PFW and UPI. He was selected to play in the Pro Bowl in 1989 and 1990.

JOHNSON, PEPPER

Pepper Johnson was a Cleveland linebacker from 1993-95. He was an Ohio State University product acquired by the Browns as a free agent on Sept. 2, 1993. He was selected to play in the Pro Bowl in 1994.

JOHNSON, WALTER

Walter Johnson was a Browns defensive tackle from 1965-76. He was a second-round draft choice by Cleveland in 1965 from California State University (Los Angeles). He was picked for the Pro Bowl from 1967-69.

JONES, DAVE

Dave Jones was Cleveland's majority owner from 1953-60.

JONES, DUB

Dub Jones was a Browns wide receiver from 1948-55. A Tulane University product, Jones was acquired by the Browns in 1948 in a trade with Brooklyn for that year's draft rights to University of Michigan All-American running back Bob Chappius. Jones's most memorable moment came Nov. 25, 1951, when he scored six touchdowns in Cleveland's 42-21 victory over the visiting Chicago Bears. Four of the touchdowns came on rushes and two on receptions. His feat set a Browns record and tied an NFL mark. On Sept. 30 of that year in a game against

Dub Jones in preseason action, 1951. Photo courtesy of the Cleveland Press Collection.

the 49ers, Jones was on the receiving end of an 81-yard pass play from Graham that went for a touchdown. He was voted to All-NFL offensive teams in 1951 by AP, NYN, and UP. He was picked for the Pro Bowl in 1951. He was a Browns assistant coach from 1963-67.

JONES, EDGAR

Edgar Jones was a Browns running back from 1946-49. He was a product of the University of Pittsburgh obtained by Cleveland as a free agent. He returned a kickoff 96 yards for a touchdown in a 66-14 rout of the Brooklyn Dodgers in the 1946 season finale Dec. 8 in Brooklyn. Jones is tied for fourth in team history for most points scored in one postseason game with 12 against Buffalo Dec. 19, 1948. His 30 postseason points rank fifth all-time for the Browns.

Edgar Jones. Photo courtesy of Ted Patterson.

JONES, HOMER

Homer Jones was a Browns wide receiver in 1970. He was a Texas Southern University product obtained by the Browns Jan. 26, 1970, in a trade with the New York Giants for Ron Johnson, Jim Kanicki, and Wayne Meylan. The majority of his action came as a kickoff returner, as he led the Browns in kickoff returns and kickoff return yards with 29 and 739, respectively, in 1970. His most memorable moment came in Cleveland Sept. 21, 1970, in the NFL's first-ever ABC *Monday Night Football* game in which Jones returned the second-half kickoff 94 yards for a touchdown that helped defeat Joe Namath and the New York Jets, 31-21.

JONES, JOE

Joe Jones was a Browns defensive end in 1970, 1971, 1973, and from 1975-78. He was a second-round draft pick of the Browns in 1970 from Tennessee State University. He missed the 1972 season due to knee surgery. He was traded to the Eagles Sept. 5, 1974, and then re-acquired via waivers Nov. 14, 1975. Jones was responsible for one of the more notable occurrences in Browns history, when early in the fourth quarter of an Oct. 10, 1976, home game against Pittsburgh, he sacked quarterback Terry Bradshaw by lifting him up and slamming him head first to the ground, causing Bradshaw to miss the next two games due to back and neck injuries.

Joe Jones closes in on Oakland's Daryle Lamonica during the Oct. 4, 1971 Monday Night Football *game. Photo courtesy of the Cleveland Press Collection.*

JONES, TONY

Tony Jones was a Browns offensive tackle from 1988-95. He was a Western Carolina University product acquired by the Browns as a free agent May 28, 1988. He was voted to the All-AFC defensive team in 1994 by PFW.

K

KANICKI, JIM

Jim Kanicki was a Browns defensive tackle from 1963-69. He was a second-round draft choice of the Browns in 1963 from Michigan State University.

KANSAS CITY CHIEFS

The Kansas City Chiefs were opponents of the Browns in the NFL from 1970-95 and have been since 1999. The last two Browns games to end in a tie came against the Chiefs. Both seasons in which these occurred, the Browns came away with seven wins and three losses. Following a 20-20 tie Dec. 2, 1973, in Kansas City, Cleveland was 7-3-2 (.667), and after a 10-10 standoff at home Nov. 19, 1989, the Browns were 7-3-1 (.682). Kansas City's all-time record against Cleveland is 7-8-2 (.471), with 6-2-1 (.722) at home and 1-6-1 (.188) on the road.

Jim Kanicki. Photo courtesy of the Cleveland Browns.

KARDIAC KIDS

The Kardiac Kids was the nickname attributed to the Browns early in the 1979 season and continued on throughout the 1980 season due to numerous games that were undecided until the final moments, most of which the Browns won.

KELLERMAN, ERNIE

Ernie Kellerman was a Cleveland defensive back from 1966-71. Kellerman was a Miami University product obtained by the Browns as a free agent in 1965. He spent that season on the practice squad. He tied for second on the team in 1967 with six interceptions.

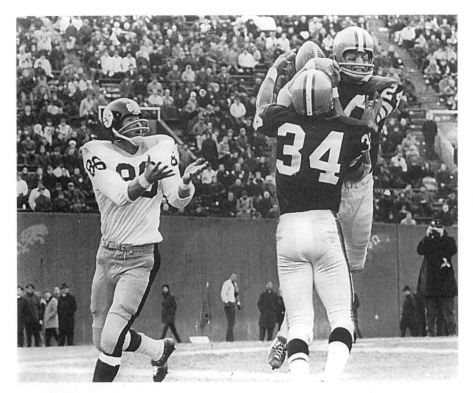

Ernie Kellerman (24) or Mike Howell appear to have an interception on the Pittsburgh goal line Nov. 5, 1967. Photo courtesy of the Cleveland Press Collection.

KELLY, LEROY

Leroy Kelly was a Browns running back from 1964-73. He was an eighth-round draft pick of the Browns in 1964 from Morgan State University. He led Cleveland in rushing yardage every season from 1966-72 and earned three straight 1,000-yard rushing seasons from 1966-68. His 1,141 yards rushing in 1966 ranked second in the NFL, 90 yards behind Chicago's Gale Sayers. His 1,205 yards on the ground in 1967, and 1,239 in 1968, led the league and rank 10th and ninth in Browns history.

Kelly caught a 46-yard touchdown pass from Bill Nelsen and scored on a 35-yard run in a 31-20 upset of the Dallas Cowboys Dec. 21, 1968, in the Eastern Conference Championship game in Cleveland. He ranks second in all-time Browns rushing yardage with 7,274. His 540 points rank fifth all-time in team history. His 120 points in 1968 rank second in Browns history. Kelly's all-time 427 postseason rushing yards rank third in team annals (#). His 12 points scored against Dallas in the 1968 Eastern Conference title game are tied for fourth all-time for the Browns.

He was effective as a receiver, totaling 190 receptions for 2,281 yards (plus 18 for 190) in postseason play in his Browns career. He ranks second all-time in team history in combined net yards with 12,329 (######). Kelly also returned punts and kickoffs on a regular basis early in his career. His 990 punt return yards rank third, and his 1,784 kickoff return yards rank fifth, all-time in team history. His 292 punt return yards in 1971 are 10th most in one Browns season.

He had three punt returns for touchdowns—a 68-yarder against the Giants Oct. 25, 1964, a 67-yarder Nov. 21, 1965, against the Cowboys, and a 56-yarder the very next week Nov. 28 against the Steelers. In addition, he returned one 74 yards in a home game against the Denver Broncos Oct. 24, 1971. Kelly's 2,014 combined net yards in 1966 rank second in Browns annals.

He was named the NFL's Most Valuable Player in 1968 by MAX. He was voted to All-NFL offensive teams in 1966 and 1967 by AP, NYN, NEA, and UPI; in 1968 by AP, NYN, NEA, PFW, FWA, and UPI; and in 1969 by NEA. He was voted to the All-AFC offensive team in 1971 by NEA. He was a Pro Bowl selection from 1966-71 and was inducted into the Pro Football Hall of Fame in 1994.

Leroy Kelly in action against the Giants Dec. 3, 1967. Photo courtesy of the Cleveland Press Collection.

KENT STATE UNIVERSITY

Kent State University was the Browns' training camp site from 1975-81. The school has had five players drafted by the Browns.

Browns assistant coach Blanton Collier works with Brian Sipe (left) and Mike Phipps during training camp at Kent State University. Photo courtesy of the Cleveland Press Collection.

KICKERS

Notable kickers in Browns annals include Lou Groza, Don Cockroft, Matt Bahr, Matt Stover and Phil Dawson.

KICKOFF LUNCHEON

The kickoff luncheon was held annually before most seasons during the 1970s and '80s at various Cleveland hotels to acquaint players and coaches with the public. The luncheon was sponsored by the Cleveland Touchdown Club and Greater Cleveland Growth Association.

KICKOFF RETURN YARDS LEADERS

Please see Individual Statistics on page 188.

KICKOFF RETURNERS

Notable Browns kickoff returners include Edgar Jones, Marion Motley, Ken Carpenter, Bobby Mitchell, Walter Roberts, Ben Davis, Bo Scott, Homer Jones, Ken Brown, Greg Pruitt, Keith Wright, Dino Hall, Glen Young, Gerald McNeil, Eric Metcalf, and Randy Baldwin.

John Kissell. Photo courtesy of the Cleveland Browns.

KISSELL, JOHN

John Kissell was a Cleveland defensive tackle from 1950-52 and 1954-56. He was a Boston College product acquired by the Browns prior to the 1950 season as part of a three-player merger with the Buffalo Bills of the folded AAFC. He played in the CFL in 1953.

KONZ, KEN

Ken Konz was a Cleveland defensive back from 1953-59. He was a first-round draft choice of the Browns in 1951 from Louisiana State University. He was in the military in 1951 and 1952. Konz led the Browns in interceptions with seven in 1954 and tied for the team lead in 1953, 1955, 1957, and 1958. He ranks fifth in Cleveland history with 30 interceptions. He also returned punts, and ranks eighth in team annals with 556 return yards. Konz was selected to play in the Pro Bowl in 1955.

KOSAR, BERNIE

Bernie Kosar was a Browns quarterback from 1985-93. He was a first-round supplemental draft choice of the Browns in 1985 from the University of Miami. The Browns obtained the rights to choose him when they traded their Nos. 1 and 3 draft choices in 1985 and Nos. 1 and 6 draft picks in 1986 to Buffalo. Kosar went public with his desire to play for the Browns, the team he rooted for while growing up in nearby Boardman, Ohio.

He fumbled his first snap in a home game against New England Oct. 6, 1985, after starter Gary Danielson went down with a severe right shoulder injury in the second quarter. Kosar completed his first seven passes, though, and directed the Browns to a 24-20 triumph. He completed 124 of 248 passes for 1,578 yards with eight touchdowns and seven interceptions that year, sharing time with the oft-injured Danielson, as the Browns won their first AFC Central Division title in five years despite just an 8-8 record. In the AFC Divisional Playoff matchup with the Dolphins in Miami Jan. 4, 1986—a game the Browns eventually lost, 24-21—Kosar threw a 16-yard touchdown pass to Ozzie Newsome that gave the Browns a 7-3 first-quarter lead.

Bernie Kosar. Photo courtesy of the Cleveland Browns.

He became the starter once and for all the next year when Danielson went down with a season-ending injury—a fractured left ankle—in the final preseason game against the Raiders in Los Angeles Aug. 28. He passed for 3,854 yards in 1986, completing 310 of 531 attempts in leading Cleveland to a 12-4 (.750) record and the Central Division title once again. That season Kosar had his only two 400-yard passing games—414 on Nov. 23 at home against Pittsburgh and 401 two weeks earlier in a Monday night home game against Miami. In an AFC Divisional Playoff Jan. 3, 1987, in Cleveland, Kosar passed for an NFL Playoff record 489 yards as the Browns fought back from a 20-10 deficit late in the fourth quarter to defeat the New York Jets, 23-20, in double overtime. In the AFC Championship the next week—a 23-20 overtime loss to Denver at home—he completed 18 of 32 passes for 259 yards with two touchdown passes and two interceptions.

In 1987, Kosar led the AFC with a 95.4 quarterback rating. He completed 241 of 389 passes for 3,033 yards that year, with 22 touchdown passes and just nine interceptions as the Browns returned to the AFC title game but lost to the Broncos again—this time in Denver by a 38-33 count. Kosar's 356 yards through the air in the loss to the Broncos rank second in team history. He suffered an arm injury in the opening game in Kansas City the next season when Chiefs safety Lloyd Burruss blindsided him. He was out until week eight, when he returned with flying colors and completed 25 of 43 passes for 314 yards and three touchdowns in a 29-21 victory over the Phoenix Cardinals. He injured his left knee Dec. 12 in a Monday night loss in Miami, which ended his season for good.

Kosar led the Browns back to their third meeting in four years with Denver in the conference championship game in 1989, but the Browns lost again, 37-21, in Denver. On Oct. 23 of that year, he completed a 97-yard touchdown pass to Webster Slaughter in a 27-7 Monday night victory over the Bears, the second-longest pass play in team history. Kosar struggled along with the team in 1990, and was benched for a period during the season. He wound up completing 230 of 423 passes for 2,562 yards, with 10 touchdown passes and

15 interceptions. His quarterback rating was only 65.7. The Browns finished just 3-13 (.188) that year. However, he rebounded in 1991, throwing for 3,487 yards, 18 touchdowns, and just nine interceptions while completing 307 passes in 494 attempts for a completion percentage of 62.1. He broke Bart Starr's 26-year-old NFL record for most consecutive passes without an interception that actually dated back to the 1990 season.

Kosar was injured for part of 1992, splitting time with Mike Tomczak as the starter. He was released Nov. 8, 1993, after two months of playing musical quarterbacks with ex-college teammate Vinny Testaverde, who was acquired as a free agent in the off-season. Kosar ranks third in all-time passing yards for the Browns with 21,904 and second in pass completions with 1,853. He holds four of the top 10 positions for most passing yards by a Browns quarterback in one season and four of the top 11 spots for most pass completions by a Browns quarterback in a season (1986, 1987, 1989, and 1991 for both categories). His 1,860 postseason passing yards and 146 pass completions both rank second all-time in team history. He holds the top two positions for most completions in a postseason game (33 against the Jets Jan. 3, 1987, and 26 in Denver Jan. 17, 1988) and four of the top eight spots. Kosar was voted to the Pro Bowl in 1987.

L

LAHR, WARREN

Warren Lahr was a Browns defensive back from 1948-59. A Case Western Reserve University product, Lahr was acquired by the Browns as a free agent. He returned an interception 52 yards for a touchdown for Cleveland's final score in its 31-21 victory over the Bills in an AAFC First-Round Payoff game Dec. 4, 1949, in Cleveland. His eight interceptions in 1950 are tied with six other players for eighth all-time in team history. His interception of a Joe Stydahar pass, his second pick of the day, with just seconds left in the 1950 NFL title game against the Rams preserved the Browns' 30-28 victory. Lahr's 44 interceptions all-time rank second in Browns annals. He returned five interceptions for touchdowns in his Browns career. He was named to All-NFL defensive teams in 1951 by NYN and UP. He was a Browns television broadcaster from 1963-67.

Warren Lahr. Photo courtesy of the Cleveland Browns.

LAKELAND COMMUNITY COLLEGE

Lakeland Community College was the Browns' training-camp site from 1982-91.

LAMBERT, JACK

Jack Lambert was a Pittsburgh Steelers linebacker from 1974-84. He was known for his ferocious play. He directed much of his energy towards Browns quarterback Brian Sipe, with whom he had several nasty encounters.

LANGHORNE, REGGIE

Reggie Langhorne was a Browns wide receiver from 1985-91. He was a seventh-round draft choice of the Browns in 1985 from Elizabeth City State University. He led the

Reggie Langhorne. Photo courtesy of the Cleveland Browns.

Browns in 1988 with 780 receiving yards and seven touchdown receptions (on 57 catches). He concluded his Browns career with 261 receptions for 3,597 yards and 15 touchdown catches. He totaled 26 receptions (fourth all-time in Browns history) (###) for 370 yards (fifth all-time in team history) (##) and two touchdown catches in postseason play.

LAST TIME . . ., THE

Did you know that the last time a Browns player returned a punt for a touchdown was Oct. 2, 1995, when Derrick Alexander returned one 69 yards in a 22-19 Bills victory in Cleveland? *For more last times, please see Browns Trivia on page 173.*

LAST TIME THE BROWNS BEAT (CURRENT TEAMS). . ., THE

Please see Browns Trivia on page 173.

LAVELLI, DANTE

Dante Lavelli was a wide receiver for the Browns from 1946-56. He was an Ohio State University product acquired by Cleveland as a free agent. He led the team in receptions in 1946 (40), 1951 (43), 1953 (45), and 1954 (47). He led the Browns in receiving yards in 1946 (843), 1950 (565), and 1953 (783). He was the team leader in touchdown receptions in 1946 (eight), 1947 (nine), 1951 (six), 1953 (six) and 1954 (seven), and the co-leader in touchdown catches in 1948 (five), 1949 (seven), and 1950 (five).

Lavelli ranks eighth all-time for the Browns in scoring with 372 points, second in receiving yards with 6,488, and second in receptions with 386. He caught a 72-yard touchdown pass from Otto Graham Nov. 9, 1947, in Brooklyn. He holds the second and sixth spots for most receiving yards in one game by a Browns player with 209 Oct. 14, 1949, on the road against the Los Angeles Dons, and 183 Oct. 27, 1946, at home against the San Francisco 49ers (#######).

He is tied with four other players for fifth in Browns all-time scoring in the postseason with 30 points. His 526 yards receiving in the postseason rank first all-time in team history

(##). His 30 postseason receptions rank first all-time in team annals (###). He caught 37- and 39-yard touchdown passes in Cleveland's 30-28 victory over the Rams in the 1950 NFL Championship game in Cleveland. His 12 points in that game are tied for fourth all-time in team history. Lavelli was voted to All-AAFC teams in 1946 by AP and OFF and in 1947 by OFF. He was named to All-NFL offensive teams in 1951 and 1953 by NYN and UP, and was selected to play in the Pro Bowl in 1951, 1953, and 1954. He was inducted into the Pro Football Hall of Fame in 1975.

LEFEAR, BILLY

Billy Lefear was a Browns wide receiver from 1972-75. A ninth-round draft choice of Cleveland's in 1972 from Henderson State University, Lefear was best known for his kickoff return duties, as he led the Browns in 1974 with 26 returns and 574 yards, and led the team in 1975 with 412 return yards. His 92-yard return

Dante Lavelli. Photo courtesy of the Cleveland Browns.

off the opening kickoff Nov. 23, 1975, sparked the winless Browns' upset of the red-hot Bengals in Cleveland. He ranks 10th all-time in Browns history with 1,461 kick-off return yards.

Billy Lefear scores against the Redskins in preseason action at the Stadium Aug. 24, 1974. Photo courtesy of the Cleveland Press Collection.

LERNER, AL

Al Lerner has been Cleveland's majority owner since 1999.

Cliff Lewis. Photo courtesy of the Cleveland Browns.

LEWIS, CLIFF

Cliff Lewis was a Browns quarterback from 1946-51. He was a Duke University product acquired by the Browns as a free agent. Because he was a Clevelander, he got to start in the Browns' first game Sept. 6, 1946, at home against the Miami Seahawks. Lewis played defensive back, and his nine interceptions in 1948 are tied for fourth most in one Browns season. He returned punts, too, and ranks fifth all-time in Browns history with 710 return yards. He was a Browns television broadcaster in 1961 and 1962.

LINDSEY, DALE

Dale Lindsey was a Cleveland linebacker from 1965-72. He was a seventh-round draft choice of the Browns in 1965 from Western Kentucky University. His 27-yard interception return gave the Browns a 17-10 lead en route to a 31-20 upset of Dallas in the 1968 Eastern Conference Championship game. He was a Browns assistant coach in 1974.

LINEBACKERS

Notable Browns linebackers include Tommy Thompson, Walt Michaels, Chuck Noll, Galen Fiss, Vince Costello, Jim Houston, Dale Lindsey, Billy Andrews, Charlie Hall, Bob Babich, Dick Ambrose, Clay Matthews, Eddie Johnson, Chip Banks, Tom Cousineau, Mike Johnson, David Grayson, Davis Brandon, Pepper Johnson, Jamir Miller, Wali Rainer, and Dwayne Rudd.

LOGAN, DAVE

Dave Logan was a Browns wide receiver from 1976-83. He was a third-round draft choice of Cleveland's in 1976 from the University of Colorado. He was the team leader in receptions (59) and receiving yards (982) in 1979, and in receiving yards (822) in 1980. His 1979 yardage total ranks ninth all-time in team history. His 4,247 receiving yards also rank ninth all-time in team annals. Logan totaled 262 receptions and 24 touchdown catches during his Browns career.

Dave Logan celebrates after catching a touchdown pass from Brian Sipe in the Browns' 33-30 overtime loss in Pittsburgh Nov. 25, 1979. Photo courtesy of the Cleveland Press Collection.

LOS ANGELES DONS

The Los Angeles Dons were Browns opponents in the AAFC from 1946-49. The Browns amassed their fourth-highest point total in a 61-14 blowout of the Los Angeles Oct. 14, 1949, on the West Coast. The Dons' all-time record against the Browns was 2-6 (.250), 1-3 (.250) at home and 1-3 (.250) on the road.

LOWEST-SCORING GAMES BETWEEN BOTH TEAMS, REGULAR AND POSTSEASON

Please see Team Statistics on page 204.

M

MACK, KEVIN

Kevin Mack was a Browns running back from 1985-93. He was a first-round supplemental draft choice by the Browns in 1984 from Clemson University. After one year in the USFL, he teamed with Earnest Byner in 1985 to become part of just the third running-back tandem in NFL history in which each back rushed for 1,000 yards in the same season. Mack rushed for 1,104 that year and led the team. He was second on the team in rushing touchdowns in 1985 with seven. He was tops on the team in rushing yardage in 1986, 1987 and from 1990-92, with his highest total coming in 1987 when he accumulated 735.

He led the Browns in rushing touchdowns in 1986 (10), 1990 (five), 1991 (eight), and 1992 (six). He is 10th all-time for the Browns in scoring with 324 points, and fifth in rushing yards with 5,123. His 6,725 combined net yards rank eighth all-time in team history (######). His 424 postseason rushing yards rank fourth all-time in Browns annals(#). Mack was voted AFC Rookie of the Year in 1985 by UPI. He was picked to play in the Pro Bowl that year and in 1987.

MAJORITY OWNERS

Art McBride	1946-52
Dave Jones	1953-60
Art Modell	1961-95
Al Lerner	Since 1999

MARSHALL, JIM

Jim Marshall was a Browns defensive end in 1960. He was a fourth-round draft choice of Cleveland's in 1960 from Ohio State University. He was traded to Minnesota as part of an eight-player deal Aug. 31, 1961, and enjoyed a successful career with the Vikings.

MATTHEWS, CLAY

Clay Matthews was a Browns linebacker from 1978-93. He was a Browns first-round draft choice in 1978 from the University of Southern California. His 12 sacks in 1984 ranked second on the team and are the third most in one Browns season. His nine sacks in

1992 tied for the team lead and for eighth most in one Browns season. His 63.5 career sacks are the most in team annals. Matthews was named to All-AFC defensive teams in 1984 by NEA, PFW, and SN. He was selected to play in the Pro Bowl in 1985 and from 1987-89.

MAYER, BILL

Bill Mayer was a Cleveland radio broadcaster from 1947-49 and in 1954, and a television broadcaster from 1949-51.

McBRIDE, ART

Art McBride was the Browns' majority owner from 1946-52. He was the team founder and known to almost everyone in Cleveland as "Mickey."

McCOLGAN, BILL

Bill McColgan was a Browns radio broadcaster from 1954-60 and television broadcaster in 1953.

Art McBride (center), 1948. Photo courtesy of the Cleveland Press Collection.

McCORMACK, MIKE

Mike McCormack was a Browns offensive tackle from 1954-62. He was a University of Kansas product acquired by Cleveland Mar. 26, 1953, as part of a 15-player trade with the Baltimore Colts. McCormack spent 1953 in the military. He was named to All-NFL offensive teams in 1955 by NYN and in 1957 by NEA. He was picked for the Pro Bowl in 1956 and 1957 and from 1960-62. He was inducted into the Pro Football Hall of Fame in 1984.

Mike McCormack. Photo courtesy of the Cleveland Browns.

McDONALD, PAUL

Paul McDonald was a Browns quarterback from 1980-85. He was a fourth-round draft choice of the Browns in 1980 from the University of Southern California. He backed up Brian Sipe for most of his first four seasons. He finished out the 1982 campaign as the starter in the last three games, and in an AFC First-Round Playoff game in Los Angeles, which resulted in a 27-10 loss to the Raiders. McDonald was the starter for the entire 1984 season, completing 271 of 493 pass attempts for 3,472 yards with 14 touchdown passes and 23 interceptions. (Many of his picks were quite untimely.) His 1984 yardage total ranks eighth all-time in Browns history, and his completions total that year ranks ninth. His 5,269 passing yards and 411 pass completions both rank 10th all-time in team annals. McDonald's 281 passing-yard performance in the 1982 playoff game against Los Angeles ranks fifth all-time in team history.

McKAY, BOB

Bob McKay was a Cleveland offensive tackle from 1970-75. He was a first-round draft choice of the Browns in 1970 from the University of Texas.

McKENZIE, KEITH

Keith McKenzie has been a Browns defensive end since 2000. He was a Ball State University product acquired by the Browns Feb. 24, 2000, as a free agent. He was the team leader with eight sacks in 2000.

McLEAN, PHIL

Phil McLean was a Browns radio broadcaster in 1951.

Bob McKay (left) and Garry Parris wrestle Pittsburgh's Joe Greene to the ground in a 42-6 loss in Cleveland Oct. 5, 1975. Photo courtesy of the Cleveland Press Collection.

McNEIL, GERALD

Gerald McNeil was a Browns wide receiver and kickoff returner from 1986-89. He was a first-round supplemental draft choice of the Browns in 1984 from Baylor University. He played in the USFL in 1984 and 1985 before returning to the Browns. He led the team in kickoff returns and kickoff return yards in 1986. His 997 kickoff return yards that season rank third in team history. He also returned punts, and led the Browns in punt returns and punt return yardage every season from 1986-89.

He holds four of the top eight positions for most punt return yards in one Browns season. McNeil's 496 punt return yards in 1989 rank first, his 386 in 1987 take fourth, his 348 in 1986 tie for sixth, and his 315 in 1988 hold eighth. His 1,545 punt return yards rank first all-time in team

Gerald McNeil.

history. He returned a punt 84 yards for a touchdown in Cleveland's 24-21 home win over Detroit Sept. 28, 1986. A week later against the Steelers in Pittsburgh, he helped end the Three Rivers Jinx by returning a kickoff 100 yards for a score in a 27-24 triumph. Consequently, he became the first NFL player to return a punt and kickoff for a touchdown in the same season since Redskin Tony Green did so in 1978. McNeil was a Pro Bowl selection in 1987.

METCALF, ERIC

Eric Metcalf. Photo courtesy of the Cleveland Browns.

Eric Metcalf was a Browns running back from 1989-94. He was a first-round draft choice of the Browns from the University of Texas in 1989. Metcalf led Cleveland in rushing yards his rookie year with 633. He was also used as a receiver out of the backfield. He turned several simple swing passes into long gains, including a spectacular one in which he jitterbugged his way into the end zone for a short touchdown on a pass from Bernie Kosar that completely faked out two Bengals defenders along the way.

Metcalf led the Browns in receptions in 1993 with 63 (tied for 10th all-time on the team). His 177 receiving yards in Cleveland's 28-16 win in Los Angeles against the Raiders Sept. 20, 1992, are tied for eighth all-time in team history (#######). He scored all four of his team's touchdowns that day. His 297 career receptions rank ninth for the Browns. He led the Browns in kickoff returns and kickoff return yardage every season from 1989-91, and returned two for touchdowns in 1990—a 98-yarder Sept. 16 against the Jets and a 101-yarder Dec. 9 in Houston.

However, Metcalf enjoyed his greatest success as a kickoff and punt returner. He led Cleveland in punt returns and punt return yards every year from 1992-94. His 464 punt return yards in 1993 rank second all-time for the Browns. His 429 in 1992 rank third, and his 348 in 1994 tie for sixth. His 1,052 kickoff return yards in 1990 rank first for the Browns. His 1,341 punt return yards and 2,806 kickoff return yards each rank second for the most in Browns history.

Metcalf returned a kickoff 90 yards for a touchdown in the Browns' 34-30 AFC Divisional Playoff win over Buffalo at home Jan. 6, 1990, the only kickoff return for a score in Browns postseason history. His first punt return for a touchdown came Nov. 29, 1992, in a 27-14 victory over the Bears at home. Metcalf's most memorable moment was when he became the first player in NFL history to return two punts of at least 75 yards for touchdowns in the same game. He did so Oct. 24, 1993, at home against the Steelers, making a 91-yarder early in the game and a 75-yarder later that gave the Browns a 28-23 victory in a battle for first place.

He returned two punts for scores in 1994, both against the Bengals. The first was a 92-yarder in the season opener in Cincinnati, and the second was a 73-yarder Oct. 23 in Cleveland. His 1,932 combined net yards in 1993 and 1,752 in 1990 rank third and 10th for the most in one Browns season. His 9,108 combined net yards rank fourth all-time in team history (######). Metcalf was voted to All-AFC offensive teams in 1993 by AP, PFW, SN and UPI, and in 1994 by SN. He was named to the Pro Bowl in 1993 and 1994.

MIAMI DOLPHINS

The Miami Dolphins were Browns opponents in the NFL from 1970-95 and have been since 1999. They were triumphant in two postseason games against the Browns, both in the AFC Divisional Playoffs in the Orange Bowl—a 20-14 conquest Dec. 24, 1972, and a 24-21 victory Jan. 4, 1986. Miami's all-time record against Cleveland is 6-4 (.600), with 2-1 (.667) at home and 4-3 (.571) on the road. The Dolphins' all-time record in the postseason against the Browns is 2-0 (home).

MIAMI SEAHAWKS

The Miami Seahawks were opponents of the Browns in the AAFC in 1946. They were Cleveland's opponent in the team's first game Sept. 6 of that year. The franchise folded after that season. Miami's all-time record against Cleveland was 0-2, with 0-1 at home and 0-1 on the road.

MICHAELS, WALT

Walt Michaels was a Browns linebacker from 1952-61. He was a seventh-round draft choice of the Browns in 1951 from Washington & Lee University. He was traded to Green

Walt Michaels tackles the Chicago Cardinals' (and future Brown) Gern Nagler in the end zone after a 24-yard touchdown reception Oct. 12, 1958. Photo courtesy of the Cleveland Press Collection.

Bay Aug. 20, 1951, and then re-acquired April 29, 1952, as part of a four-player deal with the Packers. Michaels was voted to the All-NFL defensive team in 1959 by NYN. He was selected to play in the Pro Bowl from 1956-59.

Cleo Miller looks for a hole as Reggie Rucker looks for someone to block during a 21-17 victory over the visiting San Diego Chargers Oct. 24, 1976. Photo courtesy of the Cleveland Press Collection.

MILLER, CLEO

Cleo Miller was a Browns running back from 1975-82. An Arkansas AM&N College product, Miller was acquired by the Browns in Nov. 1975 as a free agent. He tied Greg Pruitt for the lead in Browns rushing touchdowns in 1976 with four. His 613 rushing yards were second to Pruitt. In 1977, Miller gained 756 yards on the ground via 163 carries and once again rushed for a team-leading four touchdowns. Rushing for a pair of touchdowns and making a long run in the second half, he was a key figure in Cleveland's 17-14 upset of the Oilers in a battle for first place in the AFC Central Division Nov. 30, 1980. Miller's 2,236 rushing yards rank 10th all-time in Browns history.

MILLER, JAMIR

Jamir Miller has been a Browns linebacker since 1999. He was a UCLA product obtained by the Browns May 13, 1999, as a free agent. He ranked second on the team with 4.5 sacks in 1999 and five in 2000. He became the first Brown to lead the AFC in sacks with 13 in 2001, the second most in team history. His 22.5 career sacks rank eighth in Browns annals. Miller was voted to All-NFL teams in 2001 by AP, FD (first team), PFW, and SI. He was voted to the All-AFC defensive team by PFW in 2001 and was picked for the Pro Bowl that year.

MINNESOTA VIKINGS

The Minnesota Vikings were Browns opponents in the NFL from 1961-95 and have been since 1999. Two of their more memorable games with the Browns were victories in Metropolitan Stadium in Minnesota. The first was a 51-3 shellacking Nov. 9, 1969, in which they outgained the Browns more than three yards to one (454-151). The game is tied for the worst loss ever suffered by the Browns. The second game was a 28-23 triumph Dec. 14, 1980, when the Vikings rose from the dead after trailing, 23-9, in the fourth quarter. Minnesota won when quarterback Tommy Kramer completed a 46-yard Hail Mary pass to Ahmad Rashad, who caught the ball after it was batted by defensive back Thom Darden and cradled it against his body as he backpedaled into the end zone with no time left. The Vikings and Browns met once in postseason play, a 27-7 Vikings victory Jan. 4, 1970, in the NFL Championship game in frigid Minnesota. The Vikings' all-time record against the Browns is 8-3 (.727), with 5-1 (.833) at home and 3-2 (.600) on the road. Their all-time postseason record against Cleveland is 1-0 (home).

MINNIFIELD, FRANK

Frank Minnifield was a Browns cornerback from 1984-92. He was a University of Louisville product acquired by the Browns as a free agent Apr. 3, 1984. He formed half of the famed Corner Brothers duo from 1985-89 (he started for part of the 1984 season) with Hanford Dixon. He tied Felix Wright for the team lead in interceptions in 1987 with four. He was second to Wright in the same category in 1988 with four. He returned an interception 48 yards for a touchdown as Cleveland's final score in the Browns' 38-21 AFC Divisional Playoff win over the Colts Jan. 9, 1988, in Cleveland. He was voted to All-AFC defensive teams in 1987 by PFW, FWA, SN, and UPI; in 1988 by AP, NEA, PFW, FWA, SN, and UPI; and in 1989 by UPI. He was selected to play in the Pro Bowl from 1986-89.

Frank Minnifield. Photo courtesy of the Cleveland Browns.

MITCHELL, BOBBY

Bobby Mitchell was a Browns running back from 1958-61. He was a seventh-round draft choice of Cleveland's in 1958 from the University of Illinois. Mitchell complemented running back Jim Brown well, finishing second to him in rushing yards all four seasons. He gained 232 yards on the ground Nov. 15, 1959, against the Redskins, which are tied for third all-time in team history. A 90-yard touchdown run was included in his total that afternoon.

His 2,297 rushing yards rank ninth all-time for the Browns. He was the team leader in receptions (45) in 1960. He also returned kickoffs, and led the Browns in returns and return yards all four seasons (he was the co-leader in returns with Preston Powell his last year). Mitchell's 1,550 kickoff return yards overall rank eighth in team annals. He returned three kickoffs for touchdowns—a 98-yarder against the Eagles Nov. 23, 1958, a 90-yarder against the Cowboys Oct. 16, 1960, and a 91-yarder against the Eagles again Nov. 19, 1961.

Bobby Mitchell carries for a short gain and is stopped by several Eagles in the Browns'
28-14 victory Nov. 23, 1958. Photo courtesy of the Cleveland Press Collection.

He also returned punts, and totaled a seventh-best 607 yards all-time for the Browns. He returned three punts for touchdowns—a 68-yarder at home against Philadelphia Nov. 23, 1958 (the same game in which he returned a kickoff 98 yards for a score); a 78-yarder against the Giants in New York Dec. 6, 1959; and a 64-yarder against the Redskins in Cleveland Oct. 8, 1961. Mitchell was traded to Washington three days prior to the 1961 season finale in a package deal for the Redskins' first-round draft selection, the top pick in the draft. The Browns selected 1961 Heisman Trophy winner Ernie Davis, a running back from Syracuse University, with the pick. Unfortunately, tragedy struck as Davis contracted leukemia and never played a game for the Browns. Mitchell was picked for the Pro Bowl in 1960. He was enshrined into the Pro Football Hall of Fame in 1983.

MODELL, ART
Art Modell was the Browns' majority owner from 1961-95.

MODZELEWSKI, DICK
Dick Modzelewski was a Browns defensive tackle from 1964-66. He was a University of Maryland product acquired by the Browns Mar. 4, 1964, in a trade with the New York

Left to right: Art Modell, Jim Brown, and Paul Brown in 1962. Photo courtesy of the Cleveland Press Collection.

Giants for wide receiver Bob Crespino. He was the younger brother of Browns running back Ed Modzelewski, who played from 1955-59. Dick Modzelewski was selected to play in the Pro Bowl in 1964. He was the Browns' head coach in 1977 for one game, the season finale in Seattle Dec. 18, a 20-19 loss (Forrest Gregg resigned Dec. 13, and Modzelewski, the team's defensive coordinator, took his place). Modzelewski's all-time record as Browns head coach was 0-1 (away). He was a Browns assistant coach from 1968-77.

MONDAY AFTERNOON GAMES

Buffalo 28, Cleveland 28 (Sept. 5, 1949, at Buffalo)
Seattle 33, Cleveland 0 (Sept. 3, 1984, at Seattle)

Overall   0-1-1 (.250)

MONDAY NIGHT FOOTBALL

(Does not include ABC *Monday Night Football* special edition games on other nights)

Cleveland 31, N.Y. Jets 21 (Sept. 21, 1970, at Cleveland)
Cleveland 21, Houston 10 (Dec. 7, 1970, at Houston)
Oakland 34, Cleveland 20 (Oct. 4, 1971, at Cleveland)
Cleveland 21, San Diego 17 (Nov. 13, 1972, at San Diego)
Miami 17, Cleveland 9 (Oct. 15, 1973, at Cleveland)
Cleveland 30, New England 27 (OT) (Sept. 26, 1977, at Cleveland)
Cleveland 26, Dallas 7 (Sept. 24, 1979, at Cleveland)
Houston 16, Cleveland 7 (Sept. 15, 1980, at Cleveland)
Cleveland 27, Chicago 21 (Nov. 3, 1980, at Cleveland)

San Diego 44, Cleveland 14 (Sept. 7, 1981, at Cleveland)
Cleveland 17, Pittsburgh 7 (Sept. 16, 1985, at Cleveland)
Cleveland 26, Miami 16 (Nov. 10, 1986, at Cleveland)
Cleveland 30, L.A. Rams 17 (Oct. 26, 1987, at Cleveland)
Cleveland 23, Indianapolis 17 (Sept. 19, 1988, at Cleveland)
Houston 24, Cleveland 17 (Nov. 7, 1988, at Houston)
Miami 38, Cleveland 31 (Dec. 12, 1988, at Miami)
Cincinnati 21, Cleveland 14 (Sept. 25, 1989, at Cincinnati)
Cleveland 27, Chicago 7 (Oct. 23, 1989, at Cleveland)
Cleveland 30, Denver 29 (Oct. 8, 1990, at Denver)
Cincinnati 34, Cleveland 13 (Oct. 22, 1990, at Cleveland)
Miami 27, Cleveland 23 (Sept. 14, 1992, at Cleveland)
Cleveland 23, San Francisco 13 (Sept. 13, 1993, at Cleveland)
Buffalo 22, Cleveland 19 (Oct. 2, 1995, at Cleveland)
Pittsburgh 20, Cleveland 3 (Nov. 13, 1995, at Pittsburgh)

Overall   13-11 (.542)
Home   10-7 (.588)
Away   3-4 (.429)

MORIN, MILT

Milt Morin was a Browns tight end from 1966-75. A first-round draft choice of Cleveland's in 1966 from the University of Massachusetts, Morin was on the receiving end of an 87-yard pass play from Bill Nelsen Nov. 24, 1968, against Philadelphia. He was the team leader in receiving yards in 1973 with 417. He ranks 10th all-time for the Browns with 4,208 receiving yards. He was voted to All-AFC offensive teams in 1971 by AP and UPI and was voted to the Pro Bowl in 1967, 1968, and 1971.

Milt Morin, after a six-yard touchdown pass from Bill Nelsen en route to a 38-14 victory over the Cowboys in the Eastern Conference title game, Dec. 28, 1969. Photo courtesy of the Cleveland Press Collection.

MORRISON, FRED

Fred Morrison was a Cleveland running back from 1954-56. He was an Ohio State University product acquired by the Browns July 7, 1954, in a trade with the Bears for the rights to Harry Jagade and a draft choice in 1955. He had a team high of 824 rushing yards in 1955 and was picked for the Pro Bowl that year.

Fred Morrison runs for 12 yards against the Redskins during a 62-3 home win Nov. 7, 1954. (The play was nullified, though, due to an offside penalty.) Photo courtesy of the Cleveland Press Collection.

MORROW, JOHN

John Morrow was a Browns center from 1960-66. He was a University of Michigan product acquired by Cleveland Mar. 14, 1960, in a trade with the Los Angeles Rams for Art Hunter. Morrow was picked to play in the Pro Bowl in 1961 and 1963.

MOSELEY, MARK

Mark Moseley was a kicker for Cleveland in 1986. A Stephen F. Austin University product, Moseley was acquired by the Browns Nov. 26, 1986, when regular kicker Matt Bahr

Mark Moseley. Photo courtesy of the Cleveland Browns.

went down with a season-ending injury. Moseley kicked three field goals, including the game-winning 27-yarder that came 2:02 into the second extra period in the Browns' double-overtime victory over the Jets in an AFC Divisional Playoff Jan. 3, 1987, in Cleveland.

MOST ONE-SIDED GAMES, REGULAR AND POSTSEASON

Please see Team Statistics on page 204.

MOST VALUABLE PLAYER

1947   Otto Graham (AAFC by OFF)
1948   Otto Graham (co-AAFC by OFF; AAFC by UP)
1949   Otto Graham (AAFC by OFF)
1953   Otto Graham (NFL by UP)
1954   Lou Groza (NFL by SN)
1955   Otto Graham (NFL by SN, UP)
1958   Jim Brown (NFL by NEA, UPI)
1963   Jim Brown (NFL by MAX, UPI; co-NFL by NEA)
1965   Jim Brown (NFL by NEA, SN, UPI)
1968   Leroy Kelly (NFL by MAX)
1980   Brian Sipe (NFL by FWA, SN; AFC by UPI)
1989   Michael Dean Perry (AFC Defensive by UPI)

MOTLEY, MARION

Marion Motley was a Browns running back from 1946-53. He was a product of the University of Nevada acquired by the Browns as a free agent. He led the team in rushing yards every season from 1946-50 and in 1952, totaling 601, 889, 964, 570, 810 and 444 yards, respectively. His 1946 total came on 73 carries for a remarkable average of 8.2 yards per carry. He had 47- and 68-yard touchdown runs in the Browns' 31-14 victory over the visiting Los Angeles Dons Oct. 20, 1946. Later that season on Nov. 24, Motley scored on a 76-yard run in a 42-17 romp over Buffalo at home. He rushed for 188 yards Oct. 29, 1950, against the Steelers, which tied him for the eighth-most rushing yards by a Brown in one game.

He ranks sixth all-time for the Browns in rushing yards with 4,712. He is the all-time AAFC rushing yardage leader with 3,024. Motley's 7,019 combined net yards rank seventh all-time in team history (######). His 30 postseason points tie for fifth in team history and his 512 rushing yards in the postseason rank first (#). His 18 points scored in the 1948 AAFC Championship game against Buffalo tie for the most in one game in team history. He holds two of the top five spots for rushing yards in one postseason game—133 against Buffalo Dec. 19, 1948, in the AAFC Championship game (No. 2), and 109 against New York Dec. 14, 1947, in the AAFC title game.

He played linebacker early in his career. Motley actually spent his last season playing in the NFL with Pittsburgh. He retired in 1954 before attempting a comeback as a linebacker for the Steelers in 1955. The Browns traded him to Pittsburgh Sept. 8 of that year.

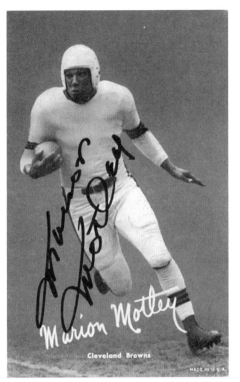

Motley was named to All-AAFC teams in 1946 by AP, NYN, OFF, and UP; in 1947 by AP, C&O, NYN, and OFF; in 1948 by AP, NYN, OFF, and SN; and in 1949 by NYN. He was voted to All-NFL offensive teams in 1950 by AP, NYN, and UP. He was picked for the Pro Bowl in 1950. He was inducted into the Pro Football Hall of Fame in 1968.

Marion Motley. Photo courtesy of the Cleveland Browns.

Trainer Leo Murphy tends to Jerry Sherk at Oakland Nov. 8, 1970. Photo courtesy of the Cleveland Press Collection.

MUELLER, JIM

Jim Mueller was a Browns radio broadcaster from 1975-95.

MURPHY, LEO

Leo Murphy was the Browns' trainer from 1950-88 and emeritus trainer in 1989.

MUSTAFAA, NAJEE

Najee Mustafaa was a Browns cornerback in 1993. A product of Georgia Tech University, Mustafaa was acquired by the Browns as a free agent Mar. 17, 1993. He returned a Scott Mitchell pass 97 yards for a touchdown Oct. 10, 1993, that gave the Browns a 14-10 lead in what turned out as a 24-14 loss to the Miami Dolphins at home. It was Mitchell's first pass of the game after replacing Dan Marino in the second quarter when Marino suffered a torn right Achilles tendon that ended his season.

N

NAGLER, GERN

Gern Nagler was a Cleveland wide receiver in 1960 and 1961. He was a 14th-round draft choice of the Browns in 1953 from Santa Clara University, but was traded to Baltimore. He played for the Chicago Cardinals from 1953-58 and the Pittsburgh Steelers in 1959. He was re-acquired Dec. 31, 1959, as part of a four-player deal with the Steelers that included future Hall of Famer Len Dawson coming to the shores of Lake Erie for a short stay. Nagler led the Browns with 616 receiving yards in 1960, including a 177-yard performance Nov. 20 in Pittsburgh, which is tied for eighth all-time for Cleveland (#######).

NATIONAL FOOTBALL LEAGUE

The National Football League was home to the Browns from 1950-95 and has been since 1999.

NBC TELEVISION NETWORK

The NBC television network broadcast Browns afternoon home games when the Browns' opponent was an AFC team, as well as all afternoon road games, from 1970-95.

NEAL, BOB

Bob Neal was a Browns radio broadcaster from 1946-51 and television broadcaster from 1948-51.

NELSEN, BILL

Bill Nelsen was a Browns quarterback from 1968-72. A product of the University of Southern California, Nelsen was acquired by the Browns May 14, 1968, as part of a five-player trade with the Pittsburgh Steelers. He was obtained when Frank Ryan began having arm troubles. Despite knee problems, Nelsen completed 152 of 293 passes for 2,366 yards, 19 touchdowns, and 10 interceptions in 1968. He started in place of the struggling Ryan

Bill Nelsen. Photo courtesy of the Cleveland Browns.

Oct. 5 against the Steelers and led the Browns to a 31-24 triumph over his former club. He connected with Milt Morin on an 87-yard pass play against the Eagles Nov. 24 that year for his longest completion as a Brown. He directed Cleveland to appearances in the NFL title game that season and in 1969. He hooked up with Paul Warfield for an 82-yard pass play that went for a touchdown in a 27-21 victory over the Cardinals in St. Louis Dec. 14, 1969. Nelsen ranks fifth all-time in Browns annals with 9,725 passing yards and 689 completions. His 839 postseason passing yards and 68 pass completions rank third all-time for the Browns. He was chosen to play in the Pro Bowl in 1969.

NEW ENGLAND PATRIOTS

The New England Patriots were opponents of the Browns in the NFL from 1970-95 and have been since 1999. The Browns defeated the Patriots, 30-0, in New England Nov. 20, 1983, becoming the second Browns team—and the first since 1951—to post consecutive shutouts (they beat the Buccaneers, 20-0, the week before). The Patriots and Browns have met once in postseason play, with the Browns coming out on top, 20-13, in an AFC Wild Card game on New Year's Day, 1995 in Cleveland. New England's all-time record against the Browns is 6-11 (.353), with 3-5 (.375) at home and 3-6 (.333) on the road. Its all-time postseason record against Cleveland is 0-1 (away).

NEW ORLEANS SAINTS

The New Orleans Saints were Browns opponents in the NFL from 1967-95 and have been since 1999. The Saints were the victims of the "new era" Browns' first win on Oct. 31, 1999, in the Superdome in New Orleans. The Browns took a 21-16 victory when Tim Couch completed a 56-yard Hail Mary pass to Kevin Johnson on the final play of the game. The Saints' all-time record against Cleveland is 3-10 (.231), with 2-6 (.250) at home and 1-4 (.200) on the road.

NEW YORK GIANTS

The New York Giants were Browns opponents in the NFL from 1950-95 and have been since 1999. They were rivals of the Browns in the American Conference from 1950-52 and Eastern Conference from 1953-69. The two teams were rivals in the Century Division in 1967 and 1969. They waged several titanic battles during the 1950s and 1960s, with Giants linebacker Sam Huff and Browns running back Jim Brown at the center of many of them. One memorable game between the teams occurred Dec. 1, 1985, in the

Pat Summerall boots the game-winning field goal that gives the New York Giants a 13-10 victory over the Browns in Cleveland Dec. 14, 1958. Photo courtesy of the Cleveland Press Collection.

Meadowlands when the Browns won a thriller, 35-33, after trailing, 33-21, late in the game. Giants kicker Eric Schubert missed a 34-yard field goal as time expired.

The Giants and Browns have met twice in the postseason, splitting the pair. Both were defensive struggles. The Browns won at home, 8-3, Dec. 17, 1950, in an American Conference playoff in 10-degree weather, when Giants' running back Eugene Roberts was tackled by Bill Willis from behind at the Browns' four-yard line late in the game. New York won, 10-0, Dec. 21, 1958, in an Eastern Conference Playoff in New York. The week before, the Giants forced the playoff with a memorable 13-10 victory in Yankee Stadium on Pat Summerall's 49-yard field goal into the wind and through the driving snow with 2:07 to play. The Giants all-time record against the Browns is 18-25-2 (.422), with 8-12-2 (.409) at home and 10-13 (.435) on the road. Their all-time postseason record against the Browns is 1-1, with 1-0 at home and 0-1 on the road.

NEW YORK JETS

The New York Jets were Browns opponents in the NFL from 1970-95 and have been since 1999. The Browns and Jets (led by Joe Namath) squared off in the first-ever *Monday Night Football* game Sept. 21, 1970, in Cleveland. The Browns won, 31-21.

Every game played between New York and Cleveland from 1978-84 went down to the wire. The six games played between the two teams during that period were decided by a total of 17 points. Every game but the 1979 affair was played in Cleveland. The Browns won four: 37-34 in overtime Dec. 10, 1978; 25-22 in overtime Sept. 2, 1979; 17-14 Dec. 7, 1980; and 10-7 Oct. 9, 1983, on Matt Bahr's 43-yard field goal as time expired. The Jets won twice: 14-13 Dec. 12, 1981, for their first-ever win against the Browns, and 24-20 Oct. 14, 1984, when three straight sacks (two by defensive end Mark Gastineau) stalled the Browns' final drive.

New York fell victim to one of the greatest comebacks in NFL history in the AFC Divisional Playoffs Jan. 3, 1987, in Cleveland when it blew a 20-10 lead late in the fourth quarter and lost, 23-20, in double overtime. The Jets' all-time record against the Browns is 6-9 (.400), with 2-2 at home and 4-7 (.363) on the road. New York's all-time record against Cleveland in the postseason is 0-1 (away).

NEW YORK YANKEES

The New York Yankees were Browns opponents in the AAFC from 1946-48. They opposed the Browns in the 1946 and '47 AAFC Championship games, losing both: 14-9 in Cleveland and 14-3 in New York, respectively. They merged with their AAFC rival Brooklyn Dodgers to become the Brooklyn-New York Yankees in 1949, the last year the conference existed. The Yankees' all-time record against Cleveland was 0-5-1 (.083), with 0-2-1 (.167) at home and 0-3 on the road. Their all-time record against the Browns in postseason play was 0-2, with 0-1 at home and 0-1 on the road.

Fans crowd around the Browns as they head to the locker room following their 14-9 victory over the visiting New York Yankees in the AAFC Championship game Dec. 22, 1946. Photo courtesy of the Cleveland Press Collection.

NEWSOME, OZZIE

Ozzie Newsome was a Browns tight end from 1978-90. He was a Browns first-round draft choice in 1978 from the University of Alabama. He had 38 receptions for 589 yards and two touchdown catches his rookie year, 55 catches for 781 yards and nine touchdown receptions in 1979, and 51 catches for 594 yards and three touchdown catches in 1980. He led the team in receptions and receiving yards every season from 1981-85, and in touchdown receptions in 1979, 1981, and from 1983-85. He was the co-leader in touchdown catches in 1982.

Newsome's 1,002 yards receiving in 1981 were the most by a Brown in 13 years and rank sixth all-time in Browns history. His 69 catches that year rank fourth in team history. In 1982, he had 49 catches for 633 yards and three touchdowns. He totaled a team-record 89 catches in both the 1983 and 1984 seasons for 970 yards (10th most in team history) in 1983 and 1,001 (seventh most all-time in Browns history) in 1984. His 191 receiving yards Oct. 14, 1984, at home against the Jets rank third in team history (#######). Newsome caught 62 passes for 711 yards in 1985. His 662 receptions all-time rank first in Browns annals and are the most by a tight end in NFL history.

His 7,980 receiving yards also rank first in team history, and his 8,147 combined net yards rank sixth for the Browns all-time (######). Newsome's 27 postseason receptions are tied for second with Mac Speedie all-time for the Browns (###). His 373 postseason receiving yards rank fourth all-time in team history (##). Newsome's 114 receiving yards in Cleveland's 23-20 double-overtime win over the Jets in the AFC Divisional Playoffs Jan. 3, 1987, in Cleveland are tied for fifth for most receiving yards in one postseason game by a

Ozzie Newsome makes a one-handed catch for a 14-yard touchdown as Miami's Norris Thomas hangs on. The Browns won the game in overtime, 30-24, Nov. 18, 1979. Photo courtesy of the Cleveland Press Collection.

Browns player (####). He was voted to All-AFC offensive teams in 1979 by FWA, SN and UPI, and in 1984 by AP, NEA, PFW, FWA, SN, and UPI. He was selected to play in the Pro Bowl in 1981, 1984, and 1985, and was inducted into the Pro Football Hall of Fame in 1999.

NICKNAMES

The following are notable nicknames of 50 Browns players:

Dick Ambrose	"Bam Bam"
Al Baker	"Bubba"
Johnny Brewer	"Tonto"
Darrell Brewster	"Pete"
Courtney Brown	"The Quiet Storm"
Orlando Brown	"Zeus"
Howard Cassady	"Hopalong"
Don Cockroft	"Donny O"
Johnny Davis	"B-1"
Doug Dieken	"Diek"
Hanford Dixon	"Top Dawg"
Ross Fichtner	"Rocky"
Frank Gatski	"Gunner"
Otto Graham	"Automatic"
Forrest Grigg	"Chubby"
Lou Groza	"The Toe"
Carl Hairston	"Big Daddy"
Chet Hanulak	"The Jet"
Kevin Johnson	"K.J."
Michael Jackson	"Thriller"
Eddie Johnson	"The Assassin"
Edgar Jones	"Special Delivery"
Joe Jones	"Turkey"
Tony Jones	"T-Bone"
William Jones	"Dub"
Jim Kanicki	"Smokey"
Bob Kolesar	"Doc"
Dante Lavelli	"Glue Fingers"
Gerald McNeil	"The Ice Cube"
Frank Minnifield	"Minnie"
Dick Modzelewski	"Little Mo"
Ed Modzelewski	"Big Mo"
Marion Motley	"The Train"
Ozzie Newsome	"The Wizard of Oz"
Jim Ninowski	"Nino"
Vito Parilli	"Babe"
Don Phelps	"Dopey"

Frank Pitts	"Riddler"
Greg Pruitt	"Do It"
Dave Puzzuoli	"Puz"
Andre Rison	"Full Moon"
Walter Roberts	"The Flea," "Mr. Rodgers"
Dick Schafrath	"Shaf"
Robert Scott	"Bo"
Jerry Sherk	"The Sheik"
Robert Sims	"Mickey"
Matt Stover	Stove Top"
Eric Turner	"E-rock"
Tommy Vardell	"Touchdown"
Lowell Wren	"Junior"

NINOWSKI, JIM

Jim Ninowski was a Browns quarterback in 1958 and 1959 and from 1962-66. He was a fourth-round draft choice of Cleveland's in 1958 from Michigan State University. He backed up Milt Plum before being traded to Detroit July 12, 1960. He was re-acquired Mar. 28, 1962, in a trade with the Lions as part of a six-player deal. Ninowski backed up Frank Ryan from 1962-66.

Jim Ninowski just gets his pass off while facing the onslaught of the New York Giants' Jim Katcavage in the season opener Sept. 16, 1962. Photo courtesy of the Cleveland Press Collection.

Chuck Noll. Photo courtesy of the Cleveland Browns.

NOLL, CHUCK

Chuck Noll was a Cleveland guard and linebacker from 1953-59. He was a 20th-round draft choice of Cleveland's in 1953 from the University of Dayton.

NOVEMBER
—25, 1951

Browns wide receiver Dub Jones set a team record, and tied a league mark for most touchdowns in one game, by scoring six times in a 42-21 rout of the visiting Chicago Bears.

—20, 1983

The Browns blanked the New England Patriots, 30-0, in New England in a crucial battle of AFC Wild Card contenders. Having shut out the Buccaneers, 20-0, the week before, Cleveland became the first Browns team to post consecutive shutouts since 1951.

—4, 1990

The Browns were battered by the Buffalo Bills, 42-0, in Cleveland in the team's second-worst shutout loss and second-worst home defeat ever. Head coach Bud Carson was fired the next day.

—8, 1993

The Browns released quarterback Bernie Kosar due to Kosar's ". . . lack of production and loss of physical skills," according to head coach Bill Belichick, as quoted from the Cleveland *Plain Dealer* Nov. 9, 1993.

—6, 1995

Browns majority owner Art Modell made the Browns' relocation to Baltimore official to the public with an announcement in Baltimore.

—4, 2001

Cleveland lost in overtime to the Chicago Bears, 27-21, at Soldier Field in a game the Browns were leading, 21-7, with little more than 30 seconds remaining. The Bears cut their deficit to 21-14 with 28 seconds left and then recovered an onside kick at the Browns' 47-yard-line with 24 seconds left. Three plays later, quarterback Shane Matthews completed a 34-yard Hail Mary pass tipped by Browns defensive back Percy Ellsworth to running back James Allen with no time left. Mike Brown returned a Tim Couch pass batted by teammate Bryan Robinson 16 yards for the winning score on the Browns' first possession of the extra period.

NUMBERS ON HELMETS

Browns players' uniform numbers appeared on their helmets from 1957-59.

OAKLAND RAIDERS

The Oakland Raiders were opponents of the Browns in the NFL from 1970-95 and have been since 1999. They were located in Los Angeles from 1982-94. One memorable Raiders victory came in the first meeting between the teams Nov. 8, 1970, in Oakland, when George Blanda kicked a 53-yard field goal with seven seconds left in a 23-20 victory. This was one of four Raiders games in a month-long stretch that produced three miracle wins and a tie when Blanda came through late. Two unforgettable Browns wins occurred in Los Angeles a year apart—Sept. 20, 1992, and Sept. 19, 1993. In the '92 game, Eric Metcalf

Leroy Kelly against the Oakland Raiders in Oakland Nov. 8, 1970. Photo courtesy of the Cleveland Press Collection.

scored all four of Cleveland's touchdowns—three on receptions, one on a run—in a 28-16 triumph. In the '93 game, Metcalf was instrumental once again, scoring on a one-yard sweep with no time left to give the Browns a 19-16 victory that capped a remarkable comeback from a 16-3 deficit late in the game. The Raiders and Browns have met twice in the postseason, with the Raiders winning both. Most notable was their 14-12 triumph in an AFC Divisional Playoff Jan. 4, 1981, in frozen Cleveland Stadium. Browns quarterback Brian Sipe was picked off by Mike Davis in the end zone with less than a minute to play. Oakland's all-time record against Cleveland is 9-4 (.692), with 5-4 (.556) at home and 4-0 on the road. The Raiders' all-time postseason record against the Browns is 2-0 (home).

OCTOBER
—25, 1981

The Browns defeated the Baltimore Colts, 42-28, in Cleveland as Brian Sipe set the Browns' single-game passing yards record by throwing for 444.

—21, 1984

The Browns lost to the Cincinnati Bengals, 12-9, in Cincinnati on a 33-yard last-second field goal by Jim Breech in a battle of 1-6 teams. Browns head coach Sam Rutigliano was fired the following day.

—4-18, 1987

The Browns played three games during this period, but with a different twist. Replacement players (for the most part) represented the Browns (and the other teams) due to an NFL players' strike that actually canceled Cleveland's long-awaited Monday night rematch against the Denver Broncos. It had been scheduled for Sept. 28 (the Broncos had beaten the Browns in the AFC title game nearly nine months earlier). The "replacement" Browns won at New England, 20-10, Oct. 4; lost at home to Houston, 15-10, Oct. 11; and routed the Bengals in Cincinnati, 34-0, Oct. 18, with help from some regular players who returned to action early.

—24, 1993

Cleveland defeated Pittsburgh, 28-23, in Cleveland as Eric Metcalf became the only player in NFL annals to return two punts for touchdowns for at least 75 yards in the same game. Metcalf's returns went for 91 and 75 yards—the second, the game-winner with 2:05 left.

—31, 1999

The Browns defeated the New Orleans Saints, 21-16, in New Orleans as quarterback Tim Couch completed a Hail Mary 56-yard touchdown pass to Kevin Johnson as time expired for the "new era" Browns' first victory.

OFFENSIVE LINEMEN

Notable offensive linemen for the Browns include Frank Gatski, Lou Groza, Lin Houston, Lou Rymkus, Abe Gibron, Mike McCormack, Jim Ray Smith, Gene Hickerson, Dick Schafrath, John Wooten, John Morrow, Monte Clark, Fred Hoaglin, John Demarie, Doug Dieken, Bob DeMarco, Tom DeLeone, Robert E. Jackson, Cody Risien, Joe DeLamielleure, Mike Baab, Paul Farren, Dan Fike, Tony Jones, Bob Dahl, Steve Everitt, Jim Pyne, Dave Wohlabaugh, and Ross Verba.

OFFENSIVE PLAYER OF THE YEAR

1980   Brian Sipe (NFL by PFW)

ONE-THOUSAND-YARD RECEIVERS

Please see Individual Statistics on page 188.

ONE-THOUSAND-YARD RUSHERS

Please see Individual Statistics on page 188.

OPENERS

For a listing of the scores of the season openers, please see Team Statistics on page 204.

ORANGE HELMETS

The Browns' helmets were orange from 1952-95 and have been since 1999.

ORANGE PANTS

The Browns wore orange pants from 1975-83.

OVERTIME

The Browns have won 12 games in overtime during the regular season, lost 10 and tied one. They have split overtime games in the postseason, winning once and losing once.

* Denotes postseason

Cleveland 30, New England 27 (Sept. 26, 1977, at Cleveland)
Cleveland 13, Cincinnati 10 (Sept. 10, 1978, at Cleveland)
Pittsburgh 15, Cleveland 9 (Sept. 24, 1978, at Pittsburgh)
Cleveland 37, N.Y. Jets 34 (Dec. 10, 1978, at Cleveland)
Cleveland 25, N.Y. Jets 22 (Sept. 2, 1979, at New York)
Cleveland 30, Miami 24 (Nov. 18, 1979, at Cleveland)

Pittsburgh 33, Cleveland 30 (Nov. 25, 1979, at Pittsburgh)
Denver 23, Cleveland 20 (Nov. 8, 1981, at Denver)
Cleveland 30, San Diego 24 (Sept. 25, 1983, at San Diego)
Cleveland 25, Houston 19 (Oct.30, 1983, at Cleveland)
Cincinnati 20, Cleveland 17 (Dec. 2, 1984, at Cleveland)
St. Louis 27, Cleveland 24 (Sept. 8, 1985, at Cleveland)
Cleveland 37, Pittsburgh 31 (Nov. 23, 1986, at Cleveland)
Cleveland 13, Houston 10 (Nov. 30, 1986, at Cleveland)
*Cleveland 23, N.Y. Jets 20 (2OT) (Jan. 3, 1987, at Cleveland)
*Denver 23, Cleveland 20 (Jan. 11, 1987, at Cleveland)
San Diego 27, Cleveland 24 (Nov. 1, 1987, at San Diego)
Miami 13, Cleveland 10 (Oct. 8, 1989, at Miami)
Cleveland 10, Kansas City 10 (Nov. 19, 1989, at Cleveland)
Indianapolis 23, Cleveland 17 (Dec. 10, 1989, at Indiana)
Cleveland 23, Minnesota 17 (Dec. 17, 1989, at Cleveland)
Cleveland 30, San Diego 24 (Oct. 20, 1991, at San Diego)
Cleveland 29, Cincinnati 26 (Oct. 29, 1995, at Cincinnati)
Chicago 27, Cleveland 21 (Nov. 4, 2001, at Chicago)
Pittsburgh 15, Cleveland 12 (Nov. 11, 2001, at Cleveland)

Overall Regular Season	12-10-1	(.543)
Home Regular Season	8-3-1	(.708)
Away Regular Season	4-7	(.364)
Postseason	1-1	(.500)

P

PALMER, CHRIS

Chris Palmer was the Browns' head coach in 1999 and 2000. His all-time record as Browns head coach was 5-27 (.156), with 2-14 (.125) at home and 3-13 (.188) on the road.

PARRISH, BERNIE

Bernie Parrish was a Browns defensive back from 1959-66. He was a ninth-round draft pick of the Browns in 1958 from the University of Florida with one year of eligibility left in school. He was the Browns' leader in interceptions in 1961 with seven. He tied for the team lead in picks in 1959 with five and 1964 with four. He ranks sixth all-time in team history with 29 interceptions. He returned three picks for touchdowns—a 37-yarder Oct. 18, 1959, against the Chicago Cardinals, a 92-yarder Dec. 11, 1960, against the Chicago Bears, and a 54-yarder off a long Don Meredith pass Oct. 18, 1964, that gave the Browns the lead for good against the Dallas Cowboys. Parrish was picked to play in the Pro Bowl in 1960 and 1963.

Bernie Parrish. Photo courtesy of the Cleveland Browns.

PARSEGHIAN, ARA

Ara Parseghian was a Browns running back in 1948 and 1949. He was a 25th-round draft choice of the Browns in 1948 from Miami University.

PASS COMPLETIONS LEADERS

Please see Individual Statistics on page 188.

PASSING YARDS LEADERS

Please see Individual Statistics on page 188.

PAUL, DON

Don Paul was a Browns defensive back from 1954-58. A Washington State University product, Paul was acquired by the Browns Aug. 30, 1954, in a trade with the Washington Redskins for rookies Dale Atkinson and Johnny Carson. He returned an interception 65 yards for a touchdown Dec. 26, 1955, against the Rams in the NFL title game in Los Angeles. He returned a fumble 89 yards for a touchdown for the Browns' final score in a 24-0 win over Pittsburgh Nov. 10, 1957. Paul was voted to the All-NFL defensive team in 1955 by UP and was picked for the Pro Bowl from 1956-58.

PAYTON, EDDIE

Eddie Payton was a Browns kickoff returner in 1977. A Jackson State University product, Payton was acquired by the Browns in 1977. He was the older brother of the NFL's all-time leading rushing yards leader Walter Payton.

PERFECT SEASON

The Browns had a perfect season in 1948, finishing with a 14-0 record—15-0 including their 49-7 demolition of Buffalo in the AAFC Championship game Dec. 19 in Cleveland. It was the second time to that point (and now third overall) in the history of pro football that a team went an entire season (regular season and postseason) undefeated and untied. The 1937 Los Angeles Bulldogs went 8-0 in winning an earlier AFL Championship (there was no postseason). The 1972 Miami Dolphins went 17-0 in winning the NFL Championship that culminated with a victory in Super Bowl VII.

PERRY, MICHAEL DEAN

Michael Dean Perry was a defensive end for Cleveland from 1988-94. He was a second-round draft choice of the Browns in 1988 from Clemson University. He was the Browns' leader with 11.5 sacks in 1990, which is fourth all-time in team history. Perry's 51.5 sacks all-time rank second in team annals. He was voted AFC Defensive Most Valuable Player in 1989 by UPI. He was voted to All-AFC defensive teams in 1989 by AP, PFW, FWA, SN, and UPI; in 1990 by AP, NEA, PFW, FWA, SN, and UPI; in 1991 by PFW and SN; in 1992 and 1993 by SN; and in 1994 by UPI. Perry was picked for the Pro Bowl from 1989-91 and in 1993 and 1994.

PHILADELPHIA EAGLES

The Philadelphia Eagles were opponents of the Browns in the NFL from 1950-95 and have been since 1999. The most famous game between the two teams occurred in the NFL's season opener on Saturday evening, Sept. 16, 1950, in Philadelphia's Municipal Stadium. As two-time defending NFL Champions, the Eagles were heavy favorites. The Browns, despite having won four straight AAFC Championships, were considered inferior because the AAFC was considered inferior to the NFL. The Browns blew away the Eagles, 35-10, in front of 71,237 fans. Philadelphia's all-time record against Cleveland is 13-31-1 (.300), with 8-14 (.364) at home and 5-17-1 (.239) on the road.

PHILCOX, TODD

Todd Philcox was a Browns quarterback from 1991-93. A Syracuse University product, he was obtained by the Browns Apr. 1, 1991, as a free agent. Philcox took over as the starter after Bernie Kosar was released Nov. 8, 1993, and played the position until Vinny Testaverde returned from a separated shoulder injury one month later.

PHIPPS, MIKE

Mike Phipps was a Browns quarterback from 1970-76. He was a first-round draft choice of the Browns in 1970 from Purdue University. The Browns traded the great Paul Warfield to Miami Jan. 26, 1970, for the Dolphins' first-round selection that was the third overall pick in the next day's draft. Phipps led the Boilermakers to 24 victories in 30 games, including a pair of AP Top 10 finishes the three previous autumns. He did not become the Browns' full-time starter until week two of the 1972 season. Veteran Bill Nelsen directed the Browns for the most part in 1970 and 1971.

Phipps's best season was 1972 when he completed 144 of 305 pass attempts for 1,994 yards, 13 touchdowns, and 16 interceptions. The Browns finished 10-4 (.714) that year, and despite Phipps's five interceptions, took the undefeated Dolphins down to the wire in an AFC Divisional Playoff game in the Orange Bowl (a 20-14 Dolphins win). Things went downhill from there. Phipps's touchdown passes/interceptions ratio was quite unimpressive for the next three seasons: 9/20, 9/17 and 4/19. He held off a challenge from Brian Sipe in the 1976 training camp and started the opening game against the New York Jets at home. He passed for

Mike Phipps is corralled by the Lions' Bobby Williams en route to a 40-24 Detroit victory Oct. 18, 1970. Photo courtesy of the Cleveland Press Collection.

three second-quarter touchdowns en route to a 21-10 halftime lead, only to suffer a separated shoulder early in the third quarter. Sipe came in and put the finishing touches on a
38-17 victory. Sipe went on to pass for 17 touchdowns and had just 14 interceptions as the
Browns improved to 9-5 (.643) after a 3-11 (.214) finish the year before, and the starting
job was his. Phipps passed for 7,700 yards overall, ranking seventh in Browns history. His
633 completions rank sixth all-time. He totaled 40 touchdown passes and 81 interceptions
in his Browns career. He was traded to the Chi-
cago Bears May 3, 1977.

PITTS, FRANK

Frank Pitts was a Browns wide receiver from
1971-73. A Southern University product, he was
acquired by the Browns Sept. 8, 1971, in a trade
with the Kansas City Chiefs for a fourth-round
draft pick in 1972 and a third-round pick in 1973.
He led the Browns in touchdown receptions in
1971 with four and was the team leader in receptions (36), receiving yards (620), and touchdown
catches (eight) in 1972. One of the 1972 touchdown receptions was a game winning 38-yarder
from Mike Phipps with less then a minute to play
on a Monday night in San Diego. Pitts was the
team leader with 31 receptions and four touchdown catches in 1973.

*Frank Pitts scores on a pass from
Mike Phipps in the Browns' 31-0
season-opening triumph at home on
Sept. 19, 1971.*

PITTSBURGH STEELERS

The Pittsburgh Steelers were Browns opponents in the NFL from 1950-95 and have
been since 1999. The Pittsburgh-Cleveland rivalry is one of the most heralded in the NFL.
The series was dominated by the Browns early on, as Cleveland won 32 of the first 41
meetings. Things turned around in the 1970s as the Steelers won 20 of the next 26 meetings. The tables then turned once again as the Browns won 10 of the next 12 encounters.
The teams were even for the most part in the early 1990s before the Steelers won the last
five games prior to the Browns' relocation to Baltimore following the 1995 season.

Pittsburgh spoiled the "new era" Browns' return in 1999 by destroying them, 43-0,
Sept.12 in brand new Cleveland Browns Stadium. The revenge-minded Browns won in
Pittsburgh two months later, 16-15, on a 39-yard field goal by Phil Dawson with 0:00
showing on the clock. Pittsburgh and Cleveland have met once in postseason play, a 29-9
Steelers victory in an AFC Divisional Playoff Jan. 7, 1995, in Pittsburgh. The Steelers' all-
time record against the Browns is 44-54 (.449), with 29-20 (.592) at home and 15-34
(.306) on the road. Their all-time postseason record against the Browns is 1-0 (home).

Jim Brown loses a yard against the Steelers. Photo courtesy of the Cleveland Press Collection.

PLAYER OF THE YEAR

1957   Jim Brown (NFL by AP)
1965   Jim Brown (NFL by AP)
1976   Jerry Sherk (NFL Defensive by NEA)
1980   Brian Sipe (NFL by AP; NFL Offensive by PFW)

PLAYERS FROM OHIO SCHOOLS REPRESENTED IN DRAFTS, MOST TO LEAST

1.	Ohio State University	35
2.	Miami University	10
3.	Bowling Green State University	9
4.	University of Toledo	8
5.	Xavier University	6
6.	John Carroll University	5
	Kent State University	5
8.	Case Western Reserve University	3
	University of Dayton	3
10.	University of Akron	2
	University of Cincinnati	2
	Heidelberg College	2
	Ohio University	2
14.	Baldwin-Wallace College	1
	Wittenberg University	1
	Youngstown State University	1

PLAYERS' STRIKES

Contractual disputes between NFL players and owners resulted in players' strikes during the 1982 and 1987 seasons. Both walkouts began two weeks into the season. The 1982 season was shortened to nine games, with one makeup game played the weekend on which the wild card games were originally scheduled. In the Browns' case, the make-up game was at Pittsburgh, originally scheduled for Oct. 24.

All postseason games other than the Super Bowl were pushed back a week, and there was only one week, rather than the usual two, in between the conference championship games and the Super Bowl. In addition, the postseason field was increased to 16 teams. The Browns finished 4-5 (.444) but still qualified for the playoffs as the eighth and final seed in the AFC. They lost to the Los Angeles Raiders, 27-10, in the Los Angeles Memorial Coliseum in the first round.

The 1987 season was shortened to 15 games, but three weeks were played largely with "replacement players."

There was also a players' strike in 1974, but it only affected training camp as it ended in August.

PLAYOFF BOWL

The Playoff Bowl was an exhibition game played between the Eastern Conference and Western Conference runners-up in the Orange Bowl in Miami after the regular season from 1960-69. The Browns played in three, losing all of them–to the Lions (17-16) Jan. 7, 1961; the Packers (40-23) Jan. 5, 1964; and the Rams (30-6) Jan. 7, 1968.

PLEASANT, ANTHONY

Anthony Pleasant was a Browns defensive end from 1990-95. He was a third-round draft choice of the Browns in 1990 from Tennessee State University. Pleasant was the Browns' leader with 11 sacks in 1993, which ties him for fifth in Browns history. His 30 all-time sacks rank sixth in team history.

PLUM, MILT

Milt Plum was a Browns quarterback from 1957-61. He was a second-round draft choice of the Browns in 1957 from Penn State University. He led the NFL in passing in 1960 and 1961. With a 110.4 rating in 1960, he completed 110 of 250 attempts for 2,297 yards, 21 touchdowns, and just five interceptions. On Oct. 23 of that year, he connected with Leon Clarke for an 86-yard pass play that went for a touchdown against the Eagles. In 1961, he completed 177 of 302 passes for 2,416 yards, 18 touchdowns and 10 interceptions, and had a 90.3 rating. Plum's 8,914 passing yards rank sixth all-time for the Browns. His 627 completions rank eighth all-time in team history. He was selected to play in the Pro Bowl in 1960 and 1961.

POSTSEASON

For a complete listing of all postseason games, please see Team Statistics on page 204.

POSTSEASON GAMES THE BROWNS LOST AND WHO THEY WOULD HAVE PLAYED HAD THEY WON

Please see Team Statistics on page 204.

POWELL, RONNIE

Ronnie Powell was a Cleveland wide receiver in 1999. He was a Northwestern State University product obtained by the Browns Apr. 23, 1999, as a free agent. Powell was best known for his kickoff return duties. He was the team leader in 1999 with 44 kickoff returns and 986 return yards, the latter ranking fourth in Browns history.

PRESEASON

The Browns' all-time record in the preseason (not including four games against the college all-stars) is 123-122-4 (.502), with 37-32-1 (.536) at home, 55-71-3 (.438) on the road, and 31-19 (.620) at neutral sites.

PRESEASON GAMES IN FOREIGN CITIES

N.Y. Jets 11, Cleveland 7 (Aug. 18, 1988, at Montreal)
Philadelphia 17, Cleveland 13 (Aug. 6, 1989, at London)
Cleveland 12, New England 9 (Aug. 14, 1993, at Toronto)

Overall   1-2 (.333)

PRESEASON GAMES AT NEUTRAL SITES IN THE UNITED STATES

The following are cities in the United States in which the Browns have played preseason games: Toledo, Ohio; Syracuse, New York; Portland, Oregon; Birmingham, Alabama; Canton, Ohio; Memphis, Tennessee; South Bend, Indiana; Ann Arbor, Michigan; Columbus, Ohio; Knoxville, Tennessee; Lincoln, Nebraska; and Stillwater, Oklahoma.

PRESEASON GAMES VS. THE BENGALS

The Browns have played the Bengals four times in the preseason, each team winning two. The first game was played Aug. 29, 1970, in Riverfront Stadium in Cincinnati, with the Bengals winning, 31-14. The last three games were played in Ohio Stadium on the campus of Ohio State University in Columbus. The Bengals won the first one, 27-21, Sept. 3, 1972. The Browns won the last two, 24-6, Aug. 19, 1973, and 21-17 Sept. 1, 1974. Interest in the game in Columbus was rabid at first but waned dramatically. Attendance at the first game was 84,816. The mark dropped to 73,421 in the second game. Only 36,326 showed up for the last game.

PRO BOWLERS

1950	Tony Adamle, Otto Graham, Lou Groza, Weldon Humble, Marion Motley, Mac Speedie, Bill Willis
1951	Tony Adamle, Ken Carpenter, Len Ford, Lou Groza, Otto Graham, Dub Jones, Dante Lavelli, Bill Willis
1952	Len Ford, Abe Gibron, Horace Gillom, Otto Graham, Lou Groza, Bill Willis
1953	Len Ford, Abe Gibron, Otto Graham, Lou Groza, Harry Jagade, Tommy James, Dante Lavelli, Ray Renfro
1954	Don Colo, Len Ford, Frank Gatski, Abe Gibron, Otto Graham, Lou Groza, Dante Lavelli
1955	Darrell Brewster, Don Colo, Abe Gibron, Lou Groza, Ken Konz, Fred Morrison
1956	Darrell Brewster, Mike McCormack, Walt Michaels, Don Paul
1957	Jim Brown, Bob Gain, Lou Groza, Mike McCormack, Walt Michaels, Don Paul, Ray Renfro
1958	Jim Brown, Don Colo, Bob Gain, Lou Groza, Walt Michaels, Don Paul, Jim Ray Smith
1959	Jim Brown, Bob Gain, Lou Groza, Art Hunter, Walt Michaels, Jim Ray Smith
1960	Jim Brown, Mike McCormack, Bobby Mitchell, Bernie Parrish, Milt Plum , Ray Renfro, Jim Ray Smith
1961	Jim Brown, Bob Gain, Mike McCormack, John Morrow, Milt Plum, Jim Ray Smith
1962	Jim Brown, Galen Fiss, Bob Gain, Bill Glass, Mike McCormack, Jim Ray Smith
1963	Jim Brown, Galen Fiss, Bill Glass, John Morrow, Bernie Parrish, Dick Schafrath
1964	Jim Brown, Bill Glass, Jim Houston, Dick Modzelewski, Frank Ryan, Dick Schafrath, Paul Warfield
1965	Jim Brown, Gary Collins, Gene Hickerson, Jim Houston, Frank Ryan, Dick Schafrath, Paul Wiggin, John Wooten
1966	Johnny Brewer, Gary Collins, Ernie Green, Gene Hickerson, Leroy Kelly, Frank Ryan, Dick Schafrath, John Wooten
1967	Bill Glass, Ernie Green, Gene Hickerson, Walter Johnson, Leroy Kelly, Milt Morin, Dick Schafrath, Paul Wiggin
1968	Erich Barnes, Gene Hickerson, Walter Johnson, Ernie Kellermann, Leroy Kelly, Milt Morin, Dick Schafrath, Paul Warfield
1969	Jack Gregory, Gene Hickerson, Fred Hoaglin, Jim Houston, Walter Johnson, Leroy Kelly, Bill Nelsen, Paul Warfield
1970	Gene Hickerson, Jim Houston, Leroy Kelly
1971	Leroy Kelly, Milt Morin
1973	Greg Pruitt, Clarence Scott, Jerry Sherk
1974	Greg Pruitt, Jerry Sherk
1975	Jerry Sherk
1976	Greg Pruitt, Jerry Sherk
1977	Greg Pruitt

1978   Thom Darden
1979   Tom DeLeone, Mike Pruitt
1980   Joe DeLamielleure, Tom DeLeone, Doug Dieken, Mike Pruitt, Brian Sipe
1981   Ozzie Newsome
1982   Chip Banks
1983   Chip Banks
1984   Ozzie Newsome
1985   Chip Banks, Bob Golic, Kevin Mack, Clay Matthews, Ozzie Newsome
1986   Chip Banks, Hanford Dixon, Bob Golic, Frank Minnifield, Cody Risien
1987   Hanford Dixon, Bob Golic, Bernie Kosar, Kevin Mack, Clay Matthews, Gerald McNeil, Frank Minnifield, Cody Risien
1988   Hanford Dixon, Clay Matthews, Frank Minnifield
1989   Mike Johnson, Clay Matthews, Frank Minnifield, Michael Dean Perry, Webster Slaughter
1990   Mike Johnson, Michael Dean Perry
1991   Michael Dean Perry
1993   Eric Metcalf, Michael Dean Perry
1994   Rob Burnett, Leroy Hoard, Pepper Johnson, Eric Metcalf, Michael Dean Perry, Eric Turner
2001   Jamir Miller

PRUITT, GREG

Greg Pruitt was a Browns running back from 1973-81. He was a second-round draft choice of the Browns in 1973 from the University of Oklahoma. Pruitt led the Browns in rushing yards every season from 1974-78. In 1975, he gained 1,067 yards and a team-leading eight touchdowns. In 1976, he gained exactly 1,000 yards and tied Cleo Miller for the team lead with four touchdowns on the ground. In 1977, he gained 1,086 yards, and in 1978 he gained 960. He ranks fourth in Browns all-time rushing yards with 5,496.

His 214 yards rushing Dec. 14, 1975, at home against the Chiefs are the sixth-most rushing yards in one game in team history. His 191 rushing yards Oct. 17, 1976, in Atlanta rank seventh in the same category. Pruitt's longest run from the line of scrimmage as a Brown was a 78-yard gain for a touchdown in a 44-7 romp over Kansas City Oct. 30, 1977. His 323 receptions rank fifth all-time in Browns annals, and his 65 in 1981 rank seventh all-time for one Browns season.

Pruitt also returned punts and kickoffs. His 659 career punt return yards rank sixth for the Browns, and his 349 in 1974 rank fifth for one season in team history. His 1,523 kickoff return yards rank ninth all-time in team annals. He led the Browns in punt returns and punt return yards each season from 1973-75, kickoff returns in 1973 and 1975, and kickoff return yards in 1973 and 1974. On Oct. 27, 1974, he returned a punt 72 yards late in the game that led to the winning touchdown in a dramatic home win over the Denver Broncos. Two weeks later, Nov. 10 in New England, he returned a kickoff 88 yards for a touchdown.

Pruitt's 1,798 combined net yards in 1975 rank sixth all-time in team history, and his 1,769 combined net yards in 1974 rank eighth all-time. His 10,700 combined net yards overall rank third all-time in team history (######). Pruitt was selected for the Pro Bowl in 1973, 1974, 1976, and 1977.

Greg Pruitt scores the winning touchdown on an eight-yard run with Steve Holden behind him in a 35-23 upset of the Bengals at home Nov. 23, 1975. Photo courtesy of the Cleveland Press Collection.

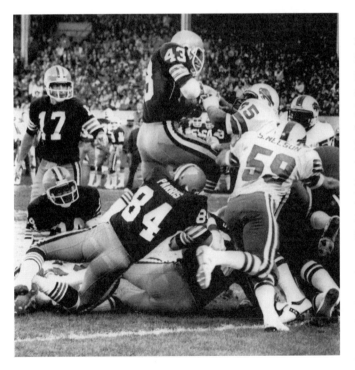

Mike Pruitt scores from a yard out at home against the Bills Oct. 29, 1978. Photo courtesy of the Cleveland Press Collection.

PRUITT, MIKE

Mike Pruitt was a running back for the Browns from 1976-84. He was a first-round draft choice of the Browns in 1976 from Purdue University. Pruitt was second on the Browns in rushing yards in 1978 with 560, but first in rushing touchdowns with five. He was the team leader in rushing yards every season from 1979-83: 1,294 in 1979, 1,034 in 1980, 1,103 in 1981, 516 in 1982, and 1,184 in 1983. His 1979 total was second in the AFC to Houston's Earl Campbell's 1,697 and ranks seventh in Cleveland history.

Pruitt led the Browns in rushing touchdowns with

nine in 1979, six in 1980, seven in 1981, and 10 in 1983. He tied Charles White in 1982 with three. His two longest runs as a Brown were a 79-yarder for a touchdown Dec. 9, 1979, in Oakland and a 71-yarder against the visiting Bills Oct. 29, 1978. His 6,540 rushing yards rank third all-time for the Browns. His 63 receptions in both 1980 and 1981 are tied with Eric Metcalf's 1993 total for 10th all-time in team annals. He also totaled 8,538 combined net yards that rank fifth all-time in Cleveland history (######). Pruitt was voted to All-AFC offensive teams in 1979 by PFW, SN, and UPI. He was picked for the Pro Bowl in 1979 and 1980.

PUNT RETURN YARDS LEADERS

Please see Individual Statistics on page 188.

PUNT RETURNERS

Notable Cleveland punt returners include Cliff Lewis, Don Phelps, Ken Carpenter, Ray Renfro, Billy Reynolds, Chet Hanulak, Don Paul, Bobby Mitchell, Jim Shofner, Walter Roberts, Leroy Kelly, Ben Davis, Reece Morrison, Greg Pruitt, Keith Wright, Dino Hall, Gerald McNeil, and Eric Metcalf.

PUNT RETURNS LEADERS

Please see Individual Statistics on page 188.

PUNTERS

Notable Browns punters include Tom Colella, Horace Gillom, Gary Collins, Don Cockroft, Johnny Evans, Steve Cox, Jeff Gossett, Bryan Wagner, Brian Hansen, Tom Tupa and Chris Gardocki.

PUNTING YARDS LEADERS

Please see Individual Statistics on page 188.

PYNE, JIM

Jim Pyne was a Browns guard in 1999 and 2000. A Virginia Tech University product, Pyne was a Browns' first-round expansion draft choice in 1999.

QUARTERBACKS

Notable Browns quarterbacks include Otto Graham, George Ratterman, Tommy O'Connell, Milt Plum, Jim Ninowski, Frank Ryan, Bill Nelsen, Mike Phipps, Brian Sipe, Paul McDonald, Gary Danielson, Bernie Kosar, Vinny Testaverde, and Tim Couch.

R

RAINER, WALI

Wali Rainer has been a Browns linebacker since 1999. He was a fourth-round draft choice of Cleveland's in 1999 from the University of Virginia.

RATTERMAN, GEORGE

George Ratterman was a Cleveland quarterback from 1952-56. He was a University of Notre Dame product acquired by Cleveland Apr. 18, 1952, in a trade with the New York Yanks for Stan Williams and Bill Forester. Ratterman backed up Otto Graham from 1952-55 and then rotated with Tommy O'Connell and Vito Parilli in 1956.

RECEIVING YARDS LEADERS

Please see Individual Statistics on page 188.

RECEPTIONS LEADERS

Please see Individual Statistics on page 188.

RED RIGHT 88

Red Right 88 was a play in which Browns quarterback Brian Sipe was intercepted by Oakland's Mike Davis with less than a minute to go on a pass intended for Ozzie Newsome. The Browns were down, 14-12, in an AFC Divisional Playoff on Jan. 4, 1981, in frozen Cleveland Stadium. All the Browns needed was a field goal, but kicker Don Cockroft was having a rough day, having missed two field goals and an extra point. The play originated from the Raiders' 13-yard-line.

Oakland Raiders safety Mike Davis intercepts a Brian Sipe pass later known as Red Right 88. Photo courtesy of the Cleveland Press Collection.

REGULAR SEASON GAMES IN JANUARY

Pittsburgh 37, Cleveland 21 (Jan. 2, 1983, at Pittsburgh)
Pittsburgh 16, Cleveland 9 (Jan. 2, 1994, at Pittsburgh)

Overall   0-2 .000 (Away)

RELOCATION TO BALTIMORE

Majority owner Art Modell moved the Browns to Baltimore in 1996 and renamed them the Ravens.

RENFRO, RAY

Ray Renfro was a Browns wide receiver from 1952-63. He was a fourth-round draft choice of the Browns in 1952 out of North Texas State College. Renfro led the Browns in rushing yards in 1953. He led the team in touchdown receptions in 1955 (eight), 1956 (four), and 1957 (six), and in receiving yards and touchdown catches in 1958 (573 and six) and 1959 (528 and six). He had highs of 48 receptions, 834 receiving yards, and six touchdown catches in 1961. He ranks fourth all-time in Browns history with 5,508 receiving yards and 10th all-time with 281 receptions. His 6,569 combined net yards all-time

(######) and 330 all-time points rank ninth in team history. He is tied for fourth in Browns annals for most points in a postseason game with 12, which occurred in Cleveland's NFL title-game rout of Detroit on Dec. 26, 1954, in Cleveland. Renfro was selected for the Pro Bowl in 1953 and 1957.

RETIRED UNIFORM NUMBERS

14   Otto Graham
32   Jim Brown
45   Ernie Davis
46   Don Fleming
76   Lou Groza

Ray Renfro. Photo courtesy of the Cleveland Browns.

REYNOLDS, BILLY

Billy Reynolds was a Browns running back in 1953, 1954, and 1957. He was a second-round draft pick by the Browns in 1953 out of the University of Pittsburgh. He was in the military in 1955 and 1956. Reynolds was known mostly for his punt and kickoff return duties as he led the Browns in punt returns in 1953 and 1957, punt return yardage all three years he played, and kickoff returns and kickoff return yards in 1954. His kickoff returns of 42 and 46 yards helped set up touchdowns in the Browns' 56-10 rout of the Lions in the 1954 NFL title game.

RISEN, CODY

Cody Risen was a Cleveland offensive tackle from 1979-83 and 1985-89. He was a seventh-round draft pick of the Browns in 1979 out of Texas A&M University. He missed the entire 1984 season due to a knee injury suffered in the final preseason game in Philadelphia. Risien was voted to All-AFC offensive teams in 1983 by UPI and in 1986 by PFW. He was voted to the Pro Bowl in 1986 and 1987.

ROAD WON-LOST-TIED RECORDS

Please see Team Statistics on page 204.

Cody Risen and assistant coach Rod Humenuik drill in offensive line techniques in 1979. Photo courtesy of the Cleveland Press Collection.

ROBERTS, WALTER

Walter Roberts was a Browns wide receiver from 1964-66. He was a San Jose State University product acquired by the Browns as a free agent in 1964. He started in place of the injured Paul Warfield for part of the 1965 season. He had an 80-yard touchdown reception from Frank Ryan that year in a season-opening win over Washington. He also saw time as a kickoff returner and punt returner. He was the Browns' leader in kickoff return yards (661) and co-leader in kickoff returns (24) in 1964. He was the team leader in kickoff returns (20) and kickoff return yards (454) in 1966. He returned a kickoff 88 yards on November 7, 1965, at home against the Eagles. He led the Browns in punt returns in 1964 and 1965. Roberts's 1,608 all-time punt return yards rank seventh in Browns history.

ROGERS, DON

Don Rogers was a Browns safety in 1984 and 1985. He was a first-round draft choice of the Browns in 1984 out of UCLA. He returned an interception of a Dan Marino pass 45 yards in an AFC Divisional Playoff loss in Miami on Jan. 4, 1986. He died tragically to a drug overdose some three-and-a-half weeks prior to the start of 1986 training camp.

ROOKIE OF THE YEAR
1957   Jim Brown (NFL by the AP, UP)
1982   Chip Banks (NFL Defensive by AP, PFW)
1985   Kevin Mack (AFC by UPI)

RUBBER BOWL
Rubber Bowl in Akron, Ohio, was the venue where the Browns played their first preseason game on Aug. 30, 1946, a 35-20 victory over the Brooklyn Dodgers.

Reggie Rucker, 1978. Photo courtesy of the Cleveland Press Collection.

RUCKER, REGGIE
Reggie Rucker was a Browns wide receiver from 1975-81. A Boston University product, Rucker was acquired by the Browns on Jan. 28, 1975, in a trade with New England for a fourth-round draft choice that year. He was the team leader in receptions in 1975, 1976, and 1978, receiving yards every year from 1975-78, and touchdown receptions in 1976 and 1978. Rucker's 177 receiving yards in the Browns' 30-24 overtime victory over the Miami Dolphins on November 18, 1979, in Cleveland are tied for eighth in team history (#######). In that game, he caught a game-winning 39-yard touchdown pass from Brian Sipe with 1:59 left on the clock to win it. He caught a 42-yard touchdown pass from Sipe for Cleveland's first score in its 27-24 AFC Central Division-clinching triumph in Cincinnati on Dec. 21, 1980. Rucker caught 310 passes for 4,953 yards as a Brown, both of which rank seventh in team history.

RUDD, DWAYNE
Dwayne Rudd has been a Cleveland linebacker since 2001. He was a University of Alabama product acquired by the Browns on Mar. 4, 2001, as a free agent.

RUNNING BACKS
Notable Browns running backs have included Edgar Jones, Marion Motley, Bill Boedeker, Rex Bumgardner, Ken Carpenter, Harry Jagade, Billy Reynolds, Maurice Bassett, Fred Morrison, Ed Modzelewski, Preston Carpenter, Jim Brown, Bobby Mitchell, Ernie Green, Leroy Kelly, Bo Scott, Greg Pruitt, Cleo Miller, Mike Pruitt, Calvin Hill, Earnest Byner, Kevin Mack, Eric Metcalf, and Leroy Hoard.

RUSHING YARDS LEADERS

Please see Individual Statistics on page 188.

Please see Individual Statistics on page 188.

RUTIGLIANO, SAM

Sam Rutigliano was the Browns' head coach from 1978-84. He was fired midway through the 1984 season the day after Cleveland's 12-9 last-second loss to the lowly Bengals in Cincinnati dropped the Browns' record to 1-7 (.125). Rutigliano led the Browns to some exciting times in the late 1970s and 1980. His Kardiac Kids won several games during that period in thrilling fashion. Rutigliano's first of two playoff games as the Browns' head man ended with his team on the losing end of a thriller—a 14-12 AFC Divisional Playoff loss to the Oakland Raiders at home on Jan. 4, 1981, in frigid Cleveland Stadium. Quarterback Brian Sipe was picked off in the end zone with less than a minute play.

Rutigliano was voted AFC Coach of the Year in 1979 and 1980 by UPI. His all-time record as the Browns' head coach was 47-50 (.485), with 28-20 (.583) at home and 19-30 (.388) on the road. His all-time postseason record as Browns head coach was 0-2, with 0-1 at home and 0-1 on the road.

Sam Rutigliano in 1978. Photo courtesy of the Cleveland Press Collection.

RYAN, FRANK

Frank Ryan was a Browns quarterback from 1962-68. He was a Rice University product acquired by the Browns on July 12, 1962, as part of a five-player trade with the Los Angeles Rams. After sharing the signal-calling duties with Jim Ninowski in 1962, Ryan completed 135 out of 256 passes for 25 touchdowns and 13 interceptions in 1963 while directing the Browns to a 10-4 (.714) record and second-place finish in the Eastern Conference.

In the season-opener at home that year against the Redskins on Sept. 15, Ryan connected with Jim Brown on an 83-yard pass play that went for a touchdown on the way to a 37-14 win. In 1964, Ryan completed 174 of 334 passes for 2,404 yards, 25 touchdowns, and 19 interceptions as the Browns won the Eastern Conference with a 10-3-1 (.750) record. Three second-half touchdown passes to Gary Collins for 18, 42, and 51 yards led Cleveland to a 27-0 upset of Baltimore in the NFL Championship game that year.

Ryan helped the Browns get off to a fine start the next year by completing an 80-yard touchdown pass to Walter Roberts in the season opener at Washington on Sept. 19. He was instrumental in the team returning to the title game, but the Browns fell in the snow and

Frank Ryan. Photo courtesy of the Cleveland Browns.

sleet of Green Bay, 23-12. Ryan passed for team records (at the time) of 2,974 yards and 29 touchdowns in 1966, and had just 14 interceptions, but the Browns failed to advance to the postseason. His 367 passing yards on Dec. 17 that year in a 38-10 rout of the Cardinals rank ninth in Browns history. His 2,026 yards passing and 20 touchdown passes helped Cleveland to a 9-5 (.643) record and the Century Division Championship in 1967. The Browns were crushed, though, 52-14 in Dallas for the Eastern Conference title.

After arm problems surfaced, Ryan was replaced as the starter in favor of Bill Nelsen four games into the 1968 season. Ryan ranks fourth all-time in Browns annals in completions (907) and yards passing (13,361). His 35 completions and 534 passing yards in postseason play also rank fourth in team history. He was a Pro Bowl selection from 1964-66.

RYMKUS, LOU

Lou Rymkus was a Browns offensive tackle from 1946-51. He was a University of Notre Dame product acquired by Cleveland as a free agent. He was named to All-AAFC teams in 1946 by SP; in 1947 by C&O, NYN, OFF, and SP; in 1948 by AP, OFF, and UP; and in 1949 by UP. He was voted to the All-AAFC offensive team in 1949 by INS.

Lou Rymkus. Photo courtesy of the Cleveland Browns.

S

SABAN, LOU

Lou Saban was a Browns linebacker from 1946-49. An Indiana University product, Saban was acquired by the Browns as a free agent. His 39-yard interception return in the fourth quarter of the 1948 AAFC Championship game was Cleveland's final touchdown in a 49-7 rout of the Buffalo Bills. He was voted to All-AAFC teams in 1948 by NYN and UP and in 1949 by AP, NYN, OFF, and UP. He was voted to the All-AAFC defensive team in 1949 by INS. Saban was a Browns television broadcaster in 1952.

SACKS LEADERS

Please see Individual Statistics on page 188.

Lou Saban. Photo courtesy of the Cleveland Browns.

SAN DIEGO CHARGERS

The San Diego Chargers were Browns opponents in the NFL from 1970-95 and have been since 1999. Their all-time record against Cleveland is 7-10-1 (.417), with 3-5-1 (.389) at home and 4-5 (.444) on the road.

SAN FRANCISCO 49ERS

The San Francisco 49ers were opponents of the Browns in the AAFC from 1946-49, and the NFL from 1950-95 and have been since 1999. The two teams have met once in the postseason—a 21-7 Browns victory in the 1949 AAFC Championship game in Cleveland. San Francisco's all-time record against Cleveland is 8-15 (.348), with 5-7 (.417) at home and 3-8 (.273) on the road. The 49ers' all-time record against Cleveland in the postseason is 0-1 (away).

John Sandusky. Photo courtesy of the Cleveland Browns.

SANDUSKY, JOHN

John Sandusky was a Browns offensive tackle from 1950-55. He was a Browns second-round draft choice in 1950 from Villanova University.

SATURDAY AFTERNOON GAMES (REGULAR SEASON)

(Local starting times of earlier than 5 p.m.)

Cleveland 14, N.Y. Giants 13 (Oct. 27, 1951, at Cleveland)
Cleveland 13, San Francisco 10 (Dec. 15, 1962, at San Francisco)
Cleveland 52, New York 20 (Dec. 12, 1964, at New York)
Cleveland 38, St. Louis 10 (Dec. 17, 1966, at St. Louis)
St. Louis 27, Cleveland 16 (Dec. 14, 1968, at St. Louis)
Dallas 6, Cleveland 2 (Dec. 12, 1970, at Cleveland)
Cleveland 27, Cincinnati 24 (Dec. 9, 1972, at Cincinnati)
Dallas 41, Cleveland 17 (Dec. 7, 1974, at Dallas)
N.Y. Jets 14, Cleveland 13 (Dec. 12, 1981, at Cleveland)
Cleveland 19, Pittsburgh 13 (Dec. 26, 1987, at Pittsburgh)
Cleveland 19, Dallas 14 (Dec. 10, 1994, at Dallas)
Cleveland 35, Seattle 9 (Dec. 24, 1994, at Cleveland)
Minnesota 27, Cleveland 11 (Dec. 9, 1995, at Minnesota)

Overall	8-5	(.615)
Home	2-2	(.500)
Away	6-3	(.667)

SATURDAY NIGHT GAMES

(Local starting times of 5 p.m. or later)

Cleveland 7, New York 0 (Oct. 12, 1946, at New York)
Cleveland 35, Philadelphia 10 (Sept. 16, 1950, at Philadelphia)
Cleveland 30, Pittsburgh 17 (Oct. 7, 1950, at Pittsburgh)
Cleveland 21, Pittsburgh 20 (Oct. 4, 1952, at Pittsburgh)
Cleveland 37, Philadelphia 13 (Oct. 10, 1953, at Cleveland)

Cleveland 23, Pittsburgh 12 (Oct. 6, 1956, at Pittsburgh)
Cleveland 23, Pittsburgh 12 (Oct. 5, 1957, at Pittsburgh)
Pittsburgh 17, Cleveland 7 (Sept. 26, 1959, at Pittsburgh)
Cleveland 35, Pittsburgh 23 (Oct. 5, 1963, at Cleveland)
Pittsburgh 23, Cleveland 7 (Oct. 10, 1964, at Cleveland)
Cleveland 24, Pittsburgh 19 (Oct. 9, 1965, at Cleveland)
Cleveland 41, Pittsburgh 10 (Oct. 8, 1966, at Cleveland)
Cleveland 21, Pittsburgh 10 (Oct. 7, 1967, at Cleveland)
Cleveland 31, Pittsburgh 24 (Oct. 5, 1968, at Cleveland)
Cleveland 42, Pittsburgh 31 (Oct. 18, 1969, at Cleveland)
Cleveland 15, Pittsburgh 7 (Oct. 3, 1970, at Cleveland)
Cleveland 24, Houston 20 (Dec. 23, 1989, at Houston)

Overall   15-2 (.882)
Home   8-1 (.889)
Away   7-1 (.875)

SATURDAY NIGHT GAMES VS. THE PITTSBURGH STEELERS
(Local starting times of 5 p.m. or later)

Cleveland 30, Pittsburgh 17 (Oct. 7, 1950, at Pit.)
Cleveland 21, Pittsburgh 20 (Oct. 4, 1952, at Pit.)
Cleveland 23, Pittsburgh 12 (Oct. 6, 1956, at Pit.)
Cleveland 23, Pittsburgh 12 (Oct. 5, 1957, at Pit.)
Pittsburgh 17, Cleveland 7 (Sept. 26, 1959, at Pit.)
Cleveland 35, Pittsburgh 23 (Oct. 5, 1963, at Cle.)
Pittsburgh 23, Cleveland 7 (Oct. 10, 1964, at Cle.)
Cleveland 24, Pittsburgh 19 (Oct. 9, 1965, at Cle.)
Cleveland 41, Pittsburgh 10 (Oct. 8, 1966, at Cle.)
Cleveland 21, Pittsburgh 10 (Oct. 7, 1967, at Cle.)
Cleveland 31, Pittsburgh 24 (Oct. 5, 1968, at Cle.)
Cleveland 42, Pittsburgh 31 (Oct. 18, 1969, at Cle.)
Cleveland 15, Pittsburgh 7 (Oct. 3, 1970, at Cle.)

Overall   11-2 .846
Home   7-1 .875
Away   4-1 .800

SCARRY, MIKE
Mike Scarry was a center for Cleveland in 1946 and 1947. He was a Waynesburg College product acquired by the Browns as a free agent. He was named to All-AAFC teams in 1946 by NYN and in 1947 by C&O.

SCHAFRATH, DICK

Dick Schafrath was a Browns guard and offensive tackle from 1959-71. He was a second-round draft choice of Cleveland's in 1959 from Ohio State University. He was voted to All-NFL offensive teams in 1963 by AP and in 1964 and 1965 by AP, NYN, and UPI. He was voted to the Pro Bowl from 1963-68.

SCHOOLS THAT HAVE HAD THE MOST PLAYERS DRAFTED (TOP TEN)

1. Ohio State University   35
2. Purdue University   23
3. University of Michigan   21
4. Michigan State University   19
5. University of Illinois   18
6. University of Notre Dame   16
7. Baylor University   14
8. University of Maryland   13
   University of North Carolina   13
   University of Southern California 13

Dick Schafrath. Photo courtesy of the Cleveland Browns.

Marty Schottenheimer. Photo courtesy of the Cleveland Browns.

SCHOTTENHEIMER, MARTY

Marty Schottenheimer was the Browns' head coach from 1984-88. He was elevated from his defensive coordinator duties to head coach when the Browns were 1-7 (.125), replacing the fired Sam Rutigliano. Schottenheimer led the Browns to a 4-4 finish that year for a 5-11 (.313) record. He led the team to AFC Central Division titles from 1985-87 and a wild card berth in 1988. The Browns lost heartbreaking AFC title games to Denver in 1986 and 1987. Philosophical differences with Browns majority owner Art Modell led to Schottenheimer's resignation following the 1988 season. He was named AFC Coach of the Year in 1986 by FWA and UPI. His all-time record as Browns head coach was 44-27 (.620), with 23-12 (.657) at home and 21-15 (.583) on the road. His all-time postseason record as Browns head coach was 2-4 (.333), with 2-2 at home and 0-2 on the road. He was a Browns assistant coach from 1980-84.

SCORING LEADERS (POINTS)

Please see Individual Statistics on page 188.

SCOTT, BO

Bo Scott was a Browns running back from 1969-74. He was a Browns third-round draft choice in 1965 from Ohio State University despite having just one season—his sophomore year— under his belt. He played in the CFL from 1965-68. Scott was second on the Browns to Leroy Kelly every year from 1970-72 in rushing attempts and rushing yards. He was the team leader with seven rushing touchdowns in 1970 and second with nine in 1971 to Kelly's 10. He led the team in receptions with 40 in 1970 and tied Gary Collins for the team lead in touchdown catches that year with four. He was a kickoff returner his rookie year in 1969, and led the Browns with 25 returns and 722 return yards. Scott's 12 points in Cleveland's victory at Dallas in the Eastern Conference title game Dec. 28, 1969, are tied for fourth all-time in Browns history.

Bo Scott. Photo courtesy of the Cleveland Browns.

SCOTT, CLARENCE

Clarence Scott was a Cleveland defensive back from 1971-83. A first-round draft choice by the Browns in 1971 from Kansas State University, Scott led the team with five interceptions in 1973 and four in 1981. He tied Charlie Hall for the team lead in picks in 1975. His 39 career interceptions with the Browns rank third all-time in team annals. He was named to the All-AFC defensive team by UPI and was a Pro Bowl selection in 1973.

Clarence Scott grabs Oakland's Fred Biletnikoff as the Raiders' wide receiver scores on an 11-yard touchdown pass from Ken Stabler. The Browns lost, 40-24, Oct. 6, 1974. Photo courtesy of the Cleveland Press Collection.

SEASON POINTS
DIFFERENTIALS

FIVE BEST

1. +286 (423-137) (1946)
2. +225 (410-185) (1947)
3. +199 (389-190) (1948)
4. +186 (348-162) (1953)
5. +179 (331-152) (1951)

FIVE WORST

1. -258 (161-419) (2000)
2. -234 (228-462) (1990)
3. -220 (217-437) (1999)
4. -154 (218-372) (1975)
5. -99 (276-375) (1981)

SEATTLE SEAHAWKS

The Seattle Seahawks were Browns opponents in the NFL from 1976-95 and have been since 1999. Their all-time record against the Browns is 10-4 (.714), with 6-3 (.667) at home and 4-1 (.800) on the road.

Mike Pruitt scores from a yard out in a 29-24 loss to Seattle in Cleveland Stadium on Nov. 11, 1979.

SEPTEMBER
—6, 1946

The Browns defeated the Miami Seahawks, 44-0, in Cleveland in the Browns' first game ever.

—16, 1950

Cleveland defeated Philadelphia, 35-10, in Philadelphia in the NFL's Saturday night season opener. The Browns were four-time defending AAFC Champions, and the NFL matched them up with the two-time defending NFL Champion Eagles right off the bat.

—21, 1970

The Browns defeated the New York Jets, 31-21, in Cleveland in the first ABC *Monday Night Football* game. Cleveland's Homer Jones returned the second-half kickoff 94 yards for a touchdown. Browns linebacker Billy Andrews put the game away when he made a diving interception of a Joe Namath pass, got up and returned it 25 yards for a touchdown with 35 seconds left.

—24, 1979

The Browns defeated the Dallas Cowboys, 26-7, in Cleveland in a battle of unbeatens on ABC *Monday Night Football*. The Browns scored 20 points in the first half of the first *quarter*. Dallas failed to record its initial first down until it trailed, 20-0.

—27-NOV. 14, 1982

NFL games during this period were cancelled due to an NFL players' strike that shortened the season to nine games, rescheduling one game for the season finale the weekend the wild card games were supposed to have been played. Because of the strike, the playoff field was expanded to 16 teams and postseason games other than the Super Bowl were pushed back one week. It also resulted in one week rather than the normal two in between the conference championship games and the Super Bowl. In the Browns' case, the rescheduled game was against the Pittsburgh Steelers and was originally planned for Oct. 24.

—3, 1984

The Browns were embarrassed by the Seattle Seahawks, 33-0, in Seattle in the season opener played on a Monday afternoon due to a scheduling conflict the day before with Major League Baseball's Seattle Mariners, who were co-tenants of the Kingdome with the Seahawks.

—7, 1986

The NFL utilized its new instant replay method of officiating questionable referees' calls during the Browns-Bears game in Soldier Field in Chicago. On the third play of the game, Browns safety Al Gross appeared to recover an errant Chicago snap in the Bears' end zone. The debate was whether or not Gross gained possession of the ball before sliding across the end line. After a review, referees ruled that Gross did indeed gain possession of the ball in time for a touchdown. Gross's score gave Cleveland a 7-0 lead, but the defending Super Bowl Champion Bears went on to win a wild one, 41-31.

—28, 1987

The Browns were to play the Denver Broncos at home on ABC *Monday Night Football*, but the game was cancelled due to the NFL players' strike. The game would have been a rematch of the Browns' AFC Championship game defeat to Denver some nine months earlier.

—10, 1989

The Browns bombed the Pittsburgh Steelers, 51-0, in Pittsburgh in the season opener, while yielding just 53 total net yards, the fewest ever given up in one game by the Browns. Cleveland forced eight Steelers turnovers and had seven sacks. This was the Browns' fourth straight win in Three Rivers Stadium after 16 consecutive losses there from 1970-85.

—4, 1994

It didn't take long for the NFL's first two-point conversion to be scored in the first year of its use. Tom Tupa earned the honors against the Bengals in Cincinnati. As the holder on Matt Stover's apparent extra point attempt following Leroy Hoard's 11-yard touchdown catch from Vinny Testaverde, he ran over the left side to give the Browns an 11-0 first-quarter lead en route to a season-opening 28-20 triumph.

—8, 1998

The NFL awarded the city of Cleveland an expansion team called the "Browns" that, beginning with its first season in 1999, would continue the history—the uniform colors and statistics—of the original Browns, who relocated to Baltimore in 1996 and became the Ravens.

—12, 1999

The Browns experienced their worst shutout and worst home loss ever in a 43-0 defeat at the hands of the Pittsburgh Steelers. The game, the first in Cleveland Browns Stadium, was the Browns' first game of the "new era" after three seasons of football-less autumns in Cleveland. Unfortunately for the Browns, the game was broadcast on national television.

—16, 2001

Because of terrorist activities against the United States five days before, the Browns game with the Steelers in Pittsburgh, along with the other NFL games that week, was cancelled and rescheduled four months later as the season finale. Originally, the Browns-Steelers game was scheduled to appear as a nationally-televised Sunday night game on ESPN. But the game was switched to an early-afternoon game and was replaced on ESPN that night by the Eagles vs. Buccaneers contest. It was the first time in NFL history that NFL games were canceled for reasons other than a players' strike.

SHANLEY, GIB

Gib Shanley was a Browns radio broadcaster from 1961-84.

SHERK, JERRY

Jerry Sherk was a Browns defensive tackle from 1970-81. A second-round draft choice of the Browns in 1970 from Oklahoma State University, Sherk was voted NFL Defensive Player of the Year in 1976 by NEA. He was named to All-AFC defensive teams in 1975 by SN and in 1976 by AP, NEA, PFW, FWA, SN, and UPI. He was selected to play in the Pro Bowl from 1973-76.

Jerry Sherk prepares to pounce on the Steelers' Terry Bradshaw. Photo courtesy of the Cleveland Press Collection.

SHOFNER, JIM

Jim Shofner was a Browns defensive back from 1958-63. He was a Browns first-round draft choice in 1958 from Texas Christian University. His eight interceptions in 1960 not only tied Bobby Franklin for the team lead but also tied for eighth in team history for most picks in one season. Shofner was elevated from his offensive coordinator duties to head coach for the last seven games of the 1990 season after Bud Carson was fired. His all-time record as head coach of the Browns was 1-6 (.143), with 1-3 (.250) at home and 0-3 on the road. He was a Browns assistant coach from 1978-80 and in 1990.

SHULA, DON

Don Shula was a Browns defensive back in 1951 and 1952. He was a ninth-round draft choice of the Browns in 1951 from John Carroll University. Shula ranked third on the team in 1951 with four interceptions.

Don Shula. Photo courtesy of the Cleveland Press Collection.

SHUTOUTS

For a list of Cleveland games in which either the Browns or the other team did not score, please see Team Statistics on page 204.

SIPE, BRIAN

Brian Sipe was a Browns quarterback from 1974-83. A 13th-round draft choice of the Browns in 1972 from San Diego State University, Sipe spent two seasons on the practice squad before making the regular roster in 1974. He filled in for the interception-prone Mike Phipps on occasion that season and was instrumental in three wins. One was a stirring comeback at home against Denver in which he scored twice—the second with 1:56 left—after relieving Phipps in the fourth quarter.

He replaced Phipps once and for all when the Browns' 1970 No. 1 draft choice went down with a separated shoulder while the Browns were leading the New York Jets, 21-10, early in the second half of the 1976 season opener. Sipe directed the Browns to victory in that game and went on to complete 178 of 312 passes that year for 2,113 yards, 17 touchdowns and 14 interceptions, becoming the first Cleveland quarterback in seven years to throw for more touchdowns than interceptions. The Browns improved to 9-5 (.643) after 4-10 (.286) and 3-11 (.214) finishes the two previous seasons, respectively.

Sipe had the starting job all to himself when the 1977 season opened with Phipps's transfer to Chicago via an off-season trade. With the Browns in first place in the AFC Central Division at 5-3, Sipe suffered a separated left shoulder in a loss to the Steelers that caused him to miss the remainder of the season. He had com-

Brian Sipe (left) and Sam Rutigliano during training camp in July 1981. Photo courtesy of the Cleveland Press Collection.

pleted 112 of 195 passes for 1,233 yards and nine touchdowns, but had thrown 14 interceptions that year. The last-place Browns finished 6-8 (.429).

In 1978, the arrival of new head coach Sam Rutigliano meant a more pass-oriented offense. Sipe passed for 2,906 yards on 222 completions out of 399 attempts, with 21 touchdown passes and 15 interceptions as the Browns improved to 8-8 in the tough AFC Central. He really started coming into his own in 1979 when he completed 286 (seventh in team history) of 535 attempts for 3,793 yards (fourth in team annals), 28 touchdown passes (tied with New England's Steve Grogan for the NFL high that year), and 26 interceptions. His feats helped lead the Browns to numerous down-to-the-wire victories and a 9-7 (.563) record, as the Browns became known as the Kardiac Kids. A late-season letdown, though, left the Browns out of the playoffs for the seventh straight year.

Sipe passed for a team record 4,132 yards on 337 completions, the most in Browns history, in 554 attempts in 1980, becoming just the second quarterback in NFL annals to pass for 4,000 yards in one season. He had an AFC high of 30 touchdown passes (tied with San Diego's Dan Fouts) and just 14 interceptions. He was the NFL's passing leader in 1980 with a 91.4 rating. On Oct. 19 of that year, he passed for 391 yards (fifth most in team history) in a 26-21 home win over Green Bay, a game in which he hit Dave Logan for a 46-yard touchdown pass with 16 seconds to go. Sipe's and the Browns' magical season, another Kardiac Kids year, came to a crushing end when he was intercepted in Oakland's end zone with less than a minute to play in a 14-12 divisional playoff loss to the Raiders in Cleveland Stadium.

Sipe completed 313, the second most in team annals, of 567 pass attempts for 3,876 yards, second most ever in one Browns season, in 1981. However, he threw for only 17 touchdowns and was picked off 25 times as the Browns fell to 5-11 (.313) and last place. He did have his moments despite a disappointing season. His 375 passing yards in the season opener in a Monday night loss to San Diego rank seventh in team history, and his 444 in a 42-28 home win over Baltimore Oct. 25 rank as the most ever by a Browns quarterback.

Rutigliano benched Sipe after six games in 1982 in favor of third-year lefty Paul McDonald, who finished out the strike-shortened season that ended with a losing record and first-round playoff elimination by the Raiders in Los Angeles. Sipe regained his starting job during the 1983 training camp and had a fine season, starting in all but two games. He completed 291 (sixth most in Browns annals) of 496 pass attempts for 3,566 yards (fifth most in team history), an AFC-high 26 touchdowns, but also 23 interceptions as the Browns wound up 9-7 (.563), barely missing the playoffs.

Sipe's 1,944 career completions and 23,713 passing yards both rank No. 1 in Browns history. In 1980, he was voted NFL Most Valuable Player by FWA and SN; NFL Player of the Year by AP; NFL Offensive Player of the Year by PFW; and AFC Most Valuable Player by UPI. He was voted to All-AFC offensive teams that year by AP, NEA, PFW, FWA, SN, and UPI, and was voted to the Pro Bowl, too.

SIX TOUCHDOWNS IN ONE GAME

Wide receiver Dub Jones accomplished this feat Nov. 25, 1951, in the Browns' 42-21 victory over the Chicago Bears in Cleveland Municipal Stadium. He broke the team record of four, set by Dante Lavelli Oct. 14, 1949, when each of his scores came on receptions in a 61-14 rout of the Los Angeles Dons. Jones matched the NFL record set by Ernie Nevers, who totaled six touchdown catches and led the Chicago Cardinals to a 40-6 thumping of the cross town Bears on Thanksgiving Day, 1929. While Lavelli and Nevers scored their touchdowns on receptions alone, Jones tallied his in the air and on the ground, scoring four on runs and two on catches. Even more remarkable, all six of his touchdowns came in the final three quarters. On top of all that, he scored the last six times he touched the ball.

SKORICH, NICK

Nick Skorich was the Browns' head coach from 1971-74. He led the Browns to 9-5 (.643) and 10-4 (.714) finishes in 1971 and 1972, respectively. The 1971 team won the AFC Central Division, and the 1972 team qualified for the playoffs as the AFC's wild card entrant. Both years, the Browns were ousted in the divisional playoffs. Skorich is the only Cleveland head coach in history who had prior NFL head coaching experience (with the Philadelphia Eagles from 1961-63). His all-time record as the Browns' head coach was 30-24-2 (.554), with 16-11-1 (.589) at home and 14-13-1 (.519) on the road. His all-time postseason record as Cleveland's head coach was 0-2, with 0-1 at home and 0-1 on the road. Skorich was a Cleveland assistant coach from 1964-70.

SLAUGHTER, WEBSTER

Webster Slaughter was a Browns wide receiver from 1986-91. He was a second-round draft choice of the Browns in 1986 from San Diego State University. He had 47 receptions for a Browns-leading 806 yards in 1987. He also led the team with seven touchdown catches that year. He had a career year in 1989, with a team-leading 65 receptions (seventh most in team history), 1,236 receiving yards (tops in team history), and a team-leading six touchdown catches. He totaled 186 and 184 receiving yards in consecutive weeks that year—Oct. 23 against the Bears and Oct. 29 against the Oilers, both in Cleveland. His 186-yard performance ranks fourth in Browns history, and his 184-yard performance ranks fifth (#######).

In the Bears game on *Monday Night Football*, Slaughter was on the receiving end of a 97-yard pass play from Bernie Kosar that went for a touchdown, the second-longest pass play in team history. His 59 receptions, 847 receiving yards, and four touchdown catches led the Browns in 1990. His 64 receptions (ninth most in team annals) and 906 receiving yards led the Browns in 1991. His

Webster Slaughter. Photo courtesy of the Cleveland Browns.

305 receptions and 4,834 receiving yards both rank eighth all-time in team history. His 30 points in the postseason are tied for fifth all-time for the Browns.

Slaughter totaled 381 postseason receiving yards with the Browns, which rank third all-time in team annals (##). He is tied for fifth for most points scored in a postseason game with 12 twice—against Houston in the 1988 AFC Wild Card game and Buffalo in a 1989 AFC Divisional Playoff affair. His 114 receiving yards in the playoff against the Bills are tied for fifth for the most in one postseason game in team history (####). Slaughter was voted to the All-AFC offensive team by UPI in 1989 and was also picked to play in the Pro Bowl that year.

SMITH, AKILI

Akili Smith has been a Cincinnati Bengals quarterback since 1999. He was nearly selected by the Browns with the No. 1 overall pick in the 1999 draft from the University of Oregon. Instead, the Browns chose University of Kentucky quarterback Tim Couch. The rivalry between Smith and Couch—Smith believed he should have been the Browns' selection—was the only thing needed to refire up the age old rivalry between the Browns and Bengals upon Cleveland's return to the NFL in 1999. Intense feelings came to a boil Oct. 10 of that year in Cleveland Browns Stadium. Smith's two-yard touchdown pass to Carl Pickens with five seconds to go lifted Cincinnati to an 18-17 victory. After the game, Smith visibly taunted Browns fans that he claimed had been overly uncouth verbally to him all afternoon. He finished the day with 25 completions in 41 pass attempts for 221 yards and two touchdowns. Couch, meanwhile, was 15 of 27 for 164 yards and an interception.

Smith led the Bengals to a 44-28 victory in Cincinnati in a rematch Dec. 12 that year. He was outplayed by Couch in a 24-7 loss to the Browns Sept. 10, 2000, in Cincinnati, completing just 15 of 43 passes for a touchdown and pair of interceptions. He quarterbacked the Bengals to a 12-3 win in Cleveland Oct. 29 that year. Smith was benched in favor of Jon Kitna before the 2001 season began and barely played against the Browns that year, attempting just two passes in the second meeting between the teams in Cleveland Nov. 25.

SMITH, JIM RAY

Jim Ray Smith was a Browns guard from 1956-62. He was a sixth-round draft choice of Cleveland's in 1954 from Baylor University with one year of eligibility left in school. He spent the 1955 season and the first half of the 1956 campaign in the military. He was voted to All-NFL offensive teams in 1959 and 1960 by AP, NYN, NEA, and UPI; in 1961 by AP, NYN, NEA, PFI, and UPI; and in 1962 by NEA. He was voted to the Pro Bowl from 1958-62.

Jim Ray Smith. Photo courtesy of the Cleveland Browns.

SONGS

Two of the more popular songs written about the Browns are *Dawg Fever* (Greg Barnhill) and *Somebody Let the Dawgs Out* (Kim Carnes).

SPEEDIE, MAC

Mac Speedie was a Browns wide receiver from 1946-52. He was a University of Utah product acquired by the Browns as a free agent. He led Cleveland in receptions in 1947 (67), 1948 (58), 1949 (62), 1950 (42), and 1952 (62). His total receptions in 1947 rank fifth all-time for the Browns. He was the team leader in receiving yards in 1947 (1,146), 1948 (816), 1949 (1,028), 1951 (589), and 1952 (911). His 1947 and 1949 totals rank second and fifth all-time in team history. Speedie's 5,602 receiving yards and 349 receptions rank third all-time in Browns annals.

Mac Speedie. Photo courtesy of the Cleveland Browns.

He was on the receiving end of several long touchdown strikes from Otto Graham, including a 78-yarder Nov. 3, 1946, against the Los Angeles Dons; a 70-yarder Sept. 26, 1947, against the Chicago Rockets; and a Browns record 99-yarder Nov. 2, 1947, against the Buffalo Bills. He also caught an 82-yard strike from Graham Nov. 23, 1947, against the New York Yankees. His 228 receiving yards at Brooklyn-New York Nov. 20, 1949, are the most ever in one game by a Browns player (#######). Speedie's 27 postseason receptions rank second all-time in team history (###). He holds two of the top six spots for most receptions in one postseason game by a Brown, as he totaled seven against Buffalo Dec. 4, 1949, and Los Angeles Dec. 23, 1951 (#####).

Speedie was voted to All-AAFC teams in 1946 by NYN and UP; in 1947 by AP, C&O, NYN, OFF, and SP; in 1948 by AP, NYN, OFF, SN, and UP; and in 1949 by AP, NYN, OFF, and UP. He was named to the All-AAFC offensive team by INS in 1949. He was voted to All-NFL teams in 1950 by NYN and UP and in 1952 by UP. He was voted to the Pro Bowl in 1950.

SPORTS ILLUSTRATED COVERS

Twelve *Sports Illustrated* covers have featured the Browns. The following are the dates and names of those who appeared:

Oct. 8, 1956	Paul Brown, George Ratterman
Sept. 26, 1960	Jim Brown

Jan. 4, 1965	Frank Ryan
Sept. 27, 1965	Frank Ryan
Nov. 21, 1966	Ross Fichtner
Aug. 30, 1982	Tom Cousineau
Aug. 26, 1985	Bernie Kosar
Jan. 12, 1987	Ozzie Newsome
Aug. 29, 1988	Bernie Kosar
Dec. 4, 1995	Art Modell
April 19, 1999	Big Dawg, Tim Couch, Akili Smith (never played for the Browns)
Sept. 1, 1999	Jim Brown, Tim Couch (a special commemorative issue honoring the return of the Browns to the NFL after three seasons without NFL football in Cleveland)

ST. LOUIS RAMS

The St. Louis Rams were opponents of the Browns in the NFL from 1950-95 and have been since 1999. The Rams were located in Los Angeles through 1994. The Browns and Rams have met three times in postseason play—all NFL Championship games. The Browns won, 30-28, Dec. 24, 1950, in Cleveland on Lou Groza's 16-yard field goal with 28 seconds left. The Rams won, 24-17, Dec. 23, 1951, in Los Angeles on a 73-yard pass play from Norm Van Brocklin to Tom Fears that broke a 17-17 fourth-quarter tie. The Browns won the rubber match, 38-14, Dec. 26, 1955, in Los Angeles as Otto Graham passed for two touchdowns and ran for two more in his final game. The Rams' all-time record against the Browns is 8-8, with 5-3 (.625) at home and 3-5 (.375) on the road. Their all-time postseason record against Cleveland is 1-2 (.333), with 1-1 at home and 0-1 on the road.

STANDING-ROOM-ONLY

Standing-room-only tickets for Browns home games were tickets that were sold for home games that allowed patrons to stand to watch games when no tickets for seats were left. Standing-room-only tickets for Browns home games were sold from 1946 through the Nov. 3,1980 Monday night game against the Chicago Bears. Sales of them ceased due to safety concerns.

STOVER, MATT

Matt Stover was a Browns kicker from 1991-95. He was a Louisiana State University product acquired by the Browns Mar. 15, 1991, as a free agent. Stover ranks sixth in all-time Browns scoring with 480 points. His 113 points in 1995 and 110 in 1994 rank fourth and fifth in team history. He failed on just two of 158 extra-point attempts as a Brown. He kicked four field goals of 50 yards or more—a 55-yarder in Houston Nov. 17, 1991, a 53-yarder in Houston Dec. 12, 1993, a 51-yarder at home against Pittsburgh Oct. 11, 1992, and a 50-yarder at home against Philadelphia Nov. 10, 1991.

STREAKS

The longest winning streak in Browns history occurred in 1948, when the Browns went 14-0 for a perfect season. The longest losing streak occurred in 1975 when the Browns lost the first nine games of the season. *For more streaks, please see Team Statistics on page 204.*

STROCK, DON

Don Strock was a Browns quarterback in 1988. He was a Virginia Tech University product acquired by the Browns Sept. 11, 1988, due to injuries to Bernie Kosar and Gary Danielson. He engineered a memorable, season-ending 28-23 comeback victory over Houston in the snow after the Browns trailed, 23-7. The win earned the team the AFC's Wild Card Playoff berth. Strock became the fourth Browns' quarterback to go down in 1988 when he injured his right hand early in the second quarter while trying to recover his own fumble in a wild card loss to Houston that was a rematch from the week before.

SUMNER, WALT

Walt Sumner was a Cleveland defensive back from 1969-74. He was a Browns seventh-round draft choice in 1969 from Florida State University. Sumner ranked second on the Browns with four interceptions in both 1969 and 1970. He was the team leader in picks in 1971 with five. He finished his Browns career with 15 interceptions. His most memorable interception was his 88-yard return of a Craig Morton pass for a touchdown in the fourth quarter of the 1969 Eastern Conference Championship game against the Cowboys in the Cotton Bowl. Sumner's return set up a touchdown on the next play, which increased the Browns' lead to 38-7 en route to a 38-14 triumph.

Walt Sumner hits the Houston Oilers' Joe Dawkins and causes a fumble. Photo courtesy of the Cleveland Press Collection.

SUNDAY NIGHT GAMES

(Local starting times of 5 p.m. or later)

Denver 24, Cleveland 14 (Sept. 16, 1984, at Cleveland)
San Francisco 38, Cleveland 24 (Nov. 29, 1987, at San Francisco)
Houston 28, Cleveland 24 (Nov. 17, 1991, at Houston)
Pittsburgh 43, Cleveland 0 (Sept. 12, 1999, at Cleveland)

Overall   0-4 (.000)
Home   0-2 (.000)
Away   0-2 (.000)

T

TAMPA BAY BUCCANEERS

The Tampa Bay Buccaneers were Browns opponents in the NFL from 1976-95 and have been since 1999. Their all-time record against Cleveland is 0-5, with 0-3 at home and 0-2 on the road.

TANNEHILL, RAY

Ray Tannehill was a Browns radio broadcaster in 1962.

TEAM TOP FIVES

For team top five statistics, please see Team Statistics on page 204.

TENNESSEE TITANS

The Tennessee Titans were Browns opponents in the NFL from 1970-95 and have been since 1999. They relocated from Houston, where they were known as the Oilers, in 1997. They were re-named "Titans" in 1999. The series was dominated by the Browns early on as Cleveland won the first nine meetings. The Titans took 10 of the next 15 games before dropping 12 of the next 15. Then they won 13 of the next 18 encounters. The teams have met once in postseason play, with the Browns falling, 24-23, in the AFC Wild Card game Christmas Eve, 1988 in Cleveland. Tennessee's all-time record against the Browns is 26-31 (.456), with 12-17 (.414) at home and 14-14 on the road. The Titans' all-time postseason mark against Cleveland is 1-0 (away).

TESTAVERDE, VINNY

Vinny Testaverde was a Browns quarterback from 1993-95. A University of Miami product who won the 1987 Heisman Trophy, he was acquired by the Browns Mar. 31, 1993, as a free agent. Testaverde was in the middle of a month-long quarterback controversy with Browns icon Bernie Kosar early in the 1993 season, in which he came off the bench to replace Kosar and lead the Browns' remarkable, last-second comeback victory over the Raiders in Los Angeles Sept. 19 to give Cleveland its first 3-0 start in 14 years. His first start as a Brown was against the Bengals in Cincinnati Oct. 17 when he passed for three touchdowns in a 28-17 victory.

He suffered a separated shoulder late in a home game against Pittsburgh a week later that sidelined him until Dec. 5. That is when, with Kosar released and Todd Philcox not cutting the mustard, he returned in the second quarter of a home game against New Orleans. He helped the Browns to a 17-13 win that snapped a four-game losing streak and preserved Cleveland's postseason hopes. Three weeks later Dec. 26 in a 42-14 rout of the Los Angeles Rams on the West Coast, Testaverde completed 21-of-23 passes for a 91.3 percent completions rate that set an NFL record for the highest completion percentage by a quarterback with at least 20 attempts in one game. Incredibly, both of Testaverde's incompletions were *intentional*.

Although the Browns failed to qualify for the playoffs, Testaverde enjoyed a fine season despite a tumultuous first half. He wound up with 130 completions in 230 attempts for 1,797 yards, 14 touchdowns, and nine interceptions. He led the Browns to their first playoff berth in five years the next season, completing 207 of 376 passes for 2,575 yards and 16 touchdowns, but also 18 interceptions. Mark Rypien relieved him for a few games due to a recurring concussion.

On Sept. 18 of that year, Testaverde hooked up with Derrick Alexander for an 81-yard pass play that went for a touchdown in a 32-0 rout of the Arizona Cardinals in Cleveland Stadium. He completed 20 of 30 passes for 268 yards and a touchdown in the Browns'

20-13 triumph over New England in an AFC Wild Card game on New Year's Day, 1995. His 20 completions against the Patriots are tied for fifth most in one postseason game in Browns history.

He completed 241 (tied for 10th in team in history) of 392 passes for 2,883 yards, 17 touchdowns, and 10 interceptions in 1995. He was replaced by rookie Eric Zeier as the starter for the Browns' Oct. 29 home game in Cincinnati even though he was leading the AFC in passing. Head coach Bill Belichick thought the change would give the team, which had lost three straight, a spark. (Zeier led the Browns to an overtime win with a strong performance, but he tailed off after that.) Testaverde returned to action midway through a 31-20 home loss to the Packers Nov. 19. He ranks eighth in passing yards (7,255) and ninth in completions (578) in Browns history. His 33 completions and 412 passing yards in the postseason rank

Vinny Testaverde. Photo courtesy of the Cleveland Browns.

fifth in team annals.

THANKSGIVING DAY GAMES

Cleveland 27, Los Angeles 17 (Nov. 27, 1947, at Los Angeles)
Cleveland 31, Los Angeles 14 (Nov. 25, 1948, at Los Angeles)
Cleveland 14, Chicago 6 (Nov. 24, 1949, at Chicago)
Dallas 26, Cleveland 14 (Nov. 24, 1966, at Dallas)
Dallas 31, Cleveland 14 (Nov. 25, 1982, at Dallas)
Detroit 13, Cleveland 10 (Nov. 23, 1989, at Detroit)

Overall   3-3 (.600)
Away   3-3 (.600)

THOMPSON, TOMMY

Tommy Thompson was a Browns linebacker from 1949-53. He was a seventh-round draft choice of the Browns in 1948 from the College of William & Mary with one year of school eligibility remaining. Thompson was voted to All-NFL defensive teams in 1953 by AP and UP.

Tommy Thompson. Photo courtesy of the Cleveland Browns.

THREE RIVERS JINX

The Three Rivers Jinx was the nickname attributed to Cleveland's 16-game losing streak in Pittsburgh's Three Rivers Stadium from 1970-85. The heart of the streak occurred from 1977-81 when five games hinged on thrilling finishes, suspect officiating calls and hard hits, as usual. The Steelers won those five games by an average of only 4.4 points per game (35-31, 15-9 [OT]; 33-30 [OT]; 16-13, 13-7, respectively).

The Browns resorted to extreme measures in trying to halt the Jinx. They traveled by plane, by bus, and by car. They even changed hotels several times. Nothing worked until Oct. 5, 1986, when Gerald McNeil's 100-yard kickoff return for a touchdown sparked the Browns' 27-24 triumph. It was the start of four straight wins for Cleveland in what had been their own personal House of Horrors. The following are the 16 games that comprised the Three Rivers Jinx:

Pittsburgh 28, Cleveland 9 (Nov. 29, 1970)
Pittsburgh 26, Cleveland 9 (Nov. 7, 1971)
Pittsburgh 30, Cleveland 0 (Dec. 3, 1972)
Pittsburgh 33, Cleveland 6 (Sept. 23, 1973)
Pittsburgh 20, Cleveland 16 (Oct. 20, 1974)
Pittsburgh 31, Cleveland 17 (Dec. 7, 1975)
Pittsburgh 31, Cleveland 14 (Sept. 19, 1976)
Pittsburgh 35, Cleveland 31 (Nov. 13, 1977)
Pittsburgh 15, Cleveland 9 (OT) (Sept. 24, 1978)
Pittsburgh 33, Cleveland 30 (OT) (Nov. 25, 1979)

Fair Hooker misses connections with a Mike Phipps pass in the Steelers' end zone during the Browns' 28-9 defeat in Pittsburgh Nov. 29, 1970. Photo courtesy of the Cleveland Press Collection.

Pittsburgh 16, Cleveland 13 (Nov. 16, 1980)
Pittsburgh 13, Cleveland 7 (Oct. 11, 1981)
Pittsburgh 37, Cleveland 21 (Jan. 2, 1983)
Pittsburgh 44, Cleveland 17 (Oct. 16, 1983)
Pittsburgh 23, Cleveland 20 (Dec. 9, 1984)
Pittsburgh 10, Cleveland 9 (Nov. 3, 1985)

THREE-THOUSAND-YARD PASSERS
For team top five statistics, please see Individual Statistics on page 188.

THURSDAY NIGHT GAMES
(Not including Thanksgiving Day games. Local starting times of 5 p.m. or later)

Houston 17, Cleveland 13 (Dec. 3, 1981, at Houston)
Cleveland 17, Cincinnati 7 (Sept. 15, 1983, at Cleveland)
Cincinnati 30, Cleveland 13 (Sept. 18, 1986, at Cleveland)
Cleveland 11, Houston 8 (Oct. 13, 1994, at Houston)

Overall   2-2 (.500)
Home   1-1 (.500)
Away   1-1 (.500)

TIES

New York 28, Cleveland 28 (Nov. 23, 1947, at New York)
Buffalo 28, Cleveland 28 (Sept. 5, 1949, at Buffalo)
Cleveland 7, Buffalo 7 (Nov. 13, 1949, at Cleveland)
New York 35, Cleveland 35 (Nov. 27, 1955, at New York)
Washington 30, Cleveland 30 (Nov. 17, 1957, at Washington)
St. Louis 17, Cleveland 17 (Nov. 27, 1960, at St. Louis)
New York 7, Cleveland 7 (Dec. 17, 1961, at New York)
Cleveland 14, Philadelphia 14 (Nov. 4, 1962, at Cleveland)
Cleveland 33, St. Louis 33 (Sept. 20, 1964, at Cleveland)
Cleveland 21, St. Louis 21 (Oct. 26, 1969, at Cleveland)
Cleveland 16, San Diego 16 (Oct. 28, 1973, at Cleveland)
Kansas City 20, Cleveland 20 (Dec. 2, 1973, at Kansas City)
Cleveland 10, Kansas City 10 (OT) (Nov. 19, 1989, at Cleveland)

TIGHT ENDS

Notable Browns tight ends include Johnny Brewer, Milt Morin, Gary Parris, Oscar Roan, and Ozzie Newsome.

TRADES

The following are five notable Browns trades:

APRIL 29, 1952

The Browns traded three players to the Green Bay Packers for linebacker Walt Michaels, who originally was a seventh-round draft choice of the Browns in 1951 but was traded to the Packers Aug. 20 of that year.

JAN. 26, 1970

The Browns traded wide receiver Paul Warfield to the Miami Dolphins for a first-round draft pick in the next day's draft. Cleveland desired to trade so it could choose Purdue University quarterback Mike Phipps.

SEPT. 1, 1980

Cleveland traded a second-round draft choice in 1981 and third-round pick in 1982 to the Buffalo Bills for guard Joe DeLamielleure.

APRIL 28, 1982

The Browns traded defensive end Lyle Alzado to the Los Angeles Raiders for a draft choice that year.

APRIL 28, 1982

The Browns traded running back Greg Pruitt to the Los Angeles Raiders for a draft choice in 1983.

TRAINING CAMP

Browns training camps have been held at the following venues in Ohio:

Bowling Green State University	1946-51
Hiram College	1952-74
Kent State University	1975-81
Lakeland Community College (Cleveland)	1982-91
Cleveland Browns Training and Administrative Complex (Berea)	1992-95, since 1999

TUESDAY NIGHT GAMES

Cleveland 34, Miami 0 (Dec. 3, 1946, at Miami)
Cleveland 14, Baltimore 10 (Oct. 5, 1948, at Baltimore)

Overall   2-0 (1.000)

TUPA, TOM

Tom Tupa was a Browns quarterback and punter from 1993-95. He was an Ohio State University product obtained by the Browns off the waiver wire Nov. 10, 1993. He was waived Nov. 24, 1993, and then re-signed Mar. 24, 1994. Tupa actually attempted (and completed for 25 yards) just one pass in his Browns career. His 6,042 punting yards rank ninth in Browns history. He has the distinction of scoring the NFL's first-ever two-point conversion in the Browns' season-opening 28-20 win over the Cincinnati Bengals Sept. 4, 1994, in Cincinnati.

TURNER, ERIC

Eric Turner was a Browns safety from 1991-95. A first-round draft choice of Cleveland's in 1991 from UCLA, he had a 42-yard interception return off Jim McMahon for a touchdown Nov. 10, 1991, at home against Philadelphia. His five interceptions in 1993 led the Browns. His nine picks in 1994 not only topped the team and tied for third-most in one Browns season, but they also tied for the league lead that year. One was a 93-yard return for a touchdown in a 32-0 rout of the Cardinals at home Sept. 18. Turner intercepted 17 passes all-time for Cleveland. He was voted to All-AFC defensive teams by AP, PFW, and UPI, and was named to the Pro Bowl, in 1994.

TWELVE DAYS OF A CLEVELAND BROWNS CHRISTMAS, THE

The Twelve Days of a Cleveland Browns Christmas was a popular song on Cleveland-area radio airwaves in Dec. 1980. It honored the Browns' first AFC Central Division title in nine years and first playoff berth in eight years.

Eric Turner. Photo courtesy of the Cleveland Browns.

TWO ONE-THOUSAND-YARD RUSHERS IN ONE SEASON

The 1985 Browns became the third team in NFL history to have two players gain at least 1,000 yards rushing in one season when Kevin Mack and Earnest Byner did it. Mack totaled 1,104 yards, Byner 1,002.

V

VS. DOMED-STADIUM TEAMS AT HOME
Please see Team Statistics on page 204.

VS. NFL CHAMPIONS (1950-69) AND SUPER BOWL
CHAMPIONS (1970-95, SINCE 1999)
OF SEASON AT HAND
Please see Team Statistics on page 204.

VS. PACIFIC TIME ZONE TEAMS AT HOME
Please see Team Statistics on page 204.

U

ULINSKI, ED

Ed Ulinski. Photo courtesy of the Cleveland Browns.

Ed Ulinski was a Browns guard from 1946-49. He was a Marshall University product obtained by the Browns as a free agent. Ulinski was a Browns assistant coach from 1954-70.

USFL

The United States Football League existed from 1983-86. Only three seasons were played, however (1983-85). The seasons were held during the spring and summer. The USFL competed with the NFL for college players and lured several, including three consecutive Heisman Trophy winners from 1983-85 and future Browns stars Kevin Mack, Gerald McNeil, and Frank Minnifield.

Prior to the 1985 season, the USFL, experiencing severe financial problems, sued the NFL and commissioner Pete Rozelle for violation of the Sherman Antitrust Act, seeking actual damages of $567 million that, when trebled, would amount to more than $1.7 billion. The league also announced it would switch to a fall season in 1986 to compete head-to-head with the NFL. At the end of the 48-day trial July 29, 1986, a United States District Court jury found the NFL liable on one of nine antitrust charges, assessing just $1 in actual damages, though, $3 when trebled. The USFL's own mismanagement was cause of its financial problems, according to the jury. More than $160 million in debt, the USFL folded Aug. 4, 1986.

W

WAGNER, BRYAN

Bryan Wagner was a Browns punter in 1989 and 1990. He was a California State University, Northridge product acquired by the Browns as a free agent Mar. 30, 1989. His 3,817 punting yards in 1989 rank fourth in Browns history. He ranks ninth in team annals in total punting yards with 6,696. Wagner is fifth in Browns career postseason punting yards with 451. His 338 yards in the 1989 AFC Championship loss to Denver rank second for Cleveland all-time.

WAITERS, VAN

Van Waiters was a Browns linebacker from 1988-91. He was a third-round draft choice of Cleveland's in 1988 from Indiana University. His most memorable moment as a Brown actually came on special teams when he caught a game-winning 14-yard touchdown pass from Mike Pagel on a fake field goal that beat the Vikings, 23-17, in overtime Dec. 17, 1989. This win in Cleveland kept the Browns' playoff hopes alive.

WALKER, NATE

Nate Walker is the Browns fan to whom the Browns' 1983 NFL Films highlights video is dedicated.

WARD, CARL

Carl Ward was a Browns defensive back in 1967 and 1968. He was a Browns fourth-round draft pick in 1967 from the University of Michigan. He also returned punts and kickoffs, including a 104-yard kickoff return for a touchdown against the Redskins Nov. 26, 1967.

WARFIELD, PAUL

Paul Warfield was a wide receiver for the Browns from 1964-69 and in 1976 and 1977. He was a first-round draft choice of the Browns in 1964 from Ohio State University.

Paul Warfield in action against the Lions Nov. 15, 1964. Photo courtesy of the Cleveland Press Collection

He was traded to the Miami Dolphins Jan. 26, 1970, for the Dolphins' first-round pick in the next day's draft. The Browns made the trade in order to draft Purdue University quarterback Mike Phipps, which they did. Warfield was reacquired in 1976 after five seasons and two Super Bowl Championships with the Dolphins, and one season—1975—in the CFL (which folded before the season was finished).

He led the Browns in receptions (52), receiving yards (920), and touchdown receptions (nine) his rookie year. His receiving yardage total that year is 10th for most receiving yards in one Browns season. Warfield was injured for most of the 1965 season. He had 36 catches for 741 yards and five touchdowns in 1966, and caught 32 balls for a team-leading 702 yards and eight touchdowns in 1967. He was the team leader in receptions (50), receiving yards (1,067), and touchdown catches (12) in 1968. His receiving yardage total that year ranks fourth all-time in team history. He became the first Browns player since 1949 to accumulate 1,000 yards receiving in one season.

Warfield caught 42 passes for a team-leading 886 yards and 10 touchdowns in 1969. Against the St. Louis Cardinals Dec. 14 that year, he was on the receiving end of an 82-yard pass play from Bill Nelsen that went for a touchdown. He averaged an incredible 20.7 yards per catch from 1964-69, a period in which the Browns appeared in four NFL title games. Warfield caught 56 balls for 864 yards and eight touchdowns in 1976 and 1977 combined.

His 5,210 receiving yards rank sixth all-time in Browns history. His 404 postseason receiving yards rank second all-time in team annals (##), and his 24 postseason receptions rank fifth (###). He had eight receptions in Dallas in the Eastern Conference Championship game Dec. 28, 1969, the most in Browns postseason history (#####). He won All-NFL offensive acclaim in 1964 by NEA; in 1968 by NEA, PFW, and UPI; and in 1969 by NEA, OFF, PFW, and SI. He was picked for the Pro Bowl in 1964, 1968, and 1969, and was enshrined into the Pro Football Hall of Fame in 1983.

WARREN, GERARD

Gerard Warren has been a Browns defensive tackle since 2001. He was a first-round draft choice of the Browns in 2001 from the University of Florida. He ranked fifth on the Browns in 2001 with five sacks.

WASHINGTON REDSKINS

The Washington Redskins were Browns opponents in the NFL from 1950-95 and have been since 1999. Their all-time record against Cleveland is 9-32-1 (.226), with 3-16-1 (.175) at home and 6-16 (.273) on the road.

WATTRICK, DON

Don Wattrick was a Cleveland television broadcaster in 1952.

WDOK-FM 102.1

WDOK-FM 102.1 was a Browns' co-flagship radio station from 1986-89, and in 1994 and 1995.

WERE-AM 1300

WERE-AM 1300 was the flagship radio station of the Browns in 1950 and 1951, and from 1962-67.

WEST COAST, ON THE

Please see Team Statistics on page 204.

WESTERN DIVISION

The Western Division was the home of the Browns from 1946-49. Cleveland won the division all four years with records of 12-2 (.857), 12-1-1 (.893), 14-0 and 9-1-2 (.833), respectively.

WGAR-AM 1220

WGAR-AM 1220 was the flagship radio station of the Browns from 1946-49, in 1954, and from 1956-61.

WHITE, CHARLES

Charles White was a Browns running back from 1980-82 and in 1984. He was a first-round draft choice by the Browns in 1980 from the University of Southern California where he won the 1979 Heisman Trophy. White missed the 1983 season due to a broken ankle suffered in the second preseason game at Buffalo Aug. 13. He was second behind Mike Pruitt in rushing yards his first three seasons. He ranked second behind Pruitt with five rushing touchdowns in 1980 and tied him for the team lead in 1982 with three.

WHITE, JAMEL

Jamel White has been a Browns running back since 2000. He was a product of the University of South Dakota acquired by the Browns via waivers Aug. 29, 2000. He was the Browns' leader with five rushing touchdowns in 2001 and was second with 443 rushing yards. He was also second on the club with 44 receptions that year. White posted a career-best 216 yards from scrimmage on 131 yards rushing—including a 51-yarder—and 85 yards receiving against Green Bay in Lambeau Field Dec. 23, 2001. The 131 rushing yards were the most by a Brown in 14 years. He also led the Browns in kickoff returns (43) and kickoff return yards (935) in 2001. His kickoff return yardage total ranks fifth in team history.

WHK-AM 1420

WHK-AM 1420 was the Browns' flagship radio station from 1968-85 and co-flagship radio station from 1990-93.

WIDE RECEIVERS

Notable wide receivers throughout Browns history include Dante Lavelli, Mac Speedie, Horace Gillom, Dub Jones, Darrell Brewster, Ray Renfro, Gary Collins, Paul Warfield, Fair Hooker, Frank Pitts, Reggie Rucker, Ricky Feacher, Dave Logan, Brian Brennan, Reggie Langhorne, Webster Slaughter, Michael Jackson, Mark Carrier, Derrick Alexander, and Kevin Johnson.

Paul Wiggin. Photo courtesy of the Cleveland Browns.

WIGGIN, PAUL

Paul Wiggin was a Browns defensive end from 1957-67. He was a sixth-round draft choice of the

Browns in 1956 from Stanford University with one year of eligibility in school remaining. He was voted to the Pro Bowl in 1965 and 1967.

WILD CARD GAMES
Houston 24, Cleveland 23 (AFC, Dec. 24, 1988, at Cleveland)
Cleveland 20, New England 13 (AFC, Jan. 1, 1995, at Cleveland)

Overall   1-1 (.500)

WILLIS, BILL
    Bill Willis was a Cleveland guard and linebacker from 1946-53. A product of Ohio State University, he was acquired by the Browns as a free agent. He saved the day in the Browns' 8-3 victory over the New York Giants in an American Conference Playoff Dec. 17, 1950, in Cleveland when he tackled fullback Eugene Roberts from behind at the Browns' four-yard line late in the game. Willis was named to All-AAFC teams in 1946 by OFF and SP; in 1947 by OFF; and in 1948 by AP, NYN, OFF, and UP. He was voted to the All-NFL offensive team in 1950 by UP. He was voted to All-NFL defensive teams in 1950 by NYN; in 1951 by AP, NYN, and UP; in 1952 by AP and NYN; and in 1953 by AP. He was selected to play in the Pro Bowl from 1950-52. He was inducted into the Pro Football Hall of Fame in 1977.

Assistant coach Fritz Heisler instructs Bill Willis (left) and Lin Houston during a practice session in Dec. 1951. Photo courtesy of the Cleveland Press Collection.

WJW-CHANNEL 8

WJW-Channel 8 was the television station that broadcast Browns road games from 1954-67.

WKNR-AM 1220

WKNR-AM 1220 was a co-flagship radio station of the Browns in 1994 and 1995.

WMJI-FM 105.7

WMJI-FM 105.7 was a Browns co-flagship radio station from 1999-2001.

WMMS-FM 100.7

WMMS-FM 100.7 was a co-flagship radio station of the Browns from 1990-93.

WOHLABAUGH, DAVE

Dave Wohlabaugh has been a Browns center since 1999. A product of Syracuse University, he was acquired by the Browns on Feb. 16, 1999, as a free agent.

WON-LOST-TIED RECORD, POSTSEASON AND PRESEASON

Please see Team Statistics on page 204.

WON-LOST-TIED RECORD, POSTSEASON AND PRE-SEASON

Please see Team Statistics on page 204.

WOOTEN, JOHN

John Wooten was a Browns guard from 1959-67. He was a fifth-round draft choice of the Browns in 1959 from the University of Colorado. He was voted to the All-NFL offensive team in 1966 by NYN, and was picked for the Pro Bowl in 1965 and 1966.

WRIGHT, FELIX

Felix Wright was a safety for the Browns from 1985-90. A product of Drake University, Wright was acquired by

John Wooten. Photo courtesy of the Cleveland Browns.

Cleveland as a free agent Apr. 13, 1985. He tied Frank Minnifield for the team lead in interceptions in 1987 with four, including a pair returned for 68 and 40 yards, respectively, in the first half against the Los Angeles Rams on *Monday Night Football* Oct. 26, the second of which went for a touchdown. Wright led the Browns in picks in 1988 with five, 1989 with nine, and 1990 with three. His 1989 total led the NFL and tied for fourth all-time in Browns annals. Wright's 26 career interceptions tie him with Hanford Dixon for ninth in Browns history.

WRIGHT, KEITH

Keith Wright was a Browns wide receiver and kickoff returner from 1978-80. He was a Browns fifth-round draft choice in 1978 from Memphis State University. He led Cleveland in kickoff return yards in 1978, and returned the opening kickoff 86 yards against the Chiefs Oct. 22 that year. His 1,767 kickoff return yards rank sixth all-time in team history. Wright also returned punts, leading the team in punt returns and punt return yardage in 1978 and 1980. His 1978 total of 789 ranks ninth in Browns history. His 467 punt return yards rank ninth all-time in team annals. He was voted to the All-AFC offensive team in 1978 by PFW.

Keith Wright follows a blocker on a kickoff return at home against the Los Angeles Rams Nov. 26, 1978. Photo courtesy of the Cleveland Press Collection.

WTAM-AM 1100

WTAM-AM 1100 was the Browns' flagship radio station in 1952, 1953 and 1955, and co-flagship radio station from 1999-2001.

WWWE-AM 1100

WWWE-AM 1100 was a Browns co-flagship radio station from 1986-89.

WXEL-CHANNEL 9

WXEL-Channel 9 was the television station that broadcast Browns road games in 1952 and 1953.

WYCHE, SAM

Sam Wyche was the Cincinnati Bengals' head coach from 1984-91 and the Tampa Bay Buccaneers' head coach from 1992-95. Many Browns fans disliked him, especially during his tenure with the Bengals. One memorable incident that added to the animosity occurred during a Bengals-Seahawks game in Cincinnati Dec. 10, 1989. That is when, while boisterous fans hurled snowballs at Seattle players, Wyche grabbed the public address microphone and shouted, "You don't live in Cleveland, you live in Cincinnati!"

X

X-RAYS IN '88

Browns quarterbacks needed several X-rays in 1988 due to a seemingly never-ending series of injuries. It all started when Bernie Kosar was blindsided by Chiefs safety Lloyd Burruss early in the second quarter of Cleveland's 6-3 opening-day win in Kansas City. Kosar suffered strained ligaments in his right elbow and missed the next six games. Gary Danielson replaced Kosar, but the next week against the New York Jets at home, he went down with a broken left ankle in the third quarter.

Danielson was replaced by Mike Pagel, who started the next four games before suffering a second-quarter shoulder separation Oct. 9 at home against Seattle while trying to tackle Paul Moyer on a blocked field goal. Don Strock, who signed Sept. 11, took over and made his first start in five years the following week at home against Philadelphia, tossing a pair of touchdown passes en route to a 19-3 victory.

Kosar made his return the next week and completed 25 of 43 passes for 314 yards and three touchdowns in a 29-21 victory over the Phoenix Cardinals in the desert. Kosar started the next seven games before suffering strained ligaments in his left knee during a 38-31 loss in Miami on Monday night, Dec. 12, leaving the game in the fourth quarter. Strock took over and performed brilliantly against his former team, completing seven of 10 passes for 70 yards, including two touchdown passes that tied the score at 31 with just 59 seconds left.

Strock started the next week in the season finale at home against Houston. In a do-or-die playoff qualifier, the veteran rallied his troops from a 16-point third-quarter deficit to a dramatic 28-23 triumph, making two touchdown passes in a driving snowstorm. During the AFC Wild Card game the next week in a rematch with the Oilers on Christmas Eve in Cleveland Stadium, Strock injured his right hand early in the second quarter while failing to recover his own fumble deep in Cleveland territory with the Browns trailing, 7-3. The Oilers scored on the very next play, upping their lead to 14-3.

Pagel came in and completed 17 of 25 passes for 179 yards and two touchdowns to rally the Browns, but they fell short, losing 24-23.

Y

YONAKOR, JOHN

John Yonakor was a Browns defensive end from 1946-49. He was a product of the University of Notre Dame acquired by the Browns as a free agent.

George Young. Photo courtesy of the Cleveland Browns.

YOUNG, GEORGE

George Young was a Cleveland defensive end from 1946-53. He was a product of the University of Georgia acquired by Cleveland as a free agent. He returned a fumble 47 yards for a touchdown in the Browns' 45-0 triumph over the Washington Redskins Oct. 14, 1951, in Cleveland Municipal Stadium.

YOUNG, GLEN

Glen Young was a Browns wide receiver in 1984, 1985, 1987, and 1988. He was a product of the University of Mississippi acquired by Cleveland as a free agent Nov. 14, 1984. He was waived in 1986, and was out of football that year. He was re-acquired as a free agent Mar. 9, 1987. Young was known mainly for his role as a kickoff returner. He was the Browns' leader in kickoff returns and kickoff return yards in 1985, 1987, and 1988. He led the AFC in 1985 when he averaged 25.7 yards per return on 35 attempts for 898 yards. His yardage total that year ranks sixth in team history. His 2,079 kickoff return yards rank third in team annals.

Z

ZEIER, ERIC

Eric Zeier was a Browns quarterback in 1995. He was a third-round draft choice of the Browns in 1995 from the University of Georgia. He saw limited playing time behind starter Vinny Testaverde but did start four games, including his first—and most impressive—performance Oct. 29 in Cincinnati when he completed 26 of 46 passes for 310 yards, and led the Browns to a dramatic 29-26 overtime win.

BROWNS
TRIVIA

FAST FACTS

Otto Graham was not the Browns' starting quarterback in their first game.

The Browns were shut out by the New York Giants, 6-0, Oct. 1, 1950, but were not bageled again until a 27-0 loss to the Denver Broncos Oct. 24, 1971.

When Dub Jones broke a Browns record, and tied an NFL mark, by scoring six touchdowns Nov. 25, 1951, against the Bears, he crossed the goal line the last five times he touched the ball.

The Browns' majority owner in the eight seasons prior to Art Modell's reign was a gentleman by the name of Dave Jones.

Marion Motley once played for the Pittsburgh Steelers.

Jim Brown missed only one half of one game in his nine-year career.

The Browns tallied 30 or more points in seven consecutive weeks during the 1968 season.

The only season the attendance figure for every Browns home game was at least 80,000 was 1969.

The first ABC *Monday Night Football* game Sept. 21, 1970, between the Browns and New York Jets drew 85,703 fans, the largest regular season or postseason crowd—home or away—in Browns history.

Mike Phipps threw more than two interceptions for every touchdown in his days with the Browns.

Despite the popular belief that the 1970s were a disastrous decade, the Browns actually won at a .507 clip.

The point total was in the 20s in each of the Browns' 10 victories in 1972.

The Browns sent no players to the Pro Bowl in 1972 despite posting a 10-4 (.714) record and earning the AFC's wild card berth.

In between Leroy Kelly's 1966-72 reign and Greg Pruitt's 1974-78 reign as the Browns' season leader in rushing yards, a player by the name of Ken Brown was the leading ground gainer in 1973.

The only two Browns tie games since 1970—in 1973 and 1989—were against the Chiefs, and both times the Browns entered play with seven wins and three defeats (though the 1973 team had a previous tie).

Forrest Gregg began his tenure as Browns head coach in 1975 0-9, and ended his tenure in 1977 1-5, but went 17-9 in between.

The Browns wore orange pants from 1975-83.

In an upset of the visiting Bengals Nov. 23, 1975, the Browns entered the game with an 0-9 record, while the Bengals came to town with an 8-1 mark.

Paul Warfield closed out his stellar career with a second stint with the Browns in 1976 and 1977.

The Browns began the 1976 season 1-0, the 1977 season 2-0, the 1978 season 3-0 and the 1979 season 4-0, yet failed to make the playoffs each year. However, when they began the 1980 season 0-2, they made the playoffs.

The average margin of defeat in the Browns' five losses in Three Rivers Stadium from 1977-81 was just 4.4 points.

The Browns once had three head coaches in a 15-day span—Forrest Gregg, Dick Modzelewski, and Sam Rutigliano from Dec. 13 to Dec. 28, 1977.

In retrospect, the Browns would have qualified for the playoffs in 1979 had they beaten the Bengals on the final Sunday by at least 33 points (due to the complicated NFL tiebreaking formula).

When Brian Sipe passed for 4,132 yards in 1980, he became just the second quarterback in NFL history to throw for 4,000 yards in one season.

Brian Sipe won Player-of-the-Year and Most Valuable Player honors in 1980, was benched during the 1982 season, then came back to lead the AFC in touchdown passes in 1983.

The attendance figure of 83,224 at the Browns' Monday night triumph over the Bears Nov. 3, 1980, was the time the team drew at least 80,000 fans at a home game. This was the last Browns home game in which standing-room-only tickets were sold, due to safety concerns.

The Browns qualified for the playoffs in 1982 despite posting a losing record, becoming just the second team in NFL history to do so (the other team, the Lions, did so the same year finishing 4-5).

The Browns' experiment of using orange numbers on brown jerseys in a preseason home game with the Pittsburgh Steelers in 1984 was a bust, as it was extremely difficult for media personnel and fans to identify players due to the excessive blending of orange and brown.

The Browns' 1984 opener in Seattle was played on a Monday afternoon.

In retrospect, had the Browns hung on to upset the Dolphins in an AFC Divisional Playoff on Jan. 4, 1986, in the Orange Bowl, they would have hosted the AFC Championship game the following week despite posting just an 8-8 record during the regular season.

The one Browns game in the strike-shortened 1987 season that was canceled was the one the entire city of Cleveland had hungered for since the schedule was published five months earlier—the home game against the Denver Broncos Sept. 28 (the Broncos had beaten the Browns in the AFC Championship game ["The Drive" game] the previous Jan. in the same venue).

In Cleveland's 37-21 defeat in Denver in the 1989 AFC title game, the Browns trailed by just three points entering the fourth quarter.

Travis Prentice is the only player to score all of Cleveland's rushing touchdowns in one season when he had seven in 2000.

THE LAST TIME ...

The last time a Browns player rushed for 100 yards in a game was Dec. 23, 2001, when Jamel White totaled 131 yards in a 30-7 loss in Green Bay.

... an opposing player of the Browns rushed for 100 yards in a game was Dec. 30, 2001, when Tennessee's Eddie George gained 130 yards in a 41-38 loss to the Browns in Cleveland.

... a Browns player passed for 400 yards in a game was Nov. 23, 1986, when Bernie Kosar totaled 414 in a 37-31 overtime victory over Pittsburgh in Cleveland.

... an opposing player of the Browns passed for 400 yards in a game was Dec. 23, 1989, when Houston's Warren Moon totaled 414 yards in the Oilers' 24-20 loss to the Browns in Houston.

... a Browns player was unsuccessful on an extra point attempt was Nov. 25, 2001, when Phil Dawson missed one in an 18-0 victory over the Bengals in Cleveland.

... an opposing player of the Browns was unsuccessful on an extra point attempt was Dec. 23, 2001, when Green Bay's Ryan Longwell missed one in a 30-7 victory over the Browns in Green Bay.

... a Browns player blocked a field goal was Sept. 10, 2000, when Orpheus Roye blocked a 42-yard attempt by Neil Rackers in a 24-7 victory in Cincinnati.

... an opposing player of the Browns blocked a field goal was Nov. 3, 1991, when Cincinnati's Eric Thomas blocked Matt Stover's 34-yard attempt that would have won the game for the Browns as time expired in the Bengals' 23-21 triumph in Cincinnati.

... a Cleveland player returned an interception for a touchdown was Dec. 16, 2001, when Anthony Henry returned a Mark Brunell pass 97 yards in the Browns' 15-10 loss to the Jaguars in Cleveland.

... an opposing player of Cleveland's returned an interception for a touchdown was Dec. 23, 2001, when Green Bay's Tyrone Williams returned a Tim Couch pass 69 yards for a touchdown in a 30-7 win over the Browns in Green Bay.

... a Browns player returned a fumble for a touchdown was Nov. 4, 2001, when Courtney Brown returned a Shane Matthews fumble 25 yards in a 27-21 overtime loss to the Bears in Chicago.

... an opposing defensive player of the Browns returned a fumble for a touchdown was Jan. 6, 2002, when Pittsburgh's Troy Edwards returned a Ben Gay fumble on the second-half kickoff 32 yards that helped the Steelers to a 28-7 victory over the Browns in Pittsburgh.

... a Browns player blocked a punt was Oct. 10, 1999, when James Williams blocked one by Cincinnati's Will Brice in an 18-17 Cincinnati victory in Cleveland.

... an opposing player of the Browns blocked a punt was Nov. 21, 1993, when Houston's Bubba McDowell blocked one by Brian Hansen in the Oilers' 27-20 victory in Cleveland.

... a Browns player returned a punt for a touchdown was Oct. 2, 1995, when Derrick Alexander returned one by Chris Mohr 69 yards in a 22-19 Bills victory in Cleveland.

... an opposing player of the Browns returned a punt for a touchdown was Dec. 9, 2001, when New England's Troy Brown returned a Chris Gardocki punt 85 yards in a 27-16 victory over Cleveland in New England.

... a Browns player returned a kickoff for a touchdown was Sept. 4, 1994, when Randy Baldwin returned one from Lee Johnson 85 yards in a 28-20 win in Cincinnati

...an opposing player of the Browns returned a kickoff for a touchdown was Sept. 7, 1986, when the Bears' Dennis Gentry returned one 91 yards in Chicago's 41-31 victory in Chicago.

... a Browns player scored a safety was Nov. 11, 2001, when Orpheus Roye tackled

Jerome Bettis in the end zone despite the Browns' 15-12 overtime loss to the Pittsburgh Steelers in Cleveland.

... an opposing player of the Browns scored a safety was Oct. 29, 2000, when Cincinnati benefitted from a holding penalty against the Browns in the end zone in a 12-3 Bengals win in Cleveland.

... the Browns gained 500 total net yards in one game was Nov. 23, 1986, when they totaled 536 against Pittsburgh in a 37-31 overtime win in Cleveland.

... a Browns opponent gained 500 total net yards in one game was Jan. 2, 1983, when the Steelers totaled 521 in a 37-21 victory over the Browns in Pittsburgh.

... the Browns posted a shutout was Nov. 25, 2001, when they bageled the Bengals, 18-0, in Cleveland.

... a Browns opponent posted a shutout was Dec. 17, 2000, when the Titans beat the Browns, 24-0, in Cleveland.

THE LAST TIME THE BROWNS BEAT (CURRENT TEAMS)
* Denotes only victory

TEAM	AT HOME	AWAY
Arizona	Sept. 18, 1994	Oct. 23, 1988
Atlanta	Dec. 16, 1990	Nov. 18, 1984
Baltimore	Oct. 21, 2001	Nov. 18, 2001
Buffalo	Nov. 15, 1987	Dec. 7, 1986
Carolina	Never	Never played
Chicago	Nov. 29, 1992	Nov. 30, 1969
Cincinnati	Nov. 25, 2001	Sept. 10, 2000
Dallas	Dec. 4, 1988	Dec. 10, 1994
Denver	Oct. 1, 1989	Oct. 8, 1990
Detroit	Sept. 23, 2001	*Sept. 11, 1983
Green Bay	Oct. 18, 1992	Nov. 4, 1956
Indianapolis	Sept. 19, 1988	Sept. 25, 1994
Jacksonville	Never	Sept. 30, 2001
Kansas City	Sept. 24, 1995	Sept. 4, 1988
Miami	Nov. 10, 1986	*Oct. 25, 1970
Minnesota	Dec. 17, 1989	*Oct. 26, 1986
New England	Nov. 6, 1994	Oct. 25, 1992
New Orleans	Dec. 5, 1993	Oct. 31, 1999
New York Giants	Sept. 30, 1973	Dec. 1, 1985
New York Jets	Oct. 2, 1994	Sept. 2, 1979
Oakland	Never	Sept. 19, 1993
Philadelphia	Oct. 16, 1988	Nov. 13, 1994
Pittsburgh	Sept. 17, 2000	Nov. 14, 1999
St. Louis	Oct. 26, 1987	Dec. 26, 1993
San Diego	Oct. 7, 2001	Oct. 20, 1991
San Francisco	Sept. 13, 1993	Nov. 15, 1981
Seattle	*Dec. 24, 1994	Nov. 12, 1989
Tampa Bay	Sept. 10, 1995	Nov. 5, 1989
Tennessee	Nov. 27, 1994	Dec. 30, 2001
Washington	Sept. 28, 1969	Nov. 27, 1988

COACHES AND
ASSISTANT COACHES

HEAD COACHES
Paul Brown (1946-62)
Blanton Collier (1963-70)
Nick Skorich (1971-74)
Forrest Gregg (1975-77)
Dick Modzelewski (1977)
Sam Rutigliano (1978-84)
Marty Schottenheimer (1984-88)
Bud Carson (1989-90)
Jim Shofner (1990)
Bill Belichick (1991-95)
Chris Palmer (1999)
Butch Davis (2001)

ASSISTANT COACHES
John Brickels (1946-48)
Blanton Collier (1946-53, 1962, 1975-76)
William (Red) Conkright (1946)
Fritz Heisler (1946-70)
Bob Voigts (1946)
Bill Edwards (1947, 1948)
Dick Gallagher (1947-49, 1955-59)
Weeb Ewbank (1949-53)
Timmy Temerario (1950, 1951)
Howard Brinker (1952-73)
Paul Bixler (1954-62)
Ed Ulinski (1954-70)
Dick Evans (1960-63)
Dub Jones (1963-67)
Nick Skorich (1964-70)
Bob Nussbaumer (1966-71)
Dick Modzelewski (1968-77)

Howard Keys (1970, 1971)
Richie McCabe (1971-75)
Ray Prochaska (1971, 1972)
Jerry Williams (1971)
John David Crow (1972, 1973)
Fran Polsfoot (1972-74)
Al Tabor (1972-77)
Jerry Smith (1973)
Forrest Gregg (1974)
Dale Lindsey (1974)
Dick Wood (1974)
Walt Corey (1975-77)
Doug Gerhart (1975)
Rod Humenuik (1975-82)
George Sefcik (1975-77, 1989-90)
Raymond Berry (1976, 1977)
Billy Kinard (1976, 1977)
Buck Buchanan (1978)
Jim Garrett (1978-84)
Rich Kotite (1978-82)
Dick MacPherson (1978-80)
John Petercuskie (1978-84)
Jim Shofner (1978-80, 1990)
Chuck Weber (1978, 1979)
Dave Adolph (1979-84, 1986-88)
Len Fontes (1980-82)
Marty Schottenheimer (1980-84)
Paul Hackett (1981, 1982)
Tom Pratt (1981-88)
Dave Redding (1982-88)
Joe Scannella (1982-84)
Joe Daniels (1983-84)

Howard Mudd (1983-88)
Darvin Wallis (1983-88)
Larrye Weaver (1983)
Keith Rowen (1984)
Tom Bettis (1985)
Bill Cowher (1985-88)
Steve Crosby (1985, 1991-95)
Greg Landry (1985)
Richard Mann (1985-93)
Tom Olivadotti (1985-86)
Joe Pendry (1985-88)
Charlie Davis (1986-87)
Lindy Infante (1986-87)
Kurt Schottenheimer (1987-88)
Ray Braun (1988)
Marc Trestman (1988-89)
Jed Hughes (1989)
Hal Hunter (1989-92)
Stan Jones (1989-90)
Paul Lanham (1989-90)
Joe Popp (1989-90)
Dan Radakovich (1989-90)
Lionel Taylor (1989-90)
John Teerlinck (1989-90)
Gary Wroblewski (1989-90)
Zeke Bratkowski (1990)
Mike Faulkiner (1990)
Jim Vechiarella (1990)
Ernie Adams (1991-95)
Jim Bates (1991-93, 1995)
Don Blackmon (1991)
John Mitchell (1991-93)
Scott O'Brien (1991-95)
Nick Saban (1991-94)
Phil Savage (1991-93)
Jerry Simmons (1991-95)
Kevin Spencer (1991-94)
Gary Tranquill (1991-93)
Al Groh (1992)
Kirk Ferentz (1993-95)
Pat Hill (1993-95)
Mike Sheppard (1993-95)
Woody Widenhofer (1993-94)

Chuck Bresnahan (1994-95)
Jacob Burney (1994-95)
Rod Dowhower (1994)
Rick Venturi (1994-95)
Eric Mangini (1995)
John Settle (1995)
Tom Spann (1995)
Clarence Brooks (1999)
Jerry Butler (1999, 2000)
Keith Butler (1999-2001)
Billy Davis (1999)
Jerry Holmes (1999, 2000)
John Hufnagel (1999, 2000)
Tim Jorgensen (1999-2001)
Mark Michaels (1999, 2000)
Bob Palcic (1999)
Ray Perkins (1999, 2000)
Dick Portee (1999)
Bob Slowik (1999)
Aril Smith (1999)
Tony Sparano (1999, 2000)
Ken Whisenhunt (1999)
Pete Carmichael (2000)
Pete Carmichael, Jr. (2000)
Romeo Crennel (2000)
John Fabris (2000)
Joe Kim (2000)
Mike Pitts (2000)
Bruce Arians (2001)
Phil Banko (2001)
Todd Bowles (2001)
Foge Fazio (2001)
Pete Garcia (2001)
Steve Hagen (2001)
Ray Hamilton (2001)
Todd McNair (2001)
Chuck Pagano (2001)
Rob Phillips (2001)
Terry Robiskie (2001)
Jerry Rosburg (2001)
Carl Smith (2001)
Larry Zierlein (2001)

ATTENDANCE STATISTICS

The Browns home attendance figures were based on the number of tickets purchased from 1946-72, and the number of tickets used from 1973-95 and have been since 1999. Standing-room-only (SRO) tickets for home games were included in attendance figures from 1946 to Nov. 3, 1980, and not included from Nov. 23, 1980, to 1995 and since 1999.

REGULAR SEASON

TEN HIGHEST HOME FIGURES, 1946-NOV. 3, 1980

1. 85,703   Cleveland 31, N.Y. Jets 21 (Sept. 21, 1970)
2. 84,850   Cleveland 42, Dallas 10 (Nov. 2, 1969)
3. 84,721   Cleveland 30, Dallas 21 (Oct. 23, 1966)
4. 84,684   Cleveland 35, Pittsburgh 23 (Oct. 5, 1963)
5. 84,349   Cleveland 15, Pittsburgh 7 (Oct. 3, 1970)
6. 84,285   Oakland 34, Cleveland 20 (Oct. 4, 1971)
7. 84,213   New York 33, Cleveland 6 (Oct. 27, 1963)
8. 84,078   Cleveland 42, Pittsburgh 31 (Oct. 18, 1969)
9. 83,943   Green Bay 21, Cleveland 20 (Sept. 18, 1966)
10. 83,819   Kansas City 31, Cleveland 7 (Oct. 8, 1972)

TEN HIGHEST HOME FIGURES, NOV. 23, 1980-95

1. 79,700   Cleveland 17, Cincinnati 7 (Sept. 15, 1983)
2. 79,543   Cleveland 34, Pittsburgh 10 (Sept. 20, 1987)
3. 79,483   Houston 9, Cleveland 3 (Sept. 13, 1981)
4. 79,253   Cleveland 31, Cincinnati 7 (Nov. 23, 1980)
5. 79,147   Cleveland 23, Cincinnati 16 (Oct. 30, 1988)
6. 79,042   Cleveland 17, Pittsburgh 7 (Sept. 16, 1985)
7. 78,986   Cleveland 42, Baltimore 28 (Oct. 25, 1981)
8. 78,904   San Diego 44, Cleveland 14 (Sept. 7, 1981)
9. 78,860   Dallas 26, Cleveland 14 (Sept. 1, 1991)
10. 78,840   Pittsburgh 17, Cleveland 7 (Oct. 15, 1989)

TEN HIGHEST HOME FIGURES SINCE 1999

1. 73,218   Pittsburgh 15, Cleveland 12 (OT) (Nov. 11, 2001)
2. 73,168   Cleveland 24, Detroit 14 (Sept. 23, 2001)
3. 73,138   Pittsburgh 43, Cleveland 0 (Sept. 12, 1999)
4. 73,118   Cincinnati 12, Cleveland 3 (Oct. 29, 2000)
5. 73,048   Cincinnati 18, Cleveland 17 (Oct. 10, 1999)
6. 73,018   Cleveland 23, Pittsburgh 20 (Sept. 17, 2000)
             Baltimore 12, Cleveland 0 (Oct. 1, 2000)
             Cleveland 20, San Diego 16 (Oct. 7, 2001)
9. 72,918   Cleveland 18, Cincinnati 0 (Nov. 25, 2001)
10. 72,898   Baltimore 41, Cleveland 9 (Nov. 7, 1999)

TEN LOWEST HOME FIGURES

1. 16,506   Cleveland 35, Chicago 2 (Nov. 6, 1949)
2. 20,564   Cleveland 17, Philadelphia 14 (Dec. 2, 1956)
3. 20,621   Cleveland 21, Baltimore 0 (Sept. 11, 1949)
4. 21,908   Cleveland 20, Washington 14 (Nov. 19, 1950)
5. 22,511   Cleveland 7, Buffalo 7 (Nov. 13, 1949)
6. 22,878   Washington 20, Cleveland 17 (Nov. 25, 1956)
7. 24,101   Cleveland 31, Chi. Cardinals 7 (Oct. 10, 1954)
8. 24,499   Cleveland 27, Chi. Cardinals 16 (Nov. 29, 1953)
9. 24,559   Cleveland 7, San Francisco 0 (Dec. 1, 1974)
10. 25,158   Cleveland 62, Washington 3 (Nov. 7, 1954)

TEN HIGHEST ROAD FIGURES

1. 78,266   Buffalo 22, Cleveland 13 (Nov. 1, 1981)
2. 77,045   Cleveland 42, New Orleans 7 (Oct. 1, 1967)
3. 76,251   Cleveland 24, Dallas 17 (Nov. 21, 1965)
4. 75,891   N.Y. Giants 13, Cleveland 10 (Sept. 22, 1991)
5. 75,811   Denver 44, Cleveland 10 (Oct. 15, 2000)
6. 75,806   Denver 30, Cleveland 7 (Nov. 13, 1988)
7. 75,504   Dallas 26, Cleveland 14 (Nov. 24, 1966)
8. 75,462   Kansas City 34, Cleveland 0 (Sept. 30, 1990)
9. 75,313   Cleveland 28, Miami 0 (Oct. 25, 1970)
10. 75,283   Detroit 21, Cleveland 10 (Nov. 9, 1975)

TEN LOWEST ROAD FIGURES

1. 5,031   Cleveland 14, Chicago 6 (Nov. 24, 1949)
2. 9,083   Cleveland 34, Miami 0 (Dec. 3, 1946)
3. 9,821   Cleveland 31, Brooklyn 21 (Dec. 5, 1948)
4. 14,600   Cleveland 66, Brooklyn 14 (Dec. 8, 1946)
5. 14,830   Cleveland 20, New England 10 (Oct. 4, 1987)
6. 15,201   Cleveland 31, Baltimore 0 (Sept. 24, 1950)
7. 16,263   Cleveland 24, Philadelphia 9 (Dec. 16, 1951)

8. 18,450   Cleveland 41, Chicago 21 (Sept. 26, 1947)
9. 18,876   Cleveland 55, Brooklyn 7 (Sept. 12, 1947)
10. 19,742   Cleveland 34, Chi. Cardinals 17 (Nov. 4, 1951)

HIGHEST, LOWEST HOME FIGURES VS. EACH TEAM
* Denotes only game played.

TEAM	HIGHEST	LOWEST
Arizona Cardinals	81,186 (Oct. 26, 1969)	24,101 (Oct. 10, 1954)
Atlanta Falcons	78,283 (Sept. 27, 1981)	46,536 (Dec. 16, 1990)
Baltimore Colts (original)	44,257 (Sept. 21, 1947)	21,621 (Sept. 11, 1949)
Baltimore Ravens	73,018 (Oct. 1, 2000)	72,818 (Oct. 21, 2001)
Brooklyn Dodgers	43,713 (Oct. 6, 1946)	30,279 (Nov. 9, 1947)
Brooklyn-New York Yankees	*26,312 (Sept. 18, 1949)	*26,312 (Sept. 18, 1949)
Buffalo Bills (current)	78,409 (Nov. 15, 1987)	50,764 (Nov. 17, 1985)
Buffalo Bisons-Bills (original)	63,263 (Sept. 5, 1947)	22,511 (Nov. 13, 1949)
Carolina Panthers	*72,818 (Nov. 21, 1999)	*72,818 (Nov. 21, 1999)
Chicago Bears	83,224 (Nov. 3, 1980)	38,155 (Dec. 11, 1960)
Chicago Rockets	60,457 (Nov. 17, 1946)	16,506 (Nov. 6, 1949)
Cincinnati Bengals	83,520 (Oct. 11, 1970)	51,774 (Dec. 2, 1984)
Dallas Cowboys	84,850 (Nov. 2, 1969)	43,638 (Oct. 1, 1961)
Denver Broncos	81,065 (Oct. 5, 1980)	60,478 (Oct. 27, 1974)
Detroit Lions	83,577 (Oct. 18, 1970)	34,168 (Dec. 19, 1954)
Green Bay Packers	83,943 (Sept. 18, 1966)	51,482 (Oct. 23, 1955)
Indianapolis Colts	80,132 (Oct. 14, 1962)	42,404 (Nov. 11, 1956)
Jacksonville Jaguars	72,818 (Dec. 16, 2001)	64,405 (Oct. 22, 1995)
Kansas City Chiefs	83,819 (Oct. 8, 1972)	44,368 (Dec. 14, 1975)
Los Angeles Dons	71,134 (Oct. 20, 1946)	63,124 (Oct. 12, 1947)
Miami Dolphins	80,374 (Nov. 18, 1979)	70,225 (Nov. 25, 1990)
Miami Seahawks	*60,135 (Sept. 6, 1946)	*60,135 (Sept. 6, 1946)
Minnesota Vikings	83,505 (Oct. 31, 1965)	68,064 (Sept. 28, 1975)
New England Patriots	76,418 (Sept. 26, 1977)	48,618 (Dec. 19, 1993)
New Orleans Saints	76,059 (Oct. 18, 1981)	44,753 (Nov. 30, 1975)
New York Giants	84,213 (Oct. 27, 1963)	30,448 (Oct. 31, 1954)
New York Jets	85,703 (Sept. 21, 1970)	36,881 (Dec. 10, 1978)
New York Yankees	80,067 (Oct. 5, 1947)	46,912 (Oct. 24, 1948)
Oakland Raiders	84,285 (Oct. 4, 1971)	65,247 (Oct. 6, 1974)
Philadelphia Eagles	79,289 (Nov. 29, 1964)	20,645 (Dec. 2, 1956)
Pittsburgh Steelers	84,684 (Oct. 5, 1963)	28,064 (Dec. 12, 1954)
St. Louis Rams	82,514 (Sept. 29, 1968)	54,713 (Sept. 29, 1963)
San Diego Chargers	80,047 (Nov. 1, 1970)	54,064 (Dec. 5, 1982)
San Francisco 49ers	82,769 (Nov. 14, 1948)	24,559 (Dec. 1, 1974)
Seattle Seahawks	78,605 (Oct. 9, 1988)	54,180 (Dec. 24, 1994)
Tampa Bay Buccaneers	61,083 (Sept. 10, 1995)	56,091 (Nov. 13, 1983)
Tennessee Titans	80,243 (Sept. 15, 1980)	30,898 (Dec. 11, 1977)
Washington Redskins	82,581 (Sept. 28, 1969)	25,158 (Nov. 7, 1954)

HIGHEST, LOWEST ROAD FIGURES VS. EACH TEAM

In cases where teams relocated cities, figures are based on those teams' stays in each city. The Browns never played a road game against the Boston Patriots.

* Denotes only game played.

TEAM	HIGHEST	LOWEST
Arizona-Phoenix Cardinals	61,261 (Oct. 23, 1988)	39,148 (Oct. 8, 2000)
Atlanta Falcons	57,235 (Oct. 30, 1966)	28,280 (Nov. 18, 1984)
Baltimore Colts (original)	36,837 (Sept. 25, 1949)	15,201 (Sept. 24, 1950)
Baltimore Colts (second)	60,238 (Oct. 20, 1968)	35,235 (Nov. 2, 1975)
Baltimore Ravens	69,353 (Nov. 18, 2001)	68,361 (Nov. 26, 2000)
Brooklyn Dodgers	18,876 (Sept. 12, 1947)	9,821 (Dec. 5, 1948)
Brooklyn-New York Yankees	*50,711 (Nov. 20, 1949)	*50,711 (Nov. 20, 1949)
Buffalo Bills (current)	78,266 (Nov. 1, 1981)	33,343 (Nov. 4, 1984)
Buffalo Bisons-Bills (original)	43,167 (Nov. 2, 1947)	30,302 (Sept. 22, 1946)
Chicago Bears	66,944 (Nov. 4, 2001)	38,717 (Dec. 10, 1961)
Chicago Cardinals	38,456 (Nov. 5, 1950)	19,742 (Nov. 4, 1951)
Chicago Rockets	51,962 (Sept. 13, 1946)	5,031 (Nov. 24, 1949)
Cincinnati Bengals	64,217 (Oct. 14, 2001)	40,179 (Oct. 18, 1987)
Dallas Cowboys	76,251 (Nov. 21, 1965)	23,500 (Dec. 3, 1961)
Denver Broncos	75,811 (Oct. 15, 2000)	51,001 (Dec. 20, 1970)
Detroit Lions	75,283 (Nov. 9, 1975)	51,382 (Dec. 8, 1963)
Green Bay Packers	59,824 (Dec. 23, 2001)	28,590 (Nov. 4, 1956)
Green Bay Packers (at Milwaukee)	54,089 (Nov. 6, 1983)	22,604 (Sept. 27, 1953)
Houston Oilers	58,852 (Dec. 23, 1989)	29,746 (Dec. 11, 1983)
Indianapolis Colts	59,654 (Sept. 26, 1993)	50,766 (Sept. 6, 1992)
Jacksonville Jaguars	66,007 (Dec. 24, 1995)	51,262 (Dec. 3, 2000)
Kansas City Chiefs	75,462 (Sept. 30, 1990)	34,340 (Dec. 12, 1976)
Los Angeles Dons	60,031 (Nov. 25, 1948)	24,800 (Nov. 3, 1946)
Los Angeles Raiders	65,461 (Nov. 16, 1986)	40,275 (Dec. 20, 1987)
Los Angeles Rams	73,948 (Dec. 16, 1973)	34,155 (Dec. 26, 1993)
Miami Dolphins	75,313 (Oct. 25, 1970)	58,444 (Oct. 8, 1989)
Miami Seahawks	*9,083 (Dec. 3, 1946)	*9,083 (Dec. 3, 1946)
Minnesota Vikings	59,133 (Oct. 26, 1986)	42,202 (Dec. 14, 1980)
New England Patriots	60,292 (Dec. 9, 2001)	14,830 (Oct. 4, 1987)
New Orleans Saints	77,045 (Oct. 1, 1967)	48,817 (Oct. 31, 1999)
New York Giants	75,891 (Sept. 22, 1991)	27,707 (Dec. 9, 1956)
New York Jets	67,354 (Sept. 16, 1990)	48,472 (Sept. 2, 1979)
New York Yankees	70,060 (Nov. 23, 1947)	34,252 (Oct. 12, 1946)
Oakland Raiders	54,463 (Nov. 8, 1970)	45,702 (Sept. 24, 2000)
Philadelphia Eagles	71,237 (Sept. 16, 1950)	16,263 (Dec. 16, 1951)
Pittsburgh Steelers	60,808 (Dec. 18, 1994)	24,229 (Dec. 9, 1951)
St. Louis Cardinals	47,845 (Oct. 28, 1979)	23,256 (Oct. 21, 1962)
St. Louis Rams	*65,866 (Oct. 24, 1999)	*65,866 (Oct. 24, 1999)
San Diego Chargers	56,358 (Dec. 3, 1995)	35,683 (Nov. 3, 1974)
San Francisco 49ers	63,672 (Oct. 28, 1990)	31,359 (Nov. 3, 1968)
Seattle Seahawks	62,262 (Dec. 3, 1978)	51,435 (Dec. 20, 1981)
Tampa Bay Buccaneers	69,162 (Nov. 5, 1989)	36,390 (Nov. 21, 1976)
Tennessee Titans	68,798 (Dec. 30, 2001)	65,904 (Sept. 19, 1999)
Washington Redskins	54,715 (Oct. 13, 1991)	21,761 (Dec. 5, 1954)

FIVE HIGHEST SEASON AVERAGE HOME FIGURES, 1946-80

Although SRO tickets were not sold for the last two games of the 1980 season, that season is included since SRO tickets were sold for six of the eight home games that year.

1. 82,623 (1969)
2. 81,054 (1970)
3. 79,612 (1965)
4. 78,476 (1964)
5. 77,830 (1967)

FIVE HIGHEST SEASON AVERAGE HOME FIGURES, 1981-95

1. 77,018 (1988)
2. 76,677 (1989)
3. 75,216 (1981)
4. 72,967 (1986)
5. 71,469 (1991)

SEASON AVERAGE HOME FIGURES, HIGHEST TO LOWEST, SINCE 1999

1. 72,887 (2001)
2. 72,693 (2000)
3. 72,617 (1999)

FIVE LOWEST SEASON AVERAGE HOME FIGURES

1. 30,579 (1954)
2. 31,601 (1949)
3. 33,387 (1950)
4. 36,941 (1956)
5. 38,569 (1951)

POSTSEASON ATTENDANCE

Browns home attendance figures were based on the number of tickets purchased from 1946-72, and the number of tickets used from 1973-95 and have been since 1999. Standing-room-only (SRO) tickets for home games were included in attendance figures from 1946 to Nov. 3, 1980.

HOME FIGURES, HIGHEST TO LOWEST, 1946-79

1. 81,497   Cleveland 31, Dallas 20 (Eastern Conference Championship, Dec. 21, 1968)
2. 80,628   Baltimore 34, Cleveland 0 (NFL Championship, Dec. 29, 1968)
3. 79,544   Cleveland 27, Baltimore 0 (NFL Championship, Dec. 27, 1964)
4. 74,082   Baltimore 20, Cleveland 3 (AFC Divisional Playoff, Dec. 26, 1971)
5. 50,934   Detroit 17, Cleveland 7 (NFL Championship, Dec. 28, 1952)
6. 43,827   Cleveland 56, Detroit 10 (NFL Championship, Dec. 26, 1954)
7. 40,489   Cleveland 14, New York 9 (AAFC Championship, Dec. 22, 1946)
8. 33,054   Cleveland 8, N.Y. Giants 3 (American Conference Playoff, Dec. 17, 1950)
9. 29,751   Cleveland 30, Los Angeles 28 (NFL Championship, Dec. 24, 1950)
10. 22,981   Cleveland 49, Buffalo 7 (AAFC Championship, Dec. 19, 1948)
11. 22,550   Cleveland 21, San Francisco 7 (AAFC Championship, Dec. 11, 1949)
12. 17,270   Cleveland 31, Buffalo 21 (AAFC Playoff, Dec. 4, 1949)

HOME FIGURES, HIGHEST TO LOWEST, 1980-95 AND SINCE 1999

1. 79,915   Denver 23, Cleveland 20 (OT) (AFC Championship, Jan. 11, 1987)
2. 78,586   Cleveland 38, Indianapolis 21 (AFC Divisional Playoff, Jan. 9, 1988)
3. 78,106   Cleveland 23, N.Y. Jets 20 (2OT) (AFC Divisional Playoff, Jan. 3, 1987)
4. 77,706   Cleveland 34, Buffalo 30 (AFC Divisional Playoff, Jan. 6, 1990)
5. 77,655   Oakland 14, Cleveland 12 (AFC Divisional Playoff, Jan. 4, 1981)
6. 77,452   Cleveland 20, New England 13 (AFC Wild Card, Jan. 1, 1995)
7. 74,977   Houston 24, Cleveland 23 (AFC Wild Card, Dec. 24, 1988)

ROAD FIGURES, HIGHEST TO LOWEST

1. 87,695   Cleveland 38, Los Angeles 14 (NFL Championship, Dec. 26, 1955)
2. 80,010   Miami 20, Cleveland 14 (AFC Divisional Playoff, Dec. 24, 1972)
3. 76,046   Denver 37, Cleveland 21 (AFC Championship, Jan. 14, 1990)
4. 75,993   Denver 38, Cleveland 33 (AFC Championship, Jan. 17, 1988)
5. 75,128   Miami 24, Cleveland 21 (AFC Divisional Playoff, Jan 4, 1986)
6. 70,786   Dallas 52, Cleveland 14 (Eastern Conference Championship, Dec. 24, 1967)
7. 69,321   Cleveland 38, Dallas 14 (Eastern Conference Championship, Dec. 28, 1969)
8. 61,879   Cleveland 14, New York 3 (AAFC Championship, Dec. 14, 1947)

9. 61,174   New York 10, Cleveland 0 (Eastern Conference Playoff, Dec. 21, 1958)
10. 58,185   Pittsburgh 29, Cleveland 9 (AFC Divisional Playoff, Jan. 7, 1995)
11. 57,540   Los Angeles 24, Cleveland 17 (NFL Championship, Dec. 23, 1951)
12. 56,555   L.A. Raiders 27, Cleveland 10 (AFC First-Round, Jan. 8, 1983)
13. 55,263   Detroit 59, Cleveland 14 (NFL Championship, Dec. 21, 1957)
14. 54,577   Detroit 17, Cleveland 16 (NFL Championship, Dec. 27, 1953)
15. 50,852   Green Bay 23, Cleveland 12 (NFL Championship, Jan. 2, 1966)
16. 47,900   Minnesota 27, Cleveland 7 (NFL Championship, Jan. 4, 1970)

INDIVIDUAL STATISTICS

COMBINED NET YARD LEADERS

(Does not include fumble return yardage for various seasons)

1946	Edgar Jones	1,055		1973	Greg Pruitt	1,112
1947	Marion Motley	1,332		1974	Greg Pruitt	1,769
1948	Marion Motley	1,493		1975	Greg Pruitt	1,798
1949	Mac Speedie	1,028		1976	Greg Pruitt	1,368
1950	Marion Motley	961		1977	Greg Pruitt	1,557
1951	Dub Jones	1,062		1978	Greg Pruitt	1,283
1952	Dub Jones	921		1979	Mike Pruitt	1,666
1953	Dante Lavelli	783		1980	Mike Pruitt	1,505
1954	Maurice Bassett	813		1981	Mike Pruitt	1,545
1955	Fred Morrison	1,009		1982	Mike Pruitt	656
1956	Preston Carpenter	1,279		1983	Mike Pruitt	1,341
1957	Jim Brown	1,133		1984	Ozzie Newsome	1,001
1958	Jim Brown	1,749		1985	Earnest Byner	1,462
1959	Jim Brown	1,607		1986	Gerald McNeil	1,366
1960	Jim Brown	1,761		1987	Earnest Byner	986
1961	Jim Brown	1,917		1988	Earnest Byner	1,152
1962	Jim Brown	1,513		1989	Eric Metcalf	1,748
1963	Jim Brown	2,131		1990	Eric Metcalf	1,752
1964	Jim Brown	1,786		1991	Webster Slaughter	1,018
1965	Jim Brown	1,872		1992	Eric Metcalf	1,501
1966	Leroy Kelly	2,014		1993	Eric Metcalf	1,932
1967	Leroy Kelly	1,677		1994	Leroy Hoard	1,365
1968	Leroy Kelly	1,555		1995	Earnest Byner	1,024
1969	Leroy Kelly	1,138		1999	Terry Kirby	1,210
1970	Leroy Kelly	982		2000	Jamel White	1,180
1971	Leroy Kelly	1,420		2001	Kevin Johnson	1,214
1972	Leroy Kelly	1,055				

INDIVIDUAL TOP FIVES (CAREER) (POSTSEASON)

SCORING (POINTS)

1. Lou Groza	83
2. Matt Bahr	46
3. Otto Graham	36
Earnest Byner	36
5. Edgar Jones	30
Dante Lavelli	30
Marion Motley	30
Gary Collins	30
Webster Slaughter	30

RUSHING YARDS

(Does not include Browns games against the Buffalo Bills Dec. 4, 1949, and Los Angeles Rams Dec. 24, 1950, for Otto Graham and Marion Motley, and the Browns game against the New York Giants Dec. 17, 1950, for Motley)

1. Marion Motley	512
2. Earnest Byner	480
3. Leroy Kelly	427
4. Kevin Mack	424
5. Otto Graham	247

PASSING YARDS

1. Otto Graham	2,001
2. Bernie Kosar	1,860
3. Bill Nelsen	839
4. Frank Ryan	534
5. Vinny Testaverde	412

PASS COMPLETIONS

1. Otto Graham	159
2. Bernie Kosar	146
3. Bill Nelsen	68
4. Frank Ryan	35
5. Vinny Testaverde	33

RECEIVING YARDS

(Does not include Browns games against the New York Giants Dec. 17, 1950, and Los Angeles Rams Dec. 24, 1950, and a portion of the Browns game against the Buffalo Bills Dec. 4, 1949)

1. Dante Lavelli	526
2. Paul Warfield	404
3. Webster Slaughter	381
4. Ozzie Newsome	373
5. Reggie Langhorne	370

RECEPTIONS

(Does not include the Browns game against the New York Giants Dec. 17, 1950, and a portion of Browns games against the Buffalo Bills Dec. 4, 1949, and Los Angeles Rams Dec. 24, 1950)

1. Horace Gillom	1,943
2. Don Cockroft	965
3. Jeff Gossett	792
4. Gary Collins	595
5. Bryan Wagner	451

1. Dante Lavelli	30
2. Mac Speedie	27
Ozzie Newsome	27
4. Reggie Langhorne	26
5. Paul Warfield	24

PUNTING YARDS

INDIVIDUAL TOP FIVES (GAME) (POSTSEASON)

vs.   Denotes home

SCORING (POINTS)

1. Marion Motley	18 (Dec. 19, 1948, vs. Buffalo)
Otto Graham	18 (Dec. 26, 1954, vs. Detroit)
Gary Collins	18 (Dec. 27, 1964, vs. Baltimore)
4. Edgar Jones	12 (Dec. 19, 1948, vs. Buffalo)
Dante Lavelli	12 (Dec. 24, 1950, vs. Los Angeles)
Ray Renfro	12 (Dec. 26, 1954, vs. Detroit)
Otto Graham	12 (Dec. 26, 1955, at Los Angeles)
Leroy Kelly	12 (Dec. 21, 1968, vs. Dallas)
Bo Scott	12 (Dec. 28, 1969, at Dallas)
Earnest Byner	12 (Jan. 4, 1986, at Miami)
Earnest Byner	12 (Jan. 9, 1988, vs. Indianapolis)
Earnest Byner	12 (Jan. 17, 1988, at Denver)
Webster Slaughter	12 (Dec. 24, 1988, vs. Houston)
Webster Slaughter	12 (Jan. 6, 1990, vs. Buffalo)
Brian Brennan	12 (Jan. 14, 1990, at Denver)

RUSHING YARDS

1. Earnest Byner	161 (Jan. 4, 1986, at Miami)
2. Marion Motley	133 (Dec. 19, 1948, vs. Buffalo)
3. Earnest Byner	122 (Jan. 9, 1988, vs. Indianapolis)
4. Jim Brown	114 (Dec. 27, 1964, vs. Baltimore)
5. Marion Motley	109 (Dec. 14, 1947, at New York)

PASSING YARDS

1. Bernie Kosar	489 (Jan. 3, 1987, vs. New York Jets)
2. Bernie Kosar	356 (Jan. 17, 1988, at Denver)
3. Otto Graham	326 (Dec. 4, 1949, vs. Buffalo)
4. Otto Graham	298 (Dec. 24, 1950, vs. Los Angeles)
5. Paul McDonald	281 (Jan. 8, 1983, at Los Angeles Raiders)

PASS COMPLETIONS

1. Bernie Kosar	33 (Jan. 3, 1987, vs. New York Jets)
2. Bernie Kosar	26 (Jan. 17, 1988, at Denver)
3. Otto Graham	22 (Dec. 4, 1949, vs. Buffalo)
Otto Graham	22 (Dec. 24, 1950, vs. Los Angeles)
5. Otto Graham	20 (Dec. 28, 1952, vs. Detroit)
Bernie Kosar	20 (Jan. 9, 1988, vs. Indianapolis)
Bernie Kosar	20 (Jan. 6, 1990, vs. Buffalo)
Vinny Testaverde	20 (Jan. 1, 1995, vs. New England)

RECEIVING YARDS

(Does not include a portion of Browns games against the Buffalo Bills Dec. 4, 1949, and Los Angeles Rams Dec. 24, 1950)

1. Gary Collins	130 (Dec. 27, 1964, vs. Baltimore)
2. Ricky Feacher	124 (Jan. 8, 1983, at Los Angeles Raiders)
3. Michael Jackson	122 (Jan. 1, 1995, vs. New England)
4. Earnest Byner	120 (Jan. 17, 1988, at Denver)
5. Ozzie Newsome	114 (Jan. 3, 1987, vs. New York Jets)
Webster Slaughter	114 (Jan. 6, 1990, vs. Buffalo)

RECEPTIONS

(Does not include the Browns game against the Los Angeles Rams Dec. 24, 1950, and a portion of the Browns game against the Buffalo Bills Dec. 4, 1949)

1. Paul Warfield	8 (Dec. 28, 1969, at Dallas)
2. Mac Speedie	7 (Dec. 4, 1949, vs. Buffalo)
Mac Speedie	7 (Dec. 23, 1951, at Los Angeles)
Herman Fontenot	7 (Jan. 11, 1987, vs. Denver)
Earnest Byner	7 (Jan. 17, 1988, at Denver)
Michael Jackson	7 (Jan. 1, 1995, vs. New England)

PUNTING YARDS

1. Horace Gillom   363 (Dec. 17, 1950, vs. New York)
2. Bryan Wagner   338 (Jan. 14, 1990, at Denver)
3. Jeff Gossett   310 (Jan. 3, 1987, vs. New York Jets)
4. Dick Deschaine   304 (Dec. 21, 1958, at New York)
5. Steve Cox   291 (Jan. 8, 1983, at Los Angeles Raiders)

INDIVIDUAL TOP TENS (CAREER)

SCORING (POINTS)

1. Lou Groza	1,608
2. Don Cockroft	1,080
3. Jim Brown	756
4. Matt Bahr	677
5. Leroy Kelly	540
6. Matt Stover	480
7. Gary Collins	420
8. Dante Lavelli	372
9. Ray Renfro	330
10. Kevin Mack	324

RUSHING YARDS

1. Jim Brown	12,312
2. Leroy Kelly	7,274
3. Mike Pruitt	6,540
4. Greg Pruitt	5,496
5. Kevin Mack	5,123
6. Marion Motley	4,712
7. Earnest Byner	3,364
8. Ernie Green	3,204
9. Bobby Mitchell	2,297
10. Cleo Miller	2,286

PASSING YARDS

1. Brian Sipe	23,713
2. Otto Graham	23,584
3. Bernie Kosar	21,904
4. Frank Ryan	13,361
5. Bill Nelsen	9,725
6. Milt Plum	8,914
7. Mike Phipps	7,700
8. Vinny Testaverde	7,255
9. Tim Couch	6,970
10. Paul McDonald	5,269

PASS COMPLETIONS

1. Brian Sipe   1,944
2. Bernie Kosar   1,853
3. Otto Graham   1,464
4. Frank Ryan   907
5. Bill Nelsen   689
6. Mike Phipps   633
7. Tim Couch   632
8. Milt Plumb   627
9. Vinny Testaverde   578
10. Paul McDonald   411

RECEIVING YARDS

1. Ozzie Newsome   7,980
2. Dante Lavelli   6,488
3. Mac Speedie   5,602
4. Ray Renfro   5,508
5. Gary Collins   5,299
6. Paul Warfield   5,210
7. Reggie Rucker   4,953
8. Webster Slaughter   4,834
9. Dave Logan   4,247
10. Milt Morin   4,208

RECEPTIONS

1. Ozzie Newsome   662
2. Dante Lavelli   386
3. Mac Speedie   349
4. Gary Collins   331
5. Greg Pruitt   323
6. Brian Brennan   315
7. Reggie Rucker   310
8. Webster Slaughter   305
9. Eric Metcalf   297
10. Ray Renfro   281

INTERCEPTIONS

1. Thom Darden   45
2. Warren Lahr   44
3. Clarence Scott   39
4. Tommy James   34
5. Ken Konz   30
6. Bernie Parrish   29
7. Ross Fichtner   27
   Mike Howell   27
9. Hanford Dixon   26
   Felix Wright   26

SACKS

1. Clay Matthews   63.5
2. Michael Dean Perry   51.5
3. Rob Burnett   40.5
4. Carl Hairston   37.5
5. Reggie Camp   35.5
6. Anthony Pleasant   30
7. Chip Banks   28
8. Jamir Miller   22.5
9. Al Baker   14.5
10. Bob Golic   13.5

PUNTING YARDS

1. Don Cockroft   26,362
2. Horace Gillom   21,207
3. Chris Gardocki   13,813
4. Gary Collins   13,764
5. Jeff Gossett   10,307
6. Brian Hansen   10,112
7. Johnny Evans   8,463
8. Steve Cox   7,984
9. Bryan Wagner   6,696
10. Tom Tupa   6,042

PUNT RETURN YARDS

1. Gerald McNeil   1,545
2. Eric Metcalf   1,341
3. Leroy Kelly   990
4. Dino Hall   901
5. Cliff Lewis   710
6. Greg Pruitt   659
7. Bobby Mitchell   607
8. Ken Konz   556
9. Keith Wright   467
10. Brian Brennan   435

KICKOFF RETURN YARDS

1. Dino Hall	3,185
2. Eric Metcalf	2,806
3. Glen Young	2,079
4. Randy Baldwin	1,872
5. Leroy Kelly	1,784
6. Keith Wright	1,767
7. Walter Roberts	1,608
8. Bobby Mitchell	1,550
9. Greg Pruitt	1,523
10. Billy Lefear	1,461

COMBINED NET YARDS

(Does not include fumble return yardage for part of Browns history)

1. Jim Brown	15,459
2. Leroy Kelly	12,329
3. Greg Pruitt	10,700
4. Eric Metcalf	9,108
5. Mike Pruitt	8,538
6. Ozzie Newsome	8,147
7. Marion Motley	7,019
8. Kevin Mack	6,725
9. Ray Renfro	6,569
10. Earnest Byner	6,564

INDIVIDUAL TOP TENS (GAME)

vs.–Denotes home

RUSHING YARDS

1. Jim Brown	237 (Nov. 24, 1957, vs. Los Angeles)
Jim Brown	237 (Nov. 19, 1961, vs. Philadelphia)
3. Bobby Mitchell	232 (Nov. 15, 1959, at Washington)
Jim Brown	232 (Sept. 22, 1963, at Dallas)
5. Jim Brown	223 (Nov. 3, 1963, at Pittsburgh)
6. Greg Pruitt	214 (Dec. 14, 1975, vs. Kansas City)
7. Greg Pruitt	191 (Oct. 17, 1976, at Atlanta)
8. Marion Motley	188 (Oct. 29, 1950, vs. Pittsburgh)
Jim Brown	188 (Oct. 18, 1964, at Dallas)
Earnest Byner	188 (Dec. 16, 1984, at Houston)

PASSING YARDS

1. Brian Sipe	444 (Oct. 25, 1981, vs. Baltimore)
2. Bernie Kosar	414 (Nov. 23, 1986, vs. Pittsburgh)
3. Otto Graham	401 (Oct. 4, 1952, at Pittsburgh)
Bernie Kosar	401 (Nov. 10, 1986, vs. Miami)
5. Brian Sipe	391 (Oct. 19, 1980, vs. Green Bay)
6. Otto Graham	382 (Nov. 20, 1949, at Brooklyn-New York)
7. Brian Sipe	375 (Sept. 7, 1981, vs. San Diego)

8. Otto Graham   369 (Oct. 15, 1950, vs. Chicago Cardinals)
9. Frank Ryan   367 (Dec. 17, 1966, at St. Louis)
10. Otto Graham   362 (Oct. 14, 1949, at Los Angeles)

RECEIVING YARDS

(Does not include Browns games against the Brooklyn Dodgers Dec. 8, 1946, and Baltimore Colts Dec. 7, 1947)

1. Mac Speedie   228 (Nov. 20, 1949, at Brooklyn-New York)
2. Dante Lavelli   209 (Oct. 14, 1949, at Los Angeles)
3. Ozzie Newsome   191 (Oct. 14, 1984, vs. New York Jets)
4. Webster Slaughter   186 (Oct. 23, 1989, vs. Chicago)
5. Webster Slaughter   184 (Oct. 29, 1989, vs. Houston)
6. Dante Lavelli   183 (Oct. 27, 1946, vs. San Francisco)
7. Pete Brewster   182 (Dec. 6, 1953, vs. New York
8. Gern Nagler   177 (Nov. 20, 1960, at Pittsburgh)
   Reggie Rucker   177 (Nov. 18, 1979, vs. Miami)
   Eric Metcalf   177 (Sept. 20, 1992, at Los Angeles Raiders)

INDIVIDUAL TOP TENS (SEASON)

SCORING (POINTS)

1. Jim Brown   126 (1965)
2. Leroy Kelly   120 (1968)
3. Lou Groza   115 (1964)
4. Matt Stover   113 (1995)
5. Matt Stover   110 (1994)
6. Lou Groza   108 (1953)
   Jim Brown   108 (1958)
   Jim Brown   108 (1962)
9. Matt Bahr   104 (1988)
10. Matt Bahr   101 (1983)

RUSHING YARDS

1. Jim Brown   1,863 (1963)
2. Jim Brown   1,544 (1965)
3. Jim Brown   1,527 (1958)
4. Jim Brown   1,446 (1964)
5. Jim Brown   1,408 (1961)
6. Jim Brown   1,329 (1959)
7. Mike Pruitt   1,294 (1979)
8. Jim Brown   1,257 (1960)
9. Leroy Kelly   1,239 (1968)
10. Leroy Kelly   1,205 (1967)

PASSING YARDS

1. Brian Sipe   4,132 (1980)
2. Brian Sipe   3,876 (1981)
3. Bernie Kosar   3,854 (1986)
4. Brian Sipe   3,793 (1979)
5. Brian Sipe   3,566 (1983)
6. Bernie Kosar   3,533 (1989)
7. Bernie Kosar   3,487 (1991)
8. Paul McDonald   3,472 (1984)
9. Tim Couch   3,040 (2001)
10. Bernie Kosar   3,033 (1987)

PASS COMPLETIONS

1. Brian Sipe	337 (1980)
2. Brian Sipe	313 (1981)
3. Bernie Kosar	310 (1986)
4. Bernie Kosar	307 (1991)
5. Bernie Kosar	303 (1989)
6. Brian Sipe	291 (1983)
7. Brian Sipe	286 (1979)
8. Tim Couch	272 (2001)
9. Paul McDonald	271 (1984)
10. Bernie Kosar	241 (1987)
Vinny Testaverde	241 (1995)

RECEIVING YARDS

1. Webster Slaughter	1,236 (1989)
2. Mac Speedie	1,146 (1947)
3. Kevin Johnson	1,097 (2001)
4. Paul Warfield	1,067 (1968)
5. Mac Speedie	1,028 (1949)
6. Ozzie Newsome	1,002 (1981)
7. Ozzie Newsome	1,001 (1984)
8. Kevin Johnson	986 (1999)
9. Dave Logan	982 (1979)
10. Ozzie Newsome	970 (1983)

RECEPTIONS

1. Ozzie Newsome	89 (1983)
Ozzie Newsome	89 (1984)
3. Kevin Johnson	84 (2001)
4. Ozzie Newsome	69 (1981)
5. Mac Speedie	67 (1947)
6. Kevin Johnson	66 (1999)
7. Greg Pruitt	65 (1981)
Webster Slaughter	65 (1989)
9. Webster Slaughter	64 (1991)
10. Mike Pruitt	63 (1980)
Mike Pruitt	63 (1981)
Eric Metcalf	63 (1993)

INTERCEPTIONS

1. Tom Colella	10 (1946)
Thom Darden	10 (1978)
Anthony Henry	10 (2001)
4. Cliff Lewis	9 (1948)
Tommy James	9 (1950)
Felix Wright	9 (1989)
Eric Turner	9 (1994)
8. Warren Lahr	8 (1950)
Bobby Franklin	8 (1960)
Jim Shofner	8 (1960)
Ross Fichtner	8 (1966)
Mike Howell	8 (1966)
Ben Davis	8 (1968)
Thom Darden	8 (1974)

SACKS

1. Reggie Camp	14 (1984)
2. Jamir Miller	13 (2001)
3. Clay Matthews	12 (1984)
4. Michael Dean Perry	11.5 (1990)
5. Chip Banks	11 (1985)
Anthony Pleasant	11 (1993)
7. Rob Burnett	10 (1994)
8. Rob Burnett	9 (1992)
Clay Matthews	9 (1992)
Rob Burnett	9 (1993)

PUNTING YARDS

1. Chris Gardocki	4,919 (2000)
2. Chris Gardocki	4,645 (1999)
3. Chris Gardocki	4,249 (2001)
4. Bryan Wagner	3,817 (1989)
5. Don Cockroft	3,643 (1974)
6. Brian Hansen	3,632 (1993)
7. Don Cockroft	3,498 (1972)
8. Jeff Gossett	3,423 (1986)
9. Brian Hansen	3,397 (1991)
10. Horace Gillom	3,321 (1951)
Don Cockroft	3,321 (1973)

PUNT RETURN YARDS

1. Gerald McNeil	496	(1989)
2. Eric Metcalf	464	(1993)
3. Eric Metcalf	429	(1992)
4. Gerald McNeil	386	(1987)
5. Greg Pruitt	349	(1974)
6. Gerald McNeil	348	(1986)
Eric Metcalf	348	(1994)
8. Gerald McNeil	315	(1988)
9. Dino Hall	295	(1979)
10. Leroy Kelly	292	(1971)

KICKOFF RETURN YARDS

1. Eric Metcalf	1,052	(1990)
2. Dino Hall	1,014	(1979)
3. Gerald McNeil	997	(1986)
4. Ronnie Powell	986	(1999)
5. Jamel White	935	(2000)
6. Glen Young	898	(1985)
7. Herman Fontenot	879	(1988)
8. Dino Hall	813	(1981)
9. Keith Wright	789	(1978)
10. Randy Baldwin	753	(1994)

COMBINED NET YARDS

1. Jim Brown	2,131	(1963)
2. Leroy Kelly	2,014	(1966)
3. Eric Metcalf	1,932	(1993)
4. Jim Brown	1,917	(1961)
5. Jim Brown	1,872	(1965)
6. Greg Pruitt	1,798	(1975)
7. Jim Brown	1,786	(1964)
8. Greg Pruitt	1,769	(1974)
9. Jim Brown	1,761	(1960)
10. Eric Metcalf	1,752	(1990)

INTERCEPTIONS LEADERS

1946 - Tom Colella	10	1961 - Bernie Parrish	7	1978 - Thom Darden	10
1947 - Tom Colella	6	1962 - Ross Fichtner	7	1979 - Thom Darden	5
1948 - Cliff Lewis	9	1963 - Larry Benz	7	1980 - Ron Bolton	6
1949 - Cliff Lewis	6	Vince Costello	7	1981 - Clarence Scott	4
1950 - Tommy James	9	1964 - Walter Beach	4	1982 - Hanford Dixon	4
1951 - Warren Lahr	5	Larry Benz	4	Larry Johnson	4
Cliff Lewis	5	Bernie Parrish	4	1983 - Tom Cousineau	4
1952 - Bert Rechichar	6	1965 - Larry Benz	5	1984 - Hanford Dixon	5
1953 - Tommy James	5	1966 - Ross Fichtner	8	Al Gross	5
Ken Konz	5	Mike Howell	8	1985 - Al Gross	5
Warren Lahr	5	1967 - Erich Barnes	4	1986 - Hanford Dixon	5
1954 - Ken Konz	7	Ross Fichtner	4	1987 - Frank Minnifield	4
1955 - Ken Konz	5	1968 - Ben Davis	8	Felix Wright	4
Warren Lahr	5	1969 - Mike Howell	6	1988 - Felix Wright	5
Chuck Noll	5	1970 - Erich Barnes	5	1989 - Felix Wright	9
1956 - Don Paul	7	1971 - Walt Sumner	5	1990 - Felix Wright	3
1957 - Ken Konz	4	1972 - Thom Darden	3	1991 - Stephen Braggs	3
Don Paul	4	Ben Davis	3	1992 - Vince Newsome	3
1958 - Ken Konz	4	1973 - Clarence Scott	5	1993 - Eric Turner	5
Don Paul	4	1974 - Thom Darden	8	1994 - Eric Turner	9
1959 - Bernie Parrish	5	1975 - Charlie Hall	2	1995 - Stevon Moore	5
Junior Wren	5	Clarence Scott	2	1999 - Marquez Pope	2
1960 - Bobby Franklin	8	1976 - Thom Darden	7	2000 - Corey Fuller	3
Jim Shofner	8	1977 - Thom Darden	6	2001 - Anthony Henry	10

KICKOFF RETURN YARDS LEADERS

1946 - Edgar Jones	307	1964 - Walter Roberts	661	1982 - Dino Hall	430
1947 - Marion Motley	322	1965 - Leroy Kelly	621	1983 - Dwight Walker	627
1948 - Marion Motley	337	1966 - Walter Roberts	454	1984 - Earnest Byner	415
1949 - Marion Motley	262	1967 - Ben Davis	708	1985 - Glen Young	898
1950 - Don Phelps	325	1968 - Charlie Leigh	322	1986 - Gerald McNeil	997
1951 - Ken Carpenter	196	1969 - Bo Scott	722	1987 - Glen Young	412
1952 - Ken Carpenter	234	1970 - Homer Jones	739	1988 - Glen Young	635
1953 - Ken Carpenter	367	1971 - Ken Brown	330	1989 - Eric Metcalf	718
1954 - Billy Reynolds	413	1972 - Ken Brown	473	1990 - Eric Metcalf	1,052
1955 - Bob White	400	1973 - Greg Pruitt	453	1991 - Eric Metcalf	351
1956 - Ken Carpenter	381	1974 - Greg Pruitt	606	1992 - Randy Baldwin	675
1957 - Milt Campbell	263	1975 - Billy Lefear	412	1993 - Randy Baldwin	444
1958 - Bobby Mitchell	454	1976 - Steve Holden	461	1994 - Randy Baldwin	753
1959 - Bobby Mitchell	236	1977 - Brian Duncan	298	1995 - Earnest Hunter	518
1960 - Bobby Mitchell	432	1978 - Keith Wright	789	1999 - Ronnie Powell	986
1961 - Bobby Mitchell	428	1979 - Dino Hall	1,014	2000 - Jamel White	935
1962 - Tom Wilson	307	1980 - Dino Hall	691	2001 - Ben Gay	513
1963 - Charley Scales	432	1981 - Dino Hall	813		

ONE-THOUSAND-YARD RECEIVERS

Mac Speedie	1,146 (1947)
Mac Speedie	1,028 (1949)
Paul Warfield	1,067 (1968)
Ozzie Newsome	1,002 (1981)
Ozzie Newsome	1,001 (1984)
Webster Slaughter	1,236 (1989)
Kevin Johnson	1,097 (2001)

ONE-THOUSAND-YARD RUSHERS

Jim Brown	1,527 (1958)	Greg Pruitt	1,067 (1975)
Jim Brown	1,329 (1959)	Greg Pruitt	1,000 (1976)
Jim Brown	1,257 (1960)	Greg Pruitt	1,086 (1977)
Jim Brown	1,408 (1961)	Mike Pruitt	1,294 (1979)
Jim Brown	1,863 (1963)	Mike Pruitt	1,034 (1980)
Jim Brown	1,446 (1964)	Mike Pruitt	1,103 (1981)
Jim Brown	1,544 (1965)	Mike Pruitt	1,184 (1983)
Leroy Kelly	1,205 (1967)	Kevin Mack	1,104 (1985)
Leroy Kelly	1,141 (1966)	Earnest Byner	1,002 (1985)
Leroy Kelly	1,239 (1968)		

PASS COMPLETIONS LEADERS

1946 - Otto Graham	95
1947 - Otto Graham	163
1948 - Otto Graham	173
1949 - Otto Graham	161
1950 - Otto Graham	137
1951 - Otto Graham	147
1952 - Otto Graham	181
1953 - Otto Graham	167
1954 - Otto Graham	142
1955 - Otto Graham	98
1956 - Tommy O'Connell	42
1957 - Tommy O'Connell	63
1958 - Milt Plum	102
1959 - Milt Plum	156
1960 - Milt Plum	151
1961 - Milt Plum	177
1962 - Frank Ryan	112
1963 - Frank Ryan	135
1964 - Frank Ryan	174
1965 - Frank Ryan	119
1966 - Frank Ryan	200
1967 - Frank Ryan	136
1968 - Bill Nelsen	152
1969 - Bill Nelsen	190
1970 - Bill Nelsen	159
1971 - Bill Nelsen	174
1972 - Mike Phipps	144
1973 - Mike Phipps	148
1974 - Mike Phipps	117
1975 - Mike Phipps	162
1976 - Brian Sipe	178
1977 - Brian Sipe	112
1978 - Brian Sipe	222
1979 - Brian Sipe	286
1980 - Brian Sipe	337
1981 - Brian Sipe	313
1982 - Brian Sipe	101
1983 - Brian Sipe	291
1984 - Paul McDonald	271
1985 - Bernie Kosar	124
1986 - Bernie Kosar	310
1987 - Bernie Kosar	241
1988 - Bernie Kosar	156
1989 - Bernie Kosar	303
1990 - Bernie Kosar	230
1991 - Bernie Kosar	307
1992 - Mike Tomczak	120
1993 - Vinny Testaverde	130
1994 - Vinny Testaverde	207
1995 - Vinny Testaverde	241
1999 - Tim Couch	223
2000 - Tim Couch	137
2001 - Tim Couch	272

PASSING YARDS LEADERS

Year	Player	Yards
1946 - Otto Graham	1,834
1947 - Otto Graham	2,753
1948 - Otto Graham	2,713
1949 - Otto Graham	2,785
1950 - Otto Graham	1,943
1951 - Otto Graham	2,205
1952 - Otto Graham	2,816
1953 - Otto Graham	2,722
1954 - Otto Graham	2,092
1955 - Otto Graham	1,721
1956 - Tommy O'Connell	551
1957 - Tommy O'Connell	1,229
1958 - Milt Plum	1,619
1959 - Milt Plum	1,992
1960 - Milt Plum	2,297
1961 - Milt Plum	2,416
1962 - Frank Ryan	1,541
1963 - Frank Ryan	2,026
1964 - Frank Ryan	2,404
1965 - Frank Ryan	1,751
1966 - Frank Ryan	2,974
1967 - Frank Ryan	2,026
1968 - Bill Nelsen	2,366
1969 - Bill Nelsen	2,743
1970 - Bill Nelsen	2,156
1971 - Bill Nelsen	2,319
1972 - Mike Phipps	1,994
1973 - Mike Phipps	1,719
1974 - Mike Phipps	1,384
1975 - Mike Phipps	1,749
1976 - Brian Sipe	2,113
1977 - Brian Sipe	1,233
1978 - Brian Sipe	2,906
1979 - Brian Sipe	3,793
1980 - Brian Sipe	4,132
1981 - Brian Sipe	3,876
1982 - Brian Sipe	1,064
1983 - Brian Sipe	3,566
1984 - Paul McDonald	3,472
1985 - Bernie Kosar	1,578
1986 - Bernie Kosar	3,854
1987 - Bernie Kosar	3,033
1988 - Bernie Kosar	1,890
1989 - Bernie Kosar	3,533
1990 - Bernie Kosar	2,562
1991 - Bernie Kosar	3,487
1992 - Mike Tomczak	1,693
1993 - Vinny Testaverde	1,797
1994 - Vinny Testaverde	2,575
1995 - Vinny Testaverde	2,883
1999 - Tim Couch	2,447
2000 - Tim Couch	1,483
2001 - Tim Couch	3,040

PUNT RETURN YARDS LEADERS

1946 - Tom Colella	172	1964 - Leroy Kelly	171	1982 - Dwight Walker	101
1947 - Otto Graham	121	1965 - Leroy Kelly	265	1983 - Dino Hall	284
1948 - Cliff Lewis	258	1966 - Leroy Kelly	104	1984 - Brian Brennan	199
1949 - Cliff Lewis	174	1967 - Ben Davis	229	1985 - Clarence Weathers	218
1950 - Don Phelps	174	1968 - Charles Leigh	76	1986 - Gerald McNeil	348
1951 - Ken Carpenter	173	1969 - Walt Sumner	72	1987 - Gerald McNeil	386
1952 - Ray Renfro	169	1970 - Reece Morrison	133	1988 - Gerald McNeil	315
1953 - Billy Reynolds	111	1971 - Leroy Kelly	292	1989 - Gerald McNeil	496
1954 - Billy Reynolds	138	1972 - Bobby Majors	96	1990 - Stefon Adams	81
1955 - Don Paul	148	1973 - Greg Pruitt	180	1991 - Webster Slaughter	112
1956 - Ken Konz	187	1974 - Greg Pruitt	349	1992 - Eric Metcalf	429
1957 - Billy Reynolds	114	1975 - Greg Pruitt	130	1993 - Eric Metcalf	464
1958 - Bobby Mitchell	65	1976 - Steve Holden	205	1994 - Eric Metcalf	348
1959 - Bobby Mitchell	177	1977 - Rolly Woolsey	290	1995 - Derrick Alexander	122
1960 - Jim Shofner	105	1978 - Keith Wright	288	1999 - Kevin Johnson	128
1961 - Bobby Mitchell	164	1979 - Dino Hall	295	2000 - Dennis Northcutt	289
1962 - Howard Cassady	47	1980 - Keith Wright	129	2001 - Kevin Johnson	117
1963 - Jim Shorter	134	1981 - Dino Hall	248		

PUNT RETURNS LEADERS

1946 - Bud Schwenk	12	1963 - Jim Shofner	9	1981 - Dino Hall 33	
1947 - Otto Graham	10	1964 - Walter Roberts	10	1982 - Dwight Walker	19
1948 - Cliff Lewis 26		1965 - Walter Roberts	18	1983 - Dino Hall 39	
1949 - Cliff Lewis 20		1966 - Leroy Kelly	13	1984 - Brian Brennan	25
1950 - Don Phelps	13	1967 - Ben Davis 18		1985 - Clarence Weathers	28
1951 - Ken Carpenter	14	1968 - Charles Leigh	14	1986 - Gerald McNeil	40
Cliff Lewis 14		1969 - Reece Morrison	11	1987 - Gerald McNeil	34
1952 - Ray Renfro	22	1970 - Reece Morrison	15	1988 - Gerald McNeil	38
1953 - Billy Reynolds	18	1971 - Leroy Kelly	30	1989 - Gerald McNeil	49
1954 - Chet Hanulak	27	1972 - Bobby Majors	16	1990 - Stefon Adams	13
1955 - Don Paul 19		1973 - Greg Pruitt	16	1991 - Webster Slaughter	17
1956 - Don Paul 17		1974 - Greg Pruitt	27	1992 - Eric Metcalf	44
1957 - Billy Reynolds	24	1975 - Greg Pruitt	13	1993 - Eric Metcalf	36
1958 - Ken Konz 18		1976 - Steve Holden	31	1994 - Eric Metcalf	35
1959 - Bobby Mitchell	17	1977 - Rolly Woolsey	32	1995 - Keenan McCardell 13	
1960 - Jim Shofner	11	1978 - Keith Wright	37	1999 - Kevin Johnson	19
1961 - Bobby Mitchell	14	1979 - Dino Hall 29		2000 - Dennis Northcutt	27
Jim Shofner	14	1980 - Keith Wright	29	2001 - Dennis Northcutt	15
1962 - Jim Shofner	8				

PUNTING YARDS LEADERS

1946 - Tom Colella	1,894	1966 - Gary Collins	2,223	1986 - Jeff Gossett	3,423
1947 - Chet Adams	2,096	1967 - Gary Collins	2,078	1987 - Jeff Gossett	779
1948 - Tom Colella	1,715	1968 - Don Cockroft	2,297	1988 - Max Runager	1,935
1949 - Horace Gillom	2,009	1969 - Don Cockroft	2,138	1989 - Bryan Wagner	3,817
1950 - Horace Gillom	2,849	1970 - Don Cockroft	3,023	1990 - Bryan Wagner	2,879
1951 - Horace Gillom	3,321	1971 - Don Cockroft	2,508	1991 - Brian Hansen	3,397
1952 - Horace Gillom	2,787	1972 - Don Cockroft	3,498	1992 - Brian Hansen	3,083
1953 - Horace Gillom	2,760	1973 - Don Cockroft	3,321	1993 - Brian Hansen	3,632
1954 - Horace Gillom	2,230	1974 - Don Cockroft	3,643	1994 - Tom Tupa	3,211
1955 - Horace Gillom	2,389	1975 - Don Cockroft	3,317	1995 - Tom Tupa	2,831
1956 - Fred Morrison	1,561	1976 - Don Cockroft	2,487	1999 - Chris Gardocki	4,645
1957 - Ken Konz	2,396	1977 - Greg Coleman	2,389	2000 - Chris Gardocki	4,919
1958 - Dick Deschaine	2,063	1978 - Johnny Evans	3,089	2001 - Chris Gardocki	4,249
1959 - Junior Wren	996	1979 - Johnny Evans	2,844		
1960 - Sam Baker	2,309	1980 - Johnny Evans	2,530		
1961 - Sam Baker	2,296	1981 - Steve Cox	2,884		
1962 - Gary Collins	1,926	1982 - Steve Cox	1,887		
1963 - Gary Collins	2,160	1983 - Jeff Gossett	2,854		
1964 - Gary Collins	2,016	1984 - Steve Cox	3,213		
1965 - Gary Collins	3,035	1985 - Jeff Gossett	3,261		

RECEIVING YARDS LEADERS

1946 - Dante Lavelli	843	1968 - Paul Warfield	1,067	1990 - Webster Slaughter	847
1947 - Mac Speedie	1,146	1969 - Paul Warfield	886	1991 - Webster Slaughter	906
1948 - Mac Speedie	816	1970 - Milt Morin	611	1992 - Michael Jackson	755
1949 - Mac Speedie	1,028	1971 - Fair Hooker	649	1993 - Michael Jackson	756
1950 - Dante Lavelli	565	1972 - Frank Pitts	620	1994 - Derrick Alexander	828
1951 - Mac Speedie	589	1973 - Milt Morin	417	1995 - Michael Jackson	714
1952 - Mac Speedie	911	1974 - Steve Holden	452	1999 - Kevin Johnson	986
1953 - Dante Lavelli	783	1975 - Reggie Rucker	770	2000 - Kevin Johnson	669
1954 - Dante Lavelli	802	1976 - Reggie Rucker	676	2001 - Kevin Johnson	1,097
1955 - Darrell Brewster	622	1977 - Reggie Rucker	565		
1956 - Darrell Brewster	417	1978 - Reggie Rucker	893		
1957 - Darrell Brewster	614	1979 - Dave Logan	982		
1958 - Ray Renfro	573	1980 - Dave Logan	822		
1959 - Ray Renfro	528	1981 - Ozzie Newsome	1,002		
1960 - Gern Nagler	616	1982 - Ozzie Newsome	633		
1961 - Ray Renfro	834	1983 - Ozzie Newsome	970		
1962 - Rich Kreitling	659	1984 - Ozzie Newsome	1,001		
1963 - Gary Collins	674	1985 - Ozzie Newsome	711		
1964 - Paul Warfield	920	1986 - Brian Brennan	838		
1965 - Gary Collins	884	1987 - Webster Slaughter	806		
1966 - Gary Collins	946	1988 - Reggie Langhorne	780		
1967 - Paul Warfield	702	1989 - Webster Slaughter	1,236		

RECEPTIONS LEADERS

1946 - Dante Lavelli	40	1964 - Paul Warfield	52	1982 - Ozzie Newsome	49
1947 - Mac Speedie	67	1965 - Gary Collins	50	1983 - Ozzie Newsome	89
1948 - Mac Speedie	58	1966 - Gary Collins	56	1984 - Ozzie Newsome	89
1949 - Mac Speedie	62	1967 - Ernie Green	39	1985 - Ozzie Newsome	62
1950 - Mac Speedie	42	1968 - Paul Warfield	50	1986 - Brian Brennan	55
1951 - Dante Lavelli	43	1969 - Gary Collins	54	1987 - Earnest Byner	52
1952 - Mac Speedie	62	1970 - Bo Scott	40	1988 - Earnest Byner	59
1953 - Dante Lavelli	45	1971 - Fair Hooker	45	1989 - Webster Slaughter	65
1954 - Dante Lavelli	47	1972 - Frank Pitts	36	1990 - Webster Slaughter	59
1955 - Darrell Brewster	34	1973 - Frank Pitts	31	1991 - Webster Slaughter	64
1956 - Darrell Brewster	28	1974 - Hugh McKinnis	32	1992 - Michael Jackson	47
1957 - Darrell Brewster	30	1975 - Reggie Rucker	60	Eric Metcalf	47
1958 - Preston Carpenter	29	1976 - Reggie Rucker	49	1993 - Eric Metcalf	63
1959 - Billy Howton	39	1977 - Cleo Miller	41	1994 - Derrick Alexander	48
1960 - Bobby Mitchell	45	1978 - Reggie Rucker	43	1995 - Earnest Byner	61
1961 - Ray Renfro	48	1979 - Dave Logan	59	1999 - Kevin Johnson	66
1962 - Jim Brown	47	1980 - Mike Pruitt	63	2000 - Kevin Johnson	57
1963 - Gary Collins	43	1981 - Ozzie Newsome	69	2001 - Kevin Johnson	84

RUSHING YARDS LEADERS

1946 - Marion Motley	601	1964 - Jim Brown	1,446	1982 - Mike Pruitt	516
1947 - Marion Motley	889	1965 - Jim Brown	1,544	1983 - Mike Pruitt	1,184
1948 - Marion Motley	964	1966 - Leroy Kelly	1,141	1984 - Boyce Green	673
1949 - Marion Motley	570	1967 - Leroy Kelly	1,205	1985 - Kevin Mack	1,104
1950 - Marion Motley	810	1968 - Leroy Kelly	1,239	1986 - Kevin Mack	665
1951 - Dub Jones	492	1969 - Leroy Kelly	817	1987 - Kevin Mack	735
1952 - Marion Motley	444	1970 - Leroy Kelly	656	1988 - Earnest Byner	576
1953 - Ray Renfro	352	1971 - Leroy Kelly	865	1989 - Eric Metcalf	633
1954 - Maurice Bassett	588	1972 - Leroy Kelly	811	1990 - Kevin Mack	702
1955 - Fred Morrison	824	1973 - Ken Brown	537	1991 - Kevin Mack	726
1956 - Preston Carpenter	756	1974 - Greg Pruitt	540	1992 - Kevin Mack	543
1957 - Jim Brown	942	1975 - Greg Pruitt	1,067	1993 - Tommy Vardell	644
1958 - Jim Brown	1,527	1976 - Greg Pruitt	1,000	1994 - Leroy Hoard	890
1959 - Jim Brown	1,329	1977 - Greg Pruitt	1,086	1995 - Leroy Hoard	547
1960 - Jim Brown	1,257	1978 - Greg Pruitt	960	1999 - Terry Kirby	452
1961 - Jim Brown	1,408	1979 - Mike Pruitt	1,294	2000 - Travis Prentice	512
1962 - Jim Brown	996	1980 - Mike Pruitt	1,034	2001 - James Jackson	554
1963 - Jim Brown	1,863	1981 - Mike Pruitt	1,103		

SACKS LEADERS

1982 - Chip Banks	5.5	1991 - Michael Dean Perry	8.5
1983 - Clay Matthews	7	1992 - Rob Burnett	9
1984 - Reggie Camp	14	Clay Matthews	9
1985 - Chip Banks	11	1993 - Anthony Pleasant	11
1986 - Carl Hairston	9	1994 - Rob Burnett	10
1987 - Carl Hairston	8	1995 - Anthony Pleasant	8
1988 - Clay Matthews	8	1999 - John Thierry	7
Michael Dean Perry	8	2000 - Keith McKenzie	8
1989 - Al Baker	7.5	2001 - Jamir Miller	13
1990 - Michael Dean Perry	11.5		

SCORING LEADERS (POINTS)

1946 - Dante Lavelli	48	1964 - Lou Groza	115	1982 - Matt Bahr	38
1947 - Marion Motley	60	1965 - Jim Brown	126	1983 - Matt Bahr	101
1948 - Edgar Jones	60	1966 - Leroy Kelly	96	1984 - Matt Bahr	97
1949 - Marion Motley	48	1967 - Leroy Kelly	78	1985 - Matt Bahr	77
1950 - Lou Groza	74	1968 - Leroy Kelly	120	1986 - Matt Bahr	90
1951 - Lou Groza	73	1969 - Don Cockroft	81	1987 - Jeff Jaeger	75
1952 - Lou Groza	89	1970 - Don Cockroft	70	1988 - Matt Bahr	104
1953 - Lou Groza	108	1971 - Don Cockroft	79	1989 - Matt Bahr	88
1954 - Lou Groza	85	1972 - Don Cockroft	94	1990 - Jerry Kauric	66
1955 - Lou Groza	77	1973 - Don Cockroft	90	1991 - Matt Stover	81
1956 - Lou Groza	51	1974 - Don Cockroft	71	1992 - Matt Stover	92
1957 - Lou Groza	77	1975 - Don Cockroft	72	1993 - Matt Stover	84
1958 - Jim Brown	108	1976 - Don Cockroft	72	1994 - Matt Stover	110
1959 - Jim Brown	84	1977 - Don Cockroft	81	1995 - Matt Stover	125
1960 - Sam Baker	80	1978 - Don Cockroft	94	1999 - Terry Kirby	54
1961 - Lou Groza	85	1979 - Don Cockroft	89	2000 - Phil Dawson	59
1962 - Jim Brown	108	1980 - Don Cockroft	87	2001 - Phil Dawson	95
1963 - Jim Brown	90	1981 - Matt Bahr	61		

THREE-THOUSAND-YARD PASSERS

Brian Sipe	3,793 (1979)
Brian Sipe	4,132 (1980)
Brian Sipe	3,876 (1981)
Brian Sipe	3,566 (1983)
Paul McDonald	3,472 (1984)
Bernie Kosar	3,854 (1986)
Bernie Kosar	3,033 (1987)
Bernie Kosar	3,533 (1989)
Bernie Kosar	3,487 (1991)
Tim Couch	3,040 (2001)

TEAM
STATISTICS

COMPOSITE MONTHLY WON-LOST-TIED RECORDS, BEST TO WORST

RANK	MONTH	WON	LOST	TIED	PCT.
1.	October	137	81	2	.627
2.	November	132	84	7	.608
3.	September	86	61	2	.584
4.	December	78	77	2	.503
5.	January	0	3	0	.000

COMPOSITE WON-LOST RECORDS VS. OTHER TEAMS, BEST TO WORST (POSTSEASON)

RANK	TEAM	WON	LOST	PCT.
1.	Buffalo Bisons/Bills (original)	2	0	1.000
	New York Yankees	2	0	1.000
	Buffalo Bills (current)	1	0	1.000
	New England Patriots	1	0	1.000
	New York Jets	1	0	1.000
	San Francisco 49ers	1	0	1.000
7.	Dallas Cowboys	2	1	.667
	St. Louis Rams	2	1	.667
9.	Indianapolis Colts	2	2	.500
	New York Giants	1	1	.500
11.	Detroit Lions	1	3	.250
12.	Green Bay Packers	0	1	.000
	Minnesota Vikings	0	1	.000
	Pittsburgh Steelers	0	1	.000
	Tennessee Titans	0	1	.000
16.	Miami Dolphins	0	2	.000
	Oakland Raiders	0	2	.000
18.	Denver Broncos	0	3	.000

COMPOSITE WON-LOST-TIED RECORDS VS. OTHER TEAMS, BEST TO WORST

RANK	TEAM	WON	LOST	TIED	PCT.
1.	Chicago Rockets	8	0	0	1.000
	Baltimore Colts (original)	7	0	0	1.000
	Brooklyn Dodgers	6	0	0	1.000
	Tampa Bay Buccaneers	5	0	0	1.000
	Brooklyn-New York Yankees	2	0	0	1.000
	Miami Seahawks	2	0	0	1.000
7.	New York Yankees	5	0	1	.917
8.	Buffalo Bisons/Bills (original)	6	0	2	.875
9.	Atlanta Falcons	8	2	0	.800
10.	New Orleans Saints	10	3	0	.769
11.	Washington Redskins	32	9	1	.774
12.	Los Angeles Dons	6	2	0	.750
13.	Arizona Cardinals	32	11	3	.728
14.	Philadelphia Eagles	31	13	1	.700
15.	Chicago Bears	8	4	0	.667
16.	San Francisco 49ers	15	8	0	.652
17.	New England Patriots	11	6	0	.647
18.	Indianapolis Colts	14	8	0	.636
	Buffalo Bills (current)	7	4	0	.636
20.	Dallas Cowboys	15	9	0	.625
21.	New York Jets	9	6	0	.600
22.	New York Giants	25	18	2	.578
23.	Pittsburgh Steelers	54	44	0	.551
24.	Tennessee Titans	31	26	0	.544
25.	Kansas City Chiefs	8	7	2	.529
26.	Cincinnati Bengals	29	28	0	.509
27.	St. Louis Rams	8	8	0	.500
28.	San Diego Chargers	7	10	1	.417
29.	Green Bay Packers	6	9	0	.400
	Miami Dolphins	4	6	0	.400
31.	Baltimore Ravens	2	4	0	.333
32.	Oakland Raiders	4	9	0	.308
33.	Seattle Seahawks	4	10	0	.286
34.	Minnesota Vikings	3	8	0	.273
35.	Denver Broncos	5	14	0	.263
36.	Detroit Lions	4	12	0	.250
37.	Jacksonville Jaguars	1	7	0	.125
38.	Carolina Panthers	0	1	0	.000

FINALES
* Denotes official finale

YEAR	HOME	AWAY
1946	Cleveland 42, Buffalo 17	*Cleveland 66, Brooklyn 14
1947	Cleveland 37, San Francisco 14	*Cleveland 42, Baltimore 0
1948	Cleveland 14, San Francisco 7	*Cleveland 31, Brooklyn 21
1949	Cleveland 7, Buffalo 7	*Cleveland 14, Chicago 6
1950	Cleveland 13, Philadelphia 7	*Cleveland 45, Washington 21
1951	Cleveland 49, Chicago Cardinals 28	*Cleveland 24, Philadelphia 9
1952	Philadelphia 28, Cleveland 20	*New York 37, Cleveland 34
1953	Cleveland 62, New York 14	*Philadelphia 42, Cleveland 27
1954	*Detroit 14, Cleveland 10	Cleveland 34, Washington 14
1955	*Cleveland 35, Chicago Cardinals 24	Cleveland 30, Pittsburgh 7
1956	*Chicago Cardinals 24, Cleveland 7	Cleveland 24, New York 7
1957	Cleveland 31, Chicago Cardinals 0	*Cleveland 34, New York 28
1958	Cleveland 21, Washington 14	*New York 13, Cleveland 10
1959	San Francisco 21, Cleveland 20	*Cleveland 28, Philadelphia 21
1960	Cleveland 42, Chicago 0	*Cleveland 48, New York 34
1961	New York 37, Cleveland 21	*New York 7, Cleveland 7
1962	Cleveland 35, Pittsburgh 14	*Cleveland 13, San Francisco 10
1963	Cleveland 27, Dallas 17	*Cleveland 27, Washington 20
1964	Cleveland 38, Philadelphia 24	*Cleveland 52, New York 20
1965	Cleveland 24, Washington 16	*Cleveland 27, St. Louis 24
1966	Cleveland 49, New York 40	*Cleveland 38, St. Louis 10
1967	Cleveland 24, New York 14	*Philadelphia 28, Cleveland 24
1968	Cleveland 45, New York 10	*St. Louis 27, Cleveland 16
1969	Cleveland 20, Green Bay 7	*New York 27, Cleveland 14
1970	Dallas 6, Cleveland 2	*Cleveland 27, Denver 13
1971	Cleveland 31, Cincinnati 27	*Cleveland 20, Washington 13
1972	Cleveland 27, Buffalo 10	*Cleveland 26, New York Jets 10
1973	Cleveland 21, Pittsburgh 16	*Los Angeles 30, Cleveland 17
1974	Cleveland 7, San Francisco 0	*Houston 28, Cleveland 24
1975	Cleveland 40, Kansas City 14	*Houston 21, Cleveland 10
1976	Cleveland 13, Houston 10	*Kansas City 39, Cleveland 14
1977	Houston 19, Cleveland 15	*Seattle 20, Cleveland 19
1978	Cleveland 37, New York Jets 34 (OT)	*Cincinnati 48, Cleveland 16
1979	Cleveland 14, Houston 7	*Cincinnati 16, Cleveland 12
1980	Cleveland 17, New York Jets 14	*Cleveland 27, Cincinnati 24
1981	New York Jets 14, Cleveland 13	*Seattle 42, Cleveland 21
1982	Cleveland 10, Pittsburgh 9	*Pittsburgh 37, Cleveland 21
1983	*Cleveland 30, Pittsburgh 17	Houston 34, Cleveland 27
1984	Cincinnati 20, Cleveland 17 (OT)	*Cleveland 27, Houston 20
1985	Cleveland 28, Houston 21	*New York Jets 37, Cleveland 10
1986	*Cleveland 47, San Diego 17	Cleveland 34, Cincinnati 3

FINALES (CONTD.)

1987	Cleveland 38, Cincinnati 24
1988	*Cleveland 28, Houston 23
1989	Cleveland 23, Minnesota 17 (OT)
1990	Cleveland 13, Atlanta 10
1991	Houston 17, Cleveland 14
1992	Houston 17, Cleveland 14
1993	New England 20, Cleveland 17
1994	*Cleveland 35, Seattle 9
1995	Cleveland 26, Cincinnati 10
1999	*Indianapolis 29, Cleveland 28
2000	*Tennessee 24, Cleveland 0
2001	Jacksonville 15, Cleveland 10

*Cleveland 19, Pittsburgh 13
Miami 38, Cleveland 31
*Cleveland 24, Houston 20
*Cincinnati 21, Cleveland 14
*Pittsburgh 17, Cleveland 10
*Pittsburgh 23, Cleveland 13
*Pittsburgh 16, Cleveland 9
Pittsburgh 17, Cleveland 7
*Jacksonville 24, Cleveland 21
Cincinnati 44, Cleveland 28
Jacksonville 48, Cleveland 0
*Pittsburgh 28, Cleveland 7

Official Finales - 26-26-1 (.500)
Official Home Finales - 5-4 (.556)
Official Away Finales - 21-22-1 (.489)
Home Finales - 37-15-1 (.708)
Away Finales - 25-27-1 (.481)

OPENERS

* Denotes official opener

YEAR	HOME	AWAY
1946	*Cleveland 44, Miami 0	Cleveland 20, Chicago 6
1947	*Cleveland 30, Buffalo 14	Cleveland 55, Brooklyn 7
1948	*Cleveland 19, Los Angeles 14	Cleveland 42, Buffalo 13
1949	Cleveland 21, Baltimore 0	*Buffalo 28, Cleveland 28
1950	New York Giants 6, Cleveland 0	*Cleveland 35, Philadelphia 10
1951	Cleveland 45, Washington 0	*San Francisco 24, Cleveland 10
1952	*Cleveland 37, Los Angeles 7	Cleveland 21, Pittsburgh 20
1953	Cleveland 37, Philadelphia 13	*Cleveland 27, Green Bay 0
1954	Cleveland 31, Chicago Cardinals 7	*Philadelphia 28, Cleveland 10
1955	*Washington 27, Cleveland 17	Cleveland 38, San Francisco 3
1956	New York 21, Cleveland 9	*Chicago Cardinals 9, Cleveland 7
1957	*New York 6, Cleveland 3	Cleveland 23, Pittsburgh 12
1958	Cleveland 35, Chicago Cardinals 28	*Cleveland 30, Los Angeles 27
1959	New York 10, Cleveland 6	*Pittsburgh 17, Cleveland 7
1960	Cleveland 28, Pittsburgh 20	*Cleveland 41, Philadelphia 24
1961	Cleveland 20, St. Louis 17	*Philadelphia 27, Cleveland 20
1962	*Cleveland 17, New York 7	Philadelphia 35, Cleveland 7
1963	*Cleveland 37, Washington 14	Cleveland 41, Dallas 24
1964	Cleveland 33, St. Louis 33	*Cleveland 27, Washington 13
1965	St. Louis 49, Cleveland 13	*Cleveland 17, Washington 7
1966	Green Bay 21, Cleveland 20	*Cleveland 36, Washington 14
1967	*Dallas 21, Cleveland 14	Detroit 31, Cleveland 14
1968	Los Angeles 24, Cleveland 6	*Cleveland 24, New Orleans 10
1969	Cleveland 27, Washington 23	*Cleveland 27, Philadelphia 20
1970	*Cleveland 31, New York Jets 21	San Francisco 34, Cleveland 31
1971	*Cleveland 31, Houston 0	Cleveland 14, Baltimore 13
1972	*Green Bay 26, Cleveland 10	Cleveland 27, Philadelphia 17
1973	*Cleveland 24, Baltimore 14	Pittsburgh 33, Cleveland 6
1974	Cleveland 20, Houston 7	*Cincinnati 33, Cleveland 7
1975	Minnesota 42, Cleveland 10	*Cincinnati 24, Cleveland 17
1976	*Cleveland 38, New York Jets 17	Pittsburgh 31, Cleveland 14
1977	Cleveland 30, New England 27 (OT)	*Cleveland 13, Cincinnati 3
1978	*Cleveland 24, San Francisco 7	Cleveland 24, Atlanta 16
1979	Cleveland 13, Baltimore 10	*Cleveland 25, New York Jets 22 (OT)
1980	Houston 16, Cleveland 7	*New England 34, Cleveland 17
1981	*San Diego 44, Cleveland 14	Cleveland 20, Cincinnati 17
1982	Philadelphia 24, Cleveland 21	*Cleveland 21, Seattle 7
1983	*Minnesota 27, Cleveland 21	Cleveland 31, Detroit 26
1984	Denver 24, Cleveland 14	*Seattle 33, Cleveland 0

OPENERS (CONTD.)

1985	*St. Louis 27, Cleveland 24 (OT)	Dallas 20, Cleveland 7
1986	Cincinnati 30, Cleveland 13	*Chicago 41, Cleveland 31
1987	Cleveland 34, Pittsburgh 10	*New Orleans 28, Cleveland 21
1988	New York Jets 23, Cleveland 3	*Cleveland 6, Kansas City 3
1989	Cleveland 38, New York Jets 24	*Cleveland 51, Pittsburgh 0
1990	*Cleveland 13, Pittsburgh 3	New York Jets 24, Cleveland 21
1991	*Dallas 26, Cleveland 14	Cleveland 20, New England 0
1992	Miami 27, Cleveland 23	*Indianapolis 14, Cleveland 3
1993	*Cleveland 27, Cincinnati 14	Cleveland 19, L.A. Raiders 16
1994	Pittsburgh 17, Cleveland 10	*Cleveland 28, Cincinnati 20
1995	Cleveland 22, Tampa Bay 6	*New England 17, Cleveland 14
1999	*Pittsburgh 43, Cleveland 0	Tennessee 26, Cleveland 9
2000	*Jacksonville 27, Cleveland 7	Cleveland 24, Cincinnati 7
2001	*Seattle 9, Cleveland 6	Cleveland 23, Jacksonville 14

Official Openers - 28-24-1 (.538)
Official Home Openers - 13-11 (.542)
Official Away Openers - 15-13-1 (.534)
Home Openers - 27-25-1 (.519)
Away Openers - 31-21-1 (.594)

GAMES IN WHICH BOTH TEAMS SCORED FEWER THAN 10 POINTS

* Denotes postseason

Cleveland 7, New York 0   (Oct. 12, 1946, at New York)
Cleveland 7, Buffalo 7   (Nov. 13, 1949, at Cleveland)
New York Giants 6, Cleveland 0   (Oct. 1, 1950, at Cleveland)
*Cleveland 8, New York Giants 3   (Dec. 17, 1950, at Cleveland)
Cleveland 7, New York 0   (Oct. 25, 1953, at New York)
Cleveland 6, Philadelphia 0   (Nov. 21, 1954, at Cleveland)
Chicago Cardinals 9, Cleveland 7   (Sept. 30, 1956, at Chicago)
Cleveland 6, New York 3   (Sept. 29, 1957, at Cleveland)
New York 7, Cleveland 7   (Dec. 17, 1961, at New York)
Pittsburgh 9, Cleveland 7   (Nov. 10, 1963, at Pittsburgh)
Dallas 6, Cleveland 2   (Dec. 12, 1970, at Cleveland)
Cleveland 7, Oakland 3   (Nov. 18, 1973, at Oakland)
Cleveland 7, San Francisco 0   (Dec. 1, 1974, at Cleveland)
Los Angeles 9, Cleveland 0   (Nov. 27, 1977, at Cleveland)
Houston 9, Cleveland 3   (Sept. 13, 1981, at Cleveland)
Indianapolis 9, Cleveland 7   (Dec. 6, 1987, at Cleveland)
Cleveland 6, Kansas City 3   (Sept. 4, 1988, at Kansas City)
Seattle 9, Cleveland 6   (Sept. 9, 2001, at Cleveland)

Overall Regular Season - 7-8-2 (.471)
Home Regular Season - 3-6-1 (.350)
Away Regular Season - 4-2-1 (.643)
Postseason - 1-0 (1.000)

HIGHEST-SCORING GAMES

TEN BY THE BROWNS

1. 66 - Cleveland 66, Brooklyn 14   (Dec. 8, 1946, at Brooklyn)
2. 62 - Cleveland 62, New York 14   (Dec. 6, 1953, at Cleveland)
   Cleveland 62, Washington 3   (Nov. 7, 1954, at Cleveland)
4. 61 - Cleveland 61, Los Angeles 14   (Oct. 14, 1949, at Los Anegles)
5. 55 - Cleveland 55, Brooklyn 7   (Sept. 12, 1947, at Brooklyn)
6. 52 - Cleveland 52, New York 20   (Dec. 12, 1964, at New York)
7. 51 - Cleveland 51, Chicago 14   (Nov. 17, 1946, at Cleveland)
   Cleveland 51, Pittsburgh 0   (Sept. 10, 1989, at Pittsburgh)
9. 49 - Cleveland 49, Chicago Cardinals 28   (Dec. 2, 1951, at Cleveland)
   Cleveland 49, Philadelphia 7   (Oct. 19, 1952, at Philadelphia)
   Cleveland 49, Atlanta 17   (Oct. 30, 1966, at Atlanta)
   Cleveland 49, New York 40   (Dec. 4, 1966, at Cleveland)

TEN BY BROWNS OPPONENTS

1. 58 - Houston 58, Cleveland 14	(Dec. 9, 1990, at Houston)
2. 56 - San Francisco 56, Cleveland 28	(Oct. 9, 1949, at San Francisco
3. 55 - Pittsburgh 55, Cleveland 27	(Oct. 17, 1954, at Pittsburgh)
Green Bay 55, Cleveland 7	(Nov. 12, 1967, at Green Bay)
5. 51 - Minnesota 51, Cleveland 3	(Nov. 9, 1969, at Minnesota)
Pittsburgh 51, Cleveland 35	(Oct. 7, 1979, at Cleveland)
7. 49 - Green Bay 49, Cleveland 17	(Oct. 15, 1961, at Cleveland)
St. Louis 49, Cleveland 13	(Sept. 26, 1965, at Cleveland)
9. 48 - New York 48, Cleveland 7	(Dec. 6, 1959, at New York)
Cincinnati 48, Cleveland 16	(Dec. 17, 1978, at Cincinnati)
Jacksonville 48, Cleveland 0	(Dec. 3, 2000, at Jacksonville)

TEN BETWEEN BOTH TEAMS

1. 89 - Cleveland 49, New York 40	(Dec. 4, 1966, at Cleveland)
2. 86 - Pittsburgh 51, Cleveland 35	(Oct. 7, 1979, at Cleveland)
3. 84 - San Francisco 56, Cleveland 28	(Oct. 9, 1949, at San Francisco)
4. 82 - Pittsburgh 55, Cleveland 27	(Oct. 17, 1954, at Pittsburgh)
Cleveland 48, New York 34	(Dec. 18, 1960, at New York)
6. 80 - Cleveland 66, Brooklyn 14	(Dec. 8, 1946, at Brooklyn)
7. 79 - Cleveland 42, Washington 37	(Nov. 26, 1967, at Cleveland)
Cleveland 41, Tennessee 38	(Dec. 30, 2001, at Tennessee)
9. 77 - Cleveland 49, Chicago Cardinals 28	(Dec. 2, 1951, at Cleveland)
10. 76 - Cleveland 62, New York 14	(Dec. 6, 1953, at Cleveland)
Cleveland 45, Los Angeles 31	(Nov. 24, 1957, at Cleveland)

HIGHEST-SCORING GAMES (POSTSEASON)

FIVE BY THE BROWNS

1. 56 - Cleveland 56, Detroit 10	(NFL Championship, Dec. 26, 1954, at Cleveland)
2. 49 - Cleveland 49, Buffalo 7	(AAFC Championship, Dec. 19, 1948, at Cleveland)
3. 38 - Cleveland 38, Los Angeles 14	(NFL Championship, Dec. 26, 1955, at Los Angeles)
Cleveland 38, Dallas 14	(Eastern Conference Championship, Dec. 28, 1969, at Dallas)
Cleveland 38, Indianapolis 21	(AFC Divisional Playoff, Jan. 9, 1988, at Cleveland)

FIVE BY BROWNS OPPONENTS

1. 59 - Detroit 59, Cleveland 14 (NFL Championship, Dec. 29, 1957, at Detroit)
2. 52 - Dallas 52, Cleveland 14   (Eastern Conference Championship, Dec. 24, 1967, at Dal.)
3. 38 - Denver 38, Cleveland 33 (AFC Championship, Jan. 17, 1988, at Denver)
4. 37 - Denver 37, Cleveland 21 (AFC Championship, Jan. 14, 1990, at Denver)
5. 34 - Baltimore 34, Cleveland 0 (NFL Championship, Dec. 29, 1968, at Cleveland)

FIVE BETWEEN BOTH TEAMS

1. 73 - Detroit 59, Cleveland 14 (NFL Championship, Dec. 29, 1957, at Detroit)
2. 71 - Denver 38, Cleveland 33 (AFC Championship, Jan. 17, 1988, at Denver)
3. 66 - Cleveland 56, Detroit 10 (NFL Championship, Dec. 26, 1954, at Cleveland)
       Dallas 52, Cleveland 14   (Eastern Conference Championship, Dec. 24, 1967, at Dal.)
5. 64 - Cleveland 34, Buffalo 30 (AFC Divisional Playoff, Jan. 6, 1990, at Cleveland)

HOME WON-LOST-TIED RECORDS

YEAR	WON	LOST	TIED	PCT.
1946	6	1	0	.857
1947	6	1	0	.857
1948	7	0	0	1.000
1949	5	0	1	.917
1950	5	1	0	.833
1951	6	0	0	1.000
1952	4	2	0	.667
1953	6	0	0	1.000
1954	5	1	0	.833
1955	5	1	0	.833
1956	1	5	0	.167
1957	6	0	0	1.000
1958	4	2	0	.667
1959	3	3	0	.500
1960	4	2	0	.667
1961	4	3	0	.571
1962	4	2	1	.643
1963	5	2	0	.714
1964	5	1	1	.786
1965	5	2	0	.714
1966	5	2	0	.714
1967	6	1	0	.857
1968	5	2	0	.714
1969	5	1	1	.786
1970	4	3	0	.571
1971	4	3	0	.571
1972	4	3	0	.571
1973	5	1	1	.786
1974	3	4	0	.429
1975	3	4	0	.429
1976	6	1	0	.857
1977	2	5	0	.286
1978	5	3	0	.625
1979	5	3	0	.625
1980	6	2	0	.750
1981	3	5	0	.375
1982	2	2	0	.500
1983	6	2	0	.750
1984	2	6	0	.250
1985	5	3	0	.625
1986	6	2	0	.750
1987	5	2	0	.714
1988	6	2	0	.750
1989	5	2	1	.688
1990	2	6	0	.250
1991	3	5	0	.375
1992	4	4	0	.500
1993	4	4	0	.500
1994	6	2	0	.750
1995	3	5	0	.375
1999	0	8	0	.000
2000	2	6	0	.250
2001	4	4	0	.500
TOTAL	**232**	**137**	**6**	**.627**

ROAD WON-LOST-TIED RECORDS

Year	Won	Lost	Tied	Pct.
1946	6	1	0	.857
1947	6	0	1	.929
1948	7	0	0	1.000
1949	4	1	1	.750
1950	5	1	0	.833
1951	5	1	0	.833
1952	4	2	0	.667
1953	5	1	0	.833
1954	4	2	0	.667
1955	4	1	1	.750
1956	4	2	0	.667
1957	3	2	1	.583
1958	5	1	0	.833
1959	4	2	0	.667
1960	4	1	1	.750
1961	4	2	1	.643
1962	3	4	0	.429
1963	5	2	0	.714
1964	5	2	0	.714
1965	6	1	0	.857
1966	4	3	0	.571
1967	3	4	0	.429
1968	5	2	0	.714
1969	5	2	0	.714
1970	3	4	0	.429
1971	5	2	0	.714
1972	6	1	0	.857
1973	2	4	1	.357
1974	1	6	0	.143
1975	0	7	0	.000
1976	3	4	0	.429
1977	4	3	0	.571
1978	3	5	0	.375
1979	4	4	0	.500
1980	5	3	0	.625
1981	2	6	0	.250
1982	2	3	0	.400
1983	3	5	0	.375
1984	3	5	0	.375
1985	3	5	0	.375
1986	6	2	0	.750
1987	5	3	0	.625
1988	4	4	0	.500
1989	4	4	0	.500
1990	1	7	0	.125
1991	3	5	0	.375
1992	3	5	0	.375
1993	3	5	0	.375
1994	5	3	0	.625
1995	2	6	0	.250
1999	2	6	0	.125
2000	1	7	0	.375
2001	3	5	0	.542
Total	**201**	**169**	**7**	**.533**

LOWEST-SCORING GAMES BETWEEN BOTH TEAMS

1. 6 - New York Giants 6, Cleveland 0 — (Oct. 1, 1950, at Cleveland)
          Cleveland 6, Philadelphia 0 — (Nov. 21, 1954, at Cleveland)
3. 7 - Cleveland 7, New York 0 — (Oct. 12, 1946, at New York)
          Cleveland 7, New York 0 — (Oct. 25, 1953, at New York)
          Cleveland 7, San Francisco 0 — (Dec. 1, 1974, at Cleveland)
6. 8 - Dallas 6, Cleveland 2 — (Dec. 12, 1970, at Cleveland)
7. 9 - Cleveland 6, New York 3 — (Sept. 29, 1957, at Cleveland)
          Los Angeles 9, Cleveland 0 — (Nov. 27, 1977, at Cleveland)
          Cleveland 6, Kansas City 3 — (Sept. 4, 1988, at Kansas City)
10. 10 - Cleveland 10, New York Giants 0 — (Nov. 18, 1951, at New York)
          Cleveland 10, Chicago Cardinals 0 — (Dec. 7, 1952, at Chicago)
          Cleveland 7, Oakland 3 — (Nov. 18, 1973, at Oakland)

LOWEST-SCORING GAMES (POSTSEASON)

FIVE BY THE BROWNS

1. 0 - New York 10, Cleveland 0 — (Eastern Conference Playoff, Dec. 21, 1958, at New York)
        Baltimore 34, Cleveland 0 — (NFL Championship, Dec. 29, 1968, at Cleveland)
3. 3 - Baltimore 20, Cleveland 3 — (AFC Divisional Playoff, Dec. 26, 1971, at Cleveland)
4. 7 - Detroit 17, Cleveland 7 — (NFL Championship, Dec. 28, 1952, at Cleveland)
        Minnesota 27, Cleveland 7 — (NFL Championship, Jan. 4, 1970, at Minnesota)

FIVE BY BROWNS OPPONENTS

1. 0 - Cleveland 27, Baltimore 0 — (NFL Championship, Dec. 27, 1964, at Cleveland)
2. 3 - Cleveland 14, New York 3 — (AAFC Championship, Dec. 14, 1947, at New York)
        Cleveland 8, New York Giants 3 — (American Conference Playoff, Dec. 17, 1950, at Cleveland)
4. 7 - Cleveland 49, Buffalo 7 — (AAFC Championship, Dec. 19, 1948, at Cleveland)
        Cleveland 21, San Francisco 7 — (AAFC Championship, Dec. 11, 1949, at Cleveland)

FIVE BETWEEN BOTH TEAMS

1.10 - New York 10, Cleveland 0 — (Eastern Conference Playoff, Dec. 21, 1958, at New York)
2. 11 - Cleveland 8, New York Giants 3 — (American Conference Playoff, Dec. 17, 1950, at Cleveland)
3. 17 - Cleveland 14, New York 3 — (AAFC Championship, Dec. 14, 1947, at New York)
4. 23 - Cleveland 14, New York 9 — (AAFC Championship, Dec. 22, 1946, at Cleveland)
        Baltimore 20, Cleveland 3 — (AFC Divisional Playoff, Dec. 26, 1971, at Cleveland)

MOST ONE-SIDED GAMES

TEN VICTORIES

1. 59 - Cleveland 62, Washington 3   (Nov. 7, 1954, at Cleveland)
2. 52 - Cleveland 66, Brooklyn 14   (Dec. 8, 1946, at Brooklyn)
3. 51 - Cleveland 51, Pittsburgh 0   (Sept. 10, 1989, at Pittsburgh)
4. 48 - Cleveland 55, Brooklyn 7   (Sept. 12, 1947, at Brooklyn)
       Cleveland 62, New York 14   (Dec. 6, 1953, at Cleveland)
6. 47 - Cleveland 61, Los Angeles 14   (Oct. 14, 1949, at Los Angeles)
7. 45 - Cleveland 45, Washington 0   (Oct. 14, 1951, at Cleveland)
8. 44 - Cleveland 44, Miami 0   (Sept. 6, 1946, at Cleveland)
9. 42 - Cleveland 42, Baltimore 0   (Dec. 7, 1947, at Baltimore)
       Cleveland 49, Philadelphia 7   (Oct. 19, 1952, at Philadelphia)
       Cleveland 42, Chicago 0   (Dec. 11, 1960, at Cleveland)

TEN DEFEATS

1. 48 - Green Bay 55, Cleveland 7   (Nov. 12, 1967, at Green Bay)
       Minnesota 51, Cleveland 3   (Nov. 9, 1969, at Minnesota)
       Jacksonville 48, Cleveland 0   (Dec. 3, 2000, at Jacksonville.)
4. 44 - Houston 58, Cleveland 14   (Dec. 9, 1990, at Houston)
5. 43 - Pittsburgh 43, Cleveland 0   (Sept. 12, 1999, at Cleveland)
6. 42 - Buffalo 42, Cleveland 0   (Nov. 4, 1990, at Cleveland)
7. 41 - New York 48, Cleveland 7   (Dec. 6, 1959, at New York)
8. 37 - Baltimore 44, Cleveland 7   (Nov. 26, 2000, at Baltimore)
9. 36 - St. Louis 49, Cleveland 13   (Sept. 26, 1965, at Cleveland)
       Pittsburgh 42, Cleveland 6   (Oct. 5, 1975, at Cleveland)

MOST ONE-SIDED GAMES (POSTSEASON)

FIVE VICTORIES

1. 46 - Cleveland 56, Detroit 10   (NFL Championship, Dec. 26, 1954, at Cleveland)
2. 42 - Cleveland 49, Buffalo 7   (AAFC Championship, Dec. 19, 1948, at Cleveland)
3. 27 - Cleveland 27, Baltimore 0 (NFL Championship, Dec. 27, 1964, at Cleveland)
4. 24 - Cleveland 38, Los Angeles 14 (NFL Championship, Dec. 26, 1955, at Los Angeles)
       Cleveland 38, Dallas 14   (Eastern Conference Championship, Dec. 28, 1969, at Dal.)

FIVE DEFEATS

1. 45 - Detroit 59, Cleveland 14   (NFL Championship, Dec. 29, 1957, at Detroit)
2. 38 - Dallas 52, Cleveland 14   (Eastern Conference Championship, Dec. 24, 1967, at Dallas)
3. 34 - Baltimore 34, Cleveland 0 (NFL Championship, Dec. 29, 1968, at Cleveland)
4. 20 - Minnesota 27, Cleveland 7 (NFL Championship, Jan. 4, 1970, at Minnesota)
       Pittsburgh 29, Cleveland 9 (AFC Divisional Playoff, Jan. 7, 1995, at Pittsburgh)

POSTSEASON

Cleveland 14, New York 9	(AAFC Championship, Dec. 22, 1946, at Cleveland)
Cleveland 14, New York 3	(AAFC Championship, Dec. 14, 1947, at New York)
Cleveland 49, Buffalo 7	(AAFC Championship, Dec. 19, 1948, at Cleveland)
Cleveland 31, Buffalo 21	(AAFC First-Round Playoff, Dec. 4, 1949, at Cleveland)
Cleveland 21, San Francisco 7	(AAFC Championship, Dec. 11, 1949, at Cleveland)
Cleveland 8, New York Giants 3	(American Conference Playoff, Dec. 17, 1950, at Cleveland)
Cleveland 30, Los Angeles 28	(NFL Championship, Dec. 24, 1950, at Cleveland)
Los Angeles 24, Cleveland 17	(NFL Championship, Dec. 23, 1951, at Los Angeles)
Detroit 17, Cleveland 7	(NFL Championship, Dec. 28, 1952, at Cleveland)
Detroit 17, Cleveland 16	(NFL Championship, Dec. 27, 1953, at Detroit)
Cleveland 56, Detroit 10	(NFL Championship, Dec. 26, 1954, at Cleveland)
Cleveland 38, Los Angeles 14	(NFL Championship, Dec. 26, 1955, at Los Angeles)
Detroit 59, Cleveland 14	(NFL Championship, Dec. 29, 1957, at Detroit)
New York 10, Cleveland 0	(Eastern Conference Playoff, Dec. 21, 1958, at New York)
Cleveland 27, Baltimore 0	(NFL Championship, Dec. 27, 1964, at Cleveland)
Green Bay 23, Cleveland 12	(NFL Championship, Jan. 2, 1966, at Green Bay)
Dallas 52, Cleveland 14	(Eastern Conference Championship, Dec. 24, 1967, at Dallas)
Cleveland 31, Dallas 20	(Eastern Conference Championship, Dec. 21, 1968, at Cleveland)
Baltimore 34, Cleveland 0	(NFL Championship, Dec. 29, 1968, at Cleveland)
Cleveland 38, Dallas 14	(Eastern Conference Championship, Dec. 28, 1969, at Dallas)
Minnesota 27, Cleveland 7	(NFL Championship, Jan. 4, 1970, at Minnesota)
Baltimore 20, Cleveland 3	(AFC Divisional Playoff, Dec. 26, 1971, at Cleveland)
Miami 20, Cleveland 14	(AFC Divisional Playoff, Dec. 24, 1972, at Miami)
Oakland 14, Cleveland 12	(AFC Divisional Playoff, Jan. 4, 1981, at Cleveland)
L.A. Raiders 27, Cleveland 10	(AFC First-Round, Jan. 8, 1983, at Los Angeles)
Miami 24, Cleveland 21	(AFC Divisional Playoff, Jan. 4, 1986, at Miami)
Cleveland 23, New York Jets 20 (2OT)	(AFC Divisional Playoff, Jan. 3, 1987, at Cleveland)
Denver 23, Cleveland 20 (OT)	(AFC Championship, Jan. 11, 1987, at Cleveland)
Cleveland 38, Indianapolis 21	(AFC Divisional Playoff, Jan. 9, 1988, at Cleveland)
Denver 38, Cleveland 33	(AFC Championship, Jan. 17, 1988, at Denver)
Houston 24, Cleveland 23	(AFC Wild Card, Dec. 24, 1988, at Cleveland)
Cleveland 34, Buffalo 30	(AFC Divisional Playoff, Jan. 6, 1990, at Cleveland)
Denver 37, Cleveland 21	(AFC Championship, Jan. 14, 1990, at Denver)
Cleveland 20, New England 13	(AFC Wild Card, Jan. 1, 1995, at Cleveland)
Pittsburgh 29, Cleveland 9	(AFC Divisional Playoff, Jan. 7, 1995, at Pittsburgh)

Overall - 16-19 (.457)   Home - 13-6 (.684)   Away - 3-13 (.188)

POSTSEASON GAMES THE BROWNS LOST AND WHO THEY WOULD HAVE PLAYED HAD THEY WON

(NFL Championship games are not included since there would not have been an opponent the next week.)

New York 10, Cleveland 0 (Eastern Conference Playoff, Dec. 21, 1958, at New York). Had the Browns won . . . vs. Baltimore in the NFL Championship at home

Dallas 52, Cleveland 14 (Eastern Conference Championship, Dec. 24, 1967, at Dallas). Had the Browns won . . . at Green Bay in the NFL Championship

Baltimore 34, Cleveland 0 (NFL Championship, Dec. 29, 1968, at Cleveland). Had the Browns won . . . vs. New York Jets in Super Bowl III in Miami

Minnesota 27, Cleveland 7 (NFL Championship, Jan. 4, 1970, at Minnesota). Had the Browns won . . . vs. Kansas City in Super Bowl IV in New Orleans

Baltimore 20, Cleveland 3 (AFC Divisional Playoff, Dec. 26, 1971, at Cleveland). Had the Browns won . . . vs. Miami in the AFC Championship at home

Miami 20, Cleveland 14 (AFC Divisional Playoff, Dec. 24, 1972, at Miami). Had the Browns won . . . at Pittsburgh in the AFC Championship

Oakland 14, Cleveland 12 (AFC Divisional Playoff, Jan. 4, 1981, at Cleveland). Had the Browns won . . . at San Diego in the AFC Championship

Los Angeles Raiders 27, Cleveland 10 (AFC First Round, Jan. 8, 1983, at Los Angeles). Had the Browns won . . . at Miami in an AFC second-round playoff

Miami 24, Cleveland 21 (AFC Divisional Playoff, Jan. 4, 1986, at Miami). Had the Browns won . . . vs. New England in the AFC Championship at home

Denver 23, Cleveland 20 (OT) (AFC Championship, Jan. 11, 1987, at Cleveland). Had the Browns won . . . vs. New York Giants in Super Bowl XXI in Pasadena, California

Denver 38, Cleveland 33 (AFC Championship, Jan. 17, 1988, at Denver). Had the Browns won . . . vs. Washington in Super Bowl XXII in San Diego

Houston 24, Cleveland 23 (AFC Wild Card, Dec. 24, 1988, at Cleveland). Had the Browns won . . . at Buffalo in an AFC divisional playoff

Denver 37, Cleveland 21 (AFC Championship, Jan. 14, 1990, at Denver). Had the Browns won . . . vs. San Francisco in Super Bowl XXIV in New Orleans

Pittsburgh 29, Cleveland 9 (AFC Divisional Playoff, Jan. 7, 1995, at Pittsburgh). Had the Browns won . . . at San Diego in the AFC Championship

DOME RECORD

Cleveland 21, Houston 10 (Dec. 7, 1970)
Cleveland 37, Houston 24 (Nov. 28, 1971)
Cleveland 23, Houston 17 (Oct. 22, 1972)
Cleveland 23, Houston 13 (Nov. 11, 1973)
Houston 28, Cleveland 24 (Dec. 15, 1974)
Detroit 21, Cleveland 10   (Nov. 9, 1975)
Houston 21, Cleveland 10 (Dec. 21, 1975)
Cleveland 21, Houston 7   (Nov. 7, 1976)
Cleveland 24, Houston 23 (Oct. 16, 1977)
Seattle 20, Cleveland 19   (Dec. 18, 1977)
Cleveland 24, New Orleans 16 (Oct. 8, 1978)
Houston 14, Cleveland 10 (Nov. 5, 1978)
Seattle 47, Cleveland 24   (Dec. 3, 1978)
Houston 31, Cleveland 10 (Sept. 30, 1979)
Cleveland 27, Seattle 3   (Oct. 12, 1980)
Cleveland 17, Houston 14 (Nov. 30, 1980)
Houston 17, Cleveland 13 (Dec. 3, 1981)
Seattle 42, Cleveland 21   (Dec. 20, 1981)
Cleveland 21, Seattle 7   (Sept. 12, 1982)
Cleveland 20, Houston 14 (Dec. 26, 1982)
Cleveland 31, Detroit 26   (Sept. 11, 1983)
Houston 34, Cleveland 27 (Dec. 11, 1983)
Seattle 33, Cleveland 0   (Sept. 3, 1984)
Cleveland 27, Houston 20 (Dec. 16, 1984)
Cleveland 21, Houston 6   (Oct. 13, 1985)
Seattle 31, Cleveland 13   (Dec. 8, 1985)
Cleveland 24, Houston 20 (Sept. 14, 1986)
Cleveland 23, Minnesota 20 (Oct. 26, 1986)

Cleveland 24, Indianapolis 9 (Nov. 2, 1986)
New Orleans 28, Cleveland 21 (Sept. 13, 1987)
Cleveland 40, Houston 7   (Nov. 22, 1987)
Houston 24, Cleveland 17 (Nov. 7, 1988)
Cleveland 17, Seattle 7   (Nov. 12, 1989)
Detroit 13, Cleveland 10   (Nov. 23, 1989)
Indianapolis 23, Cleveland 17 (OT) (Dec. 10, 1989)
Cleveland 24, Houston 20 (Dec. 23, 1989)
New Orleans 25, Cleveland 20 (Oct. 14, 1990)
Houston 58, Cleveland 14 (Dec. 9, 1990)
Houston 28, Cleveland 24 (Nov. 17, 1991)
Cleveland 31, Indianapolis 0(Dec. 1, 1991)
Indianapolis 14, Cleveland 3 (Sept. 6, 1992)
Cleveland 24, Houston 14 (Nov. 8, 1992)
Minnesota 17, Cleveland 13 (Nov. 22, 1992)
Detroit 24, Cleveland 14   (Dec. 13, 1992)
Indianapolis 23, Cleveland 10 (Sept. 26, 1993)
Seattle 22, Cleveland 5   (Nov. 14, 1993)
Atlanta 17, Cleveland 14   (Nov. 28, 1993)
Houston 19, Cleveland 17 (Dec. 12, 1993)
Cleveland 21, Indianapolis 14 (Sept. 25, 1994)
Cleveland 11, Houston 8   (Oct. 13, 1994)
Cleveland 14, Houston 7   (Sept. 17, 1995)
Detroit 38, Cleveland 20   (Oct. 8, 1995)
Minnesota 27, Cleveland 11 (Dec. 9, 1995)
St. Louis 34, Cleveland 3   (Oct. 24, 1999)
Cleveland 21, New Orleans 16 (Oct. 31, 1999)

Overall - 26-29 (.473)

SHUTOUTS

* Denotes postseason

Cleveland 44, Miami 0	(Sept. 6, 1946, at Cleveland)
Cleveland 28, Buffalo 0	(Sept. 22, 1946, at Buffalo)
Cleveland 7, New York 0	(Oct. 12, 1946, at New York)
Cleveland 34, Miami 0	(Dec. 3, 1946, at Miami)
Cleveland 28, Baltimore 0	(Sept. 21, 1947, at Cleveland)
Cleveland 42, Baltimore 0	(Dec. 7, 1947, at Baltimore)
Cleveland 21, Baltimore 0	(Sept. 11, 1949, at Cleveland)
Cleveland 31, Brooklyn-New York 0	(Nov. 20, 1949, at Brooklyn-New York)
Cleveland 31, Baltimore 0	(Sept. 24, 1950, at Baltimore.)
New York Giants 6, Cleveland 0	(Oct. 1, 1950, at Cleveland)
Cleveland 45, Washington 0	(Oct. 14, 1951, at Cleveland)
Cleveland 17, Pittsburgh 0	(Oct. 21, 1951, at Cleveland)
Cleveland 10, New York Giants 0	(Nov. 18, 1951, at New York)
Cleveland 28, Pittsburgh 0	(Dec. 9, 1951, at Pittsburgh)
Cleveland 10, Chicago Cardinals 0	(Dec. 7, 1952, at Chicago)
Cleveland 27, Green Bay 0	(Sept. 27, 1953, at Green Bay)
Cleveland 7, New York 0	(Oct. 25, 1953, at New York)
Cleveland 6, Philadelphia 0	(Nov. 21, 1954, at Cleveland)
Cleveland 16, Philadelphia 0	(Nov. 18, 1956, at Philadelphia)
Cleveland 24, Pittsburgh 0	(Nov. 10, 1957, at Cleveland)
Cleveland 31, Chicago Cardinals 0	(Dec. 1, 1957, at Cleveland)
*New York 10, Cleveland 0	(Dec. 21, 1958, at New York)
Cleveland 42, Chicago 0	(Dec. 11, 1960, at Cleveland)
*Cleveland 27, Baltimore 0	(Dec. 27, 1964, at Cleveland)
Cleveland 24, Chicago 0	(Oct. 22, 1967, at Cleveland)
*Baltimore 34, Cleveland 0	(Dec. 29, 1968, at Cleveland)
Cleveland 28, Miami 0	(Oct. 25, 1970, at Miami)
Cleveland 31, Houston 0	(Sept. 19, 1971, at Cleveland)
Denver 27, Cleveland 0	(Oct. 24, 1971, at Cleveland)
Chicago 17, Cleveland 0	(Oct. 15, 1972, at Cleveland)
Pittsburgh 30, Cleveland 0	(Dec. 3, 1972, at Pittsburgh)
Cleveland 20, Houston 0	(Nov. 5, 1972, at Cleveland)
Cleveland 7, San Francisco 0	(Dec. 1, 1974, at Cleveland)
Los Angeles 9, Cleveland 0	(Nov. 27, 1977, at Cleveland)
Cleveland 20, Tampa Bay 0	(Nov. 13, 1983, at Cleveland)
Cleveland 30, New England 0	(Nov. 20, 1983, at New England)
Seattle 33, Cleveland 0	(Sept. 3, 1984, at Seattle)
Cleveland 34, Cincinnati 0	(Oct. 18, 1987, at Cincinnati)
Cleveland 51, Pittsburgh 0	(Sept. 10, 1989, at Pittsburgh)
Cincinnati 21, Cleveland 0	(Dec. 3, 1989, at Cleveland)
Kansas City 34, Cleveland 0	(Sept. 30, 1990, at Kansas City)
Buffalo 42, Cleveland 0	(Nov. 4, 1990, at Cleveland)

Pittsburgh 35, Cleveland 0   (Dec. 23, 1990, at Pittsburgh)
Cleveland 20, New England 0   (Sept. 8, 1991, at New England)
Cleveland 31, Indianapolis 0   (Dec. 1, 1991, at Indianapolis)
Denver 12, Cleveland 0   (Sept. 27, 1992, at Cleveland)
Cleveland 32, Arizona 0   (Sept. 18, 1994, at Cleveland)
Pittsburgh 43, Cleveland 0   (Sept. 12, 1999, at Cleveland)
Baltimore 12, Cleveland 0   (Oct. 1, 2000, at Cleveland)
Pittsburgh 22, Cleveland 0   (Oct. 22, 2000, at Pittsburgh)
Jacksonville 48, Cleveland 0   (Dec. 3, 2000, at Jacksonville)
Cleveland 18, Cincinnati 0   (Nov. 25, 2001, at Cleveland)

Overall Regular Season - 34-15 (.694)
Home Regular Season - 16-9 (.640)
Away Regular Season - 18-6 (.750)
Postseason - 1-2 (.333)

STREAKS

FIVE LONGEST WINNING IN A SEASON

1. 14 games in a row—Sept. 3 to Dec. 5, 1948 (0-0 to 14-0)
2. 11 games in a row—Oct. 7-Dec. 16, 1951 (0-1 to 11-1)
             Sept. 27-Dec. 6, 1953 (0-0 to 11-0)
4. 8 games in a row—Oct. 24-Dec. 12, 1954 (1-2 to 9-2)
             Oct. 20-Dec. 8, 1968 (2-3 to 10-3)

FIVE LONGEST LOSING IN A SEASON

1. 9 games in a row—Sept. 21-Nov. 16, 1975 (0-0 to 0-9)
2. 8 games in a row—Oct. 14-Dec. 9, 1990 (2-3 to 2-11)
3. 7 games in a row—Sept. 12-Oct. 24, 1999 (0-0 to 0-7)
             Sept. 24-Nov. 5, 2000 (2-1 to 2-8)
5. 6 games in a row—Nov. 5-Dec. 9, 1995 (4-4 to 4-10)
             Nov. 21-Dec. 26, 1999 (2-8 to 2-14)

FIVE LONGEST WINNING TO START A SEASON

1. 14 games in a row—Sept. 3-Dec. 5, 1948
2. 11 games in a row—Sept. 27-Dec. 6, 1953
3. 7 games in a row—Sept. 6-Oct. 20, 1946
4. 6 games in a row—Sept. 15-Oct. 20, 1963
5. 5 games in a row—Sept. 5-Oct. 5, 1947
             Sept. 28-Oct. 26, 1958

FIVE LONGEST LOSING TO START A SEASON

1. 9 games in a row—Sept. 21-Nov. 16, 1975
2. 7 games in a row—Sept. 12-Oct. 24, 1999
3. 3 games in a row—Sept. 3-16, 1984
4. 2 games in a row—Sept. 17- 24, 1967
   Sept. 7-15, 1980
   Sept. 7-13, 1981
   Sept. 6-14, 1992

FIVE LONGEST WINNING TO END A SEASON

1. 14 games in a row—Sept. 3-Dec. 5, 1948 (0-0 to 14-0)
2. 11 games in a row—Oct. 7-Dec. 16, 1951 (0-1 to 11-1)
3. 6 games in a row—Oct. 29-Dec. 10, 1950 (4-2 to 10-2)
4. 5 games in a row—Nov. 10-Dec. 8, 1946 (7-2 to 12-2)
   Nov. 21-Dec. 19, 1971 (4-5 to 9-5)
   Nov. 23-Dec. 21, 1986 (7-4 to 12-4)

FIVE LONGEST LOSING TO END A SEASON

1. 6 games in a row—Nov. 21-Dec. 26, 1999 (2-8 to 2-14)
2. 5 games in a row—Nov. 22-Dec. 20, 1981 (5-6 to 5-11)
   Nov. 19-Dec. 17, 2000 (3-8 to 3-13)
4. 4 games in a row—Nov. 27-Dec. 18, 1977 (6-4 to 6-8)
5. 3 games in a row—Dec. 8-22, 1991 (6-7 to 6-10)
   Dec. 13-27, 1992 (7-6 to 7-9)

TEAM TOP FIVES (GAME)
(POSTSEASON)

RUSHING YARDS

1. 251 (Jan. 4, 1986, at Miami)
2. 227 (Dec. 28, 1952, vs. Detroit)
3. 218 (Dec. 29, 1957, at Detroit)
4. 217 (Dec. 11, 1949, vs. San Francisco)
5. 215 (Dec. 19, 1948, vs. Buffalo)

PASSING YARDS

1. 494 (Jan. 3, 1987, vs. New York Jets)
2. 356 (Jan. 17, 1988, at Denver)
3. 326 (Dec. 4, 1949, vs. Buffalo)
4. 298 (Dec. 24, 1950, vs. Los Angeles)
5. 281 (Jan. 8, 1983, at Los Angeles)

PASS COMPLETIONS

1. 34 (Jan. 3, 1987, vs. New York Jets)
2. 26 (Jan. 17, 1988, at Denver)
3. 22 (Dec. 4, 1949, vs. Buffalo)
   22 (Dec. 24, 1950, vs. Los Angeles)
5. 20 (Dec. 28, 1952, vs. Detroit)
   20 (Dec. 28, 1969, at Dallas)
   20 (Jan. 9, 1988, vs. Indianapolis)
   20 (Jan. 6, 1990, vs. Buffalo)
   20 (Jan. 1, 1995, vs. New England)

INTERCEPTIONS

1. 7 (Dec. 26, 1955, at Los Angeles)
2. 6 (Dec. 26, 1954, vs. Detroit)
3. 5 (Dec. 19, 1948, vs. Buffalo)
   5 (Dec. 24, 1950, vs. Los Angeles)
5. 4 (Dec. 21, 1968, vs. Dallas)

PUNTING YARDS

1. 363 (Dec. 17, 1950, vs. New York Giants)
2. 338 (Jan. 14, 1990, at Denver)
3. 310 (Jan. 3, 1987, vs. New York Jets)
4. 304 (Dec. 21, 1958, at New York)
5. 291 (Jan. 8, 1983, at Los Angeles Raiders)

PUNT RETURN YARDS
(Does not include the game against the Buffalo Bills on December 4, 1949)

1. 81 (Jan. 4, 1981, vs. Oakland)
2. 74 (Dece. 26, 1971, vs. Baltimore)
3. 65 (Jan. 3, 1987, vs. New York Jets)
4. 61 (Dec. 11, 1949, vs. San Francisco)
5. 46 (Dec. 24, 1972, at Miami)

KICKOFF RETURN YARDS

1. 180 (Jan. 6, 1990, vs. Buffalo)
2. 163 (Dec. 29, 1957, at Detroit)
3. 155 (Jan. 2, 1966, at Green Bay)
4. 132 (Dec. 23, 1951, at Los Angeles)
5. 130 (Jan. 14, 1990, at Denver)

TOTAL NET YARDS

1. 558 (Jan. 3, 1987, vs. New York Jets)
2. 464 (Jan. 17, 1988, at Denver)
3. 404 (Jan. 9, 1988, vs. Indianapolis)
4. 398 (Dec. 4, 1949, vs. Buffalo)
5. 384 (Dec. 28, 1952, vs. Detroit)

TEAM TOP FIVES (SEASON)

SCORING (POINTS)

1. 415 (1964)
2. 403 (1966)
3. 394 (1968)
4. 391 (1986)
5. 390 (1987)

RUSHING YARDS

1. 2,639 (1963)
2. 2,557 (1947)
   2,557 (1948)
4. 2,526 (1958)
5. 2,488 (1978)

PASSING YARDS

1. 4,339 (1981)
2. 4,132 (1980)
3. 4,018 (1986)
4. 3,932 (1983)
5. 3,838 (1979)

PASS COMPLETIONS

1. 348 (1981)
2. 337 (1980)

3. 324 (1983)
   324 (1995)
5. 315 (1986)

INTERCEPTIONS

1. 41 (1946)
2. 33 (2001)
3. 32 (1947)
   32 (1968)
5. 31 (1950)
   31 (1960)

SACKS

1. 48 (1992)
   48 (1993)
3. 45 (1989)
4. 44 (1985)
5. 43 (1984)
   43 (2001)

PUNTING YARDS

1. 4,645 (1999)
2. 4,919 (2000)
3. 4,249 (2001)

4. 3,822 (1989)
5. 3,645 (1974)

PUNT RETURN YARDS

1. 563 (1993)
2. 537 (1946)
3. 523 (1974)
4. 503 (1947)
5. 496 (1989)

KICKOFF RETURN YARDS

1. 1,725 (1999)
2. 1,710 (2000)
3. 1,697 (1978)
4. 1,537 (1981)
5. 1,531 (1979)

TOTAL NET YARDS

1. 5,915 (1981)
2. 5,772 (1979)
3. 5,588 (1980)
4. 5,583 (1983)
5. 5,394 (1986)

VS. DOMED-STADIUM TEAMS AT HOME
* Denotes postseason

Cleveland 28, Houston 14 (Nov. 22, 1970)
Cleveland 31, Houston 0 (Sept. 19, 1971)
Cleveland 20, Houston 0 (Nov. 5, 1972)
Cleveland 42, Houston 13 (Oct. 21, 1973)
Cleveland 20, Houston 7 (Sept. 22, 1974)
Houston 40, Cleveland 10 (Oct. 12, 1975)
Cleveland 17, New Orleans 16 (Nov. 30, 1975)
Cleveland 13, Houston 10 (Dec. 5, 1976)
Houston 19, Cleveland 15 (Dec. 11, 1977)
Houston 16, Cleveland 13 (Oct. 1, 1978)
Seattle 29, Cleveland 24 (Nov. 11, 1979)
Cleveland 14, Houston 7 (Dec. 2, 1979)
Houston 16, Cleveland 7 (Sept. 15, 1980)
Houston 9, Cleveland 3 (Sept. 13, 1981)
Cleveland 20, New Orleans 17 (Oct. 18, 1981)
Minnesota 27, Cleveland 21 (Sept. 4, 1983)
Seattle 24, Cleveland 9 (Oct. 2, 1983)
Cleveland 25, Houston 19 (OT) (Oct. 30, 1983)
New Orleans 16, Cleveland 14 (Oct. 28, 1984)
Cleveland 27, Houston 10 (Nov. 25, 1984)
Cleveland 28, Houston 21 (Dec. 15, 1985)

Cleveland 24, Detroit 21 (Sept. 28, 1986)
Cleveland 13, Houston 10 (OT) (Nov. 30, 1986)
Houston 15, Cleveland 10 (Oct. 11, 1987)
Indianapolis 9, Cleveland 7 (Dec. 6, 1987)
*Cleveland 38, Indianapolis 21 (Jan. 9, 1988)
Cleveland 23, Indianapolis 17 (Sept. 19, 1988)
Seattle 16, Cleveland 10 (Oct. 9, 1988)
Cleveland 28, Houston 23 (Dec. 18, 1988)
*Houston 24, Cleveland 23 (Dec. 24, 1988)
Cleveland 28, Houston 17 (Oct. 29, 1989)
Cleveland 23, Minnesota 17 (OT) (Dec. 17, 1989)
Houston 35, Cleveland 23 (Nov. 18, 1990)
Houston 17, Cleveland 14 (Dec. 15, 1991)
Houston 17, Cleveland 14 (Dec. 20, 1992)
Houston 27, Cleveland 20 (Nov. 21, 1993)
Cleveland 17, New Orleans 13 (Dec. 5, 1993)
Cleveland 34, Houston 10 (Nov. 27, 1994)
Cleveland 35, Seattle 9 (Dec. 24, 1994)
Houston 37, Cleveland 10 (Nov. 5, 1995)
Indianapolis 29, Cleveland 28 (Dec. 26, 1999)
Cleveland 24, Detroit 14 (Sept. 23, 2001)

Regular Season - 22-18 (.550)
Postseason - 1-1 (.500)

VS. NFL CHAMPIONS (1950-69) AND SUPER BOWL CHAMPIONS (1970-95, SINCE 1999) OF SEASON AT HAND

(Does not include the Browns' four seasons in the AAFC from 1946-49 and the 1950, 1954, 1955, and 1964 seasons since they were the champions those years)
* Denotes postseason

Cleveland 38, Los Angeles 23 (Oct. 7, 1951, at Los Angeles)
*Los Angeles 24, Cleveland 17 (Dec. 23, 1951, at Los Angeles)
Detroit 17, Cleveland 6 (Nov. 2, 1952, at Detroit)
*Detroit 17, Cleveland 7 (Dec. 28, 1952, at Cleveland)
*Detroit 17, Cleveland 16 (Dec. 27, 1953, at Detroit)
New York 21, Cleveland 9 (Oct. 14, 1956, at Cleveland)
Cleveland 24, New York 7 (Dec. 9, 1956, at New York)
Detroit 20, Cleveland 7 (Dec. 8, 1957, at Detroit)
*Detroit 59, Cleveland 14 (Dec. 29, 1957, at Detroit)
Cleveland 38, Baltimore 31 (Nov. 1, 1959, at Baltimore)
Cleveland 41, Philadelphia 24 (Sept. 25, 1960, at Philadelphia)
Philadelphia 31, Cleveland 29 (Oct. 23, 1960, at Cleveland)
Green Bay 49, Cleveland 17 (Oct. 15, 1961, at Cleveland)

*Green Bay 23, Cleveland 12 (Jan. 2, 1966, at Green Bay)
Green Bay 21, Cleveland 20 (Sept. 18, 1966, at Cleveland)
Green Bay 55, Cleveland 7 (Nov. 12, 1967, at Green Bay)
Cleveland 30, Baltimore 20 (Oct. 20, 1968, at Baltimore)
*Baltimore 34, Cleveland 0 (Dec. 29, 1968, at Cleveland)
Minnesota 51, Cleveland 3 (Nov. 9, 1969, at Minnesota)
*Minnesota 27, Cleveland 7 (Jan. 4, 1970, at Minnesota)
*Miami 20, Cleveland 14 (Dec. 24, 1972, at Miami)
Miami 17, Cleveland 9 (Oct. 15, 1973, at Cleveland)
Pittsburgh 20, Cleveland 16 (Oct. 20, 1974, at Pittsburgh)
Pittsburgh 26, Cleveland 16 (Nov. 17, 1974, at Cleveland)
Pittsburgh 42, Cleveland 6 (Oct. 5, 1975, at Cleveland)
Pittsburgh 31, Cleveland 17 (Dec. 7, 1975, at Pittsburgh)
Pittsburgh 15, Cleveland 9 (OT) (Sept. 24, 1978, at Pittsburgh)
Pittsburgh 34, Cleveland 14 (Oct. 15, 1978, at Cleveland)
Pittsburgh 51, Cleveland 35 (Oct. 7, 1979, at Cleveland)
Pittsburgh 33, Cleveland 30 (OT) (Nov. 25, 1979, at Pittsburgh)
*Oakland 14, Cleveland 12 (Jan. 4, 1981, at Cleveland)
Cleveland 15, San Francisco 12 (Nov. 15, 1981, at San Francisco)
San Francisco 41, Cleveland 7 (Nov. 11, 1984, at Cleveland)
Washington 42, Cleveland 17 (Oct. 13, 1991, at Washington)
St. Louis 34, Cleveland 3 (Oct. 24, 1999, at St. Louis)
Baltimore 12, Cleveland 0 (Oct. 1, 2000, at Cleveland)
Baltimore 44, Cleveland 7 (Nov. 26, 2000, at Baltimore)
New England 27, Cleveland 16 (Dec. 9, 2001, at New England)

Overall Regular Season - 6-23 (.207)
Home Regular Season - 0-11 (.000)
Away Regular Season - 6-12 (.333)
Postseason - 0-9 (.000) (postseason wins are not feasible)

VS. PACIFIC TIME ZONE TEAMS AT HOME

* Denotes postseason

Cleveland 31, Los Angeles 14 (Oct. 20, 1946)
San Francisco 34, Cleveland 20 (Oct. 27, 1946)
Los Angeles 13, Cleveland 10 (Oct. 12, 1947)
Cleveland 37, San Francisco 14 (Nov. 16, 1947)
Cleveland 19, Los Angeles 14 (Sept. 3, 1948)
Cleveland 14, San Francisco 7 (Nov. 14, 1948)
Cleveland 42, Los Angeles 7 (Oct. 2, 1949)
Cleveland 30, San Francisco 28 (Oct. 30, 1949)
*Cleveland 21, San Francisco 7 (Dec. 11, 1949)
Cleveland 34, San Francisco 14 (Nov. 12, 1950)
*Cleveland 30, Los Angeles 28 (Dec. 24, 1950)
Cleveland 37, Los Angeles 7 (Sept. 28, 1952)
Cleveland 23, San Francisco 21 (Nov. 15, 1953)
Cleveland 45, Los Angeles 31 (Nov. 24, 1957)
San Francisco 21, Cleveland 20 (Nov. 29, 1959)
Cleveland 20, Los Angeles 6 (Sept. 29, 1963)
Los Angeles 24, Cleveland 6 (Sept. 29, 1968)
San Diego 27, Cleveland 10 (Nov. 1, 1970)
Oakland 34, Cleveland 20 (Oct. 4, 1971)
Cleveland 16, San Diego 16 (Oct. 28, 1973)
Oakland 40, Cleveland 24 (Oct. 6, 1974)
Cleveland 7, San Francisco 0 (Dec. 1, 1974)

Cleveland 21, San Diego 17 (Oct. 24, 1976)
Oakland 26, Cleveland 10 (Oct. 9, 1977)
Los Angeles 9, Cleveland 0 (Nov. 27, 1977)
Cleveland 24, San Francisco 7 (Sept. 3, 1978)
Cleveland 30, Los Angeles 19 (Nov. 26, 1978)
Seattle 29, Cleveland 24 (Nov. 11, 1979)
*Oakland 14, Cleveland 12 (Jan. 4, 1981)
San Diego 44, Cleveland 14 (Sept. 7, 1981)
San Diego 30, Cleveland 13 (Dec. 5, 1982)
Seattle 24, Cleveland 9 (Oct. 2, 1983)
San Francisco 41, Cleveland 7 (Nov. 11, 1984)
Los Angeles Raiders 21, Cleveland 20 (Oct. 20, 1985)
Cleveland 47, San Diego 17 (Dec. 21, 1986)
Cleveland 30, Los Angeles Rams 17 (Oct. 26, 1987)
Seattle 16, Cleveland 10 (Oct. 9, 1988)
San Diego 24, Cleveland 14 (Sept. 23, 1990)
Los Angeles Rams 38, Cleveland 23 (Dec. 2, 1990)
San Diego 14, Cleveland 13 (Nov. 15, 1992)
Cleveland 23, San Francisco 13 (Sept. 13, 1993)
Cleveland 35, Seattle 9 (Dec. 24, 1994)
Seattle 9, Cleveland 6 (Sept. 9, 2001)
Cleveland 20, San Diego 16 (Oct. 7, 2001)

Regular Season - 20-20-1 (.500)
Postseason - 2-1 (.667)

WON-LOST RECORDS (POSTSEASON)

YEAR	WON	LOST	PCT.
1946	1	0	1.000
1947	1	0	1.000
1948	1	0	1.000
1949	2	0	1.000
1950	2	0	1.000
1951	0	1	.000
1952	0	1	.000
1953	0	1	.000
1954	1	0	1.000
1955	1	0	1.000
1957	0	1	.000
1958	0	1	.000
1964	1	0	1.000
1965	0	1	.000
1967	0	1	.000
1968	1	1	.500
1969	1	1	.500
1971	0	1	.000
1972	0	1	.000
1980	0	1	.000
1982	0	1	.000
1985	0	1	.000
1986	1	1	.500
1987	1	1	.500
1988	0	1	.000
1989	1	1	.500
1994	1	1	.500
TOTAL	**16**	**19**	**.457**

WON-LOST-TIED RECORDS

Year	Won	Lost	Tied	Pct.
1946	12	2	0	.857
1947	12	1	1	.893
1948	14	0	0	1.000
1949	9	1	2	.833
1950	10	2	0	.833
1951	11	1	0	.917
1952	8	4	0	.667
1953	11	1	0	.917
1954	9	3	0	.750
1955	9	2	1	.792
1956	5	7	0	.417
1957	9	2	1	.792
1958	9	3	0	.750
1959	7	5	0	.583
1960	8	3	1	.708
1961	8	5	1	.607
1962	7	6	1	.536
1963	10	4	0	.714
1964	10	3	1	.750
1965	11	3	0	.786
1966	9	5	0	.643
1967	9	5	0	.643
1968	10	4	0	.714
1969	10	3	1	.750
1970	7	7	0	.500
1971	9	5	0	.643
1972	10	4	0	.714
1973	7	5	2	.571
1974	4	10	0	.286
1975	3	11	0	.214
1976	9	5	0	.643
1977	6	8	0	.429
1978	8	8	0	.500
1979	9	7	0	.563
1980	11	5	0	.688
1981	5	11	0	.313
1982	4	5	0	.444
1983	9	7	0	.563
1984	5	11	0	.313
1985	8	8	0	.500
1986	12	4	0	.750
1987	10	5	0	.667
1988	10	6	0	.625
1989	9	6	1	.594
1990	3	13	0	.188
1991	6	10	0	.375
1992	7	9	0	.438
1993	7	9	0	.438
1994	11	5	0	.688
1995	5	11	0	.313
1999	2	14	0	.125
2000	3	13	0	.188
2001	7	9	0	.438
TOTAL	**433**	**306**	**13**	**.584**

WEST COAST, ON THE

* Denotes postseason

Los Angeles 17, Cleveland 16 (Nov. 3, 1946)
Cleveland 14, San Francisco 7 (Nov. 10, 1946)
Cleveland 14, San Francisco 7 (Oct. 26, 1947)
Cleveland 27, Los Angeles 17 (Nov. 27, 1947)
Cleveland 31, Los Angeles 14 (Nov. 25, 1948)
Cleveland 31, San Francisco 28 (Nov. 28, 1948)
San Francisco 56, Cleveland 28 (Oct. 9, 1949)
Cleveland 61, Los Angeles 14 (Oct. 14, 1949)
San Francisco 24, Cleveland 10 (Sept. 30, 1951)
Cleveland 38, Los Angeles 23 (Oct. 7, 1951)
*Los Angeles 24, Cleveland 17 (Dec. 23, 1951)
Cleveland 38, San Francisco 3 (Oct. 2, 1955)
*Cleveland 38, Los Angeles 14 (Dec. 26, 1955)
Cleveland 30, Los Angeles 27 (Sept. 28, 1958)
Cleveland 13, San Francisco 10 (Dec. 15, 1962)
Los Angeles 42, Cleveland 7 (Dec. 12, 1965)
Cleveland 33, San Francisco 21 (Nov. 3, 1968)
San Francisco 34, Cleveland 31 (Sept. 27, 1970)
Oakland 23, Cleveland 20 (Nov. 8, 1970)
Cleveland 21, San Diego 17 (Nov. 13, 1972)
Cleveland 7, Oakland 3 (Nov. 18, 1973)
Los Angeles 30, Cleveland 17 (Dec. 16, 1973)
San Diego 36, Cleveland 35 (Nov. 3, 1974)
Oakland 38, Cleveland 17 (Nov. 16, 1975)
San Diego 37, Cleveland 14 (Dec. 4, 1977)
Seattle 20, Cleveland 19 (Dec. 18, 1977)
Seattle 47, Cleveland 24 (Dec. 3, 1978)

Oakland 19, Cleveland 14 (Dec. 9, 1979)
Cleveland 27, Seattle 3 (Oct. 12, 1980)
Los Angeles 27, Cleveland 16 (Oct. 4, 1981)
Cleveland 15, San Francisco 12 (Nov. 15, 1981)
Seattle 42, Cleveland 21 (Dec. 20, 1981)
Cleveland 21, Seattle 7 (Sept. 12, 1982)
*Los Angeles Raiders 27, Cleveland 10 (Jan. 8, 1983)
Cleveland 30, San Diego 24 (OT) (Sept. 25, 1983)
Seattle 33, Cleveland 0 (Sept. 3, 1984)
Los Angeles Rams 20, Cleveland 17 (Sept. 9, 1984)
Cleveland 21, San Diego 7 (Sept. 29, 1985)
Seattle 31, Cleveland 13 (Dec. 8, 1985)
Los Angeles Raiders 27, Cleveland 14 (Nov. 16, 1986)
San Diego 27, Cleveland 24 (OT) (Nov. 1, 1987)
San Francisco 38, Cleveland 24 (Nov. 29, 1987)
Cleveland 24, Los Angeles Raiders 17 (Dec. 20, 1987)
Cleveland 17, Seattle 7 (Nov. 12, 1989)
San Francisco 20, Cleveland 17 (Oct. 28, 1990)
Cleveland 30, San Diego 24 (OT) (Oct. 20, 1991)
Cleveland 28, Los Angeles Raiders 16 (Sept. 20, 1992)
Cleveland 19, Los Angeles Raiders 16 (Sept. 19, 1993)
Seattle 22, Cleveland 5 (Nov. 14, 1993)
Cleveland 42, Los Angeles Rams 14 (Dec. 26, 1993)
San Diego 31, Cleveland 13 (Dec. 3, 1995)
San Diego 23, Cleveland 10 (Dec. 5, 1999)
Oakland 36, Cleveland 10 (Sept. 24, 2000)

Regular Season - 24-26 (.480)
Postseason - 1-2 (.333)

Celebrate the Heroes of Ohio Sports
in These Other Acclaimed Titles from Sports Publishing!

Ohio State's Unforgettables
by Bruce Hooley
- 8.5 x 11 hardcover
- 225 pages
- 150+ color and b/w photos
- $29.95
- *2002 release!*

The Cleveland Indians Encyclopedia:
Second Edition
by Russell Schneider
- 8.5 x 11 hardcover
- 600 pages
- 700+ photos throughout
- $49.95

Tales from the Tribe Dugout
by Russell Schneider
- 5.5 x 8.25 hardcover
- 200 pages
- caricatures throughout
- $19.95
- *2002 release!*

Jim O'Brien:
Bucking the Odds
by Ralph Paulk
- 6 x 9 hardcover
- 225 pages
- $22.95

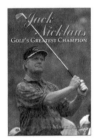

Jack Nicklaus:
Golf's Greatest Champion
by Mark Shaw
- 6 x 9 softcover
- 250 pages
- photo section
- $14.95
- *2002 release!*

The Ohio State Football Encyclopedia
by Jack Park
- 8.5 x 11 hardcover
- 400 pages
- 200+ photos throughout
- $39.95

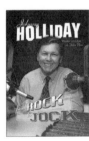

Johnny Holliday:
From Rock to Jock
by Johnny Holliday
with Stephen Moore
- 6 x 9 hardcover
- 225+ pages
- eight-page photo section
- $22.95
- *2002 release!*

Talking on Air:
A Broadcaster's Life in Sports
by Ken Coleman
and Dan Valenti
- 6 x 9 hardcover
- 216 pages
- eight-page photo section
- $22.95

To order at any time, please call toll-free **877-424-BOOK (2665)**.
For fast service and quick delivery, order on-line at

www.SportsPublishingLLC.com.